"'Teach us to pray,' the disciples of Jesus asked him. Today many of the contemporary disciples of Jesus ask the same thing. We cannot learn to pray as we can learn to swim or to run a business. We have to be taught constantly to pray by the Lord himself. We are always beginners who humbly ask the Lord to teach us to pray. Prayer is always gift and grace. And the Lord in his immense mercy will always give us this grace, if we are open and responsive to him. This precious book can help many people enter into the wonderful world of prayer. They can receive the help and instruction they need in order to long for a deep, prayerful relationship with Our Lord himself. It is my hope that many readers will be inspired to keep saying to the Lord: 'Teach us to pray.'"

—ANDERS CARDINAL ARBORELIUS, OCD
Bishop of Stockholm, Sweden

"In a sense, this is a 'how to' book of the best sort: a simple, practical guide for learning how to pray. But it's also vastly more than that: an eloquent, intimate, and deeply persuasive invitation to seek out a personal relationship with the Father who made us, and to master the art of immersing ourselves in the love of God."

—ARCHBISHOP CHARLES J. CHAPUT, OFM CAP
Archbishop of Philadelphia

"*Personal Prayer* is one of the finest contemporary books on prayer. Frs. Acklin and Hicks treat the subject in a way that is both profound and simultaneously down-to-earth. The authors weave in the writings of the saints and mystical doctors with contemporary examples in such a way that a clear path is presented for growing in our relationship with Jesus Christ. The reader will rediscover the depths of the Father's love for us as well as our own need to be transparent, vulnerable, and poor before Him if we desire to grow in intimacy with Him. I would highly recommend this book to anyone who hungers for deeper communion with the Blessed Trinity."

—Bishop Thomas J. Olmsted
Bishop of Phoenix

"Fr. Acklin and Fr. Hicks describe the 'one thing [that] is needful,' the intimacy with God for which the human heart longs. In *Personal Prayer*, their description of the human experience of prayer is so true to life and beautifully integrated with Sacred Scripture and sound theology. This practical book will serve as a valuable guide for those who wish to grow in their life of prayer toward a deeper union with God. I pray that this book will bring many souls closer to God."

—Sr. Mary Grace Lamsam, CP
Directress of Formation, Passionist Nuns,
Our Lady of Sorrows Monastery, Pittsburgh

"Like seasoned and dedicated teachers, and as concerned fathers, Frs. Acklin and Hicks take your hand and accompany you through the radically human experience of prayer. With the wisdom of the Church, manifested in her Scripture and her saints, they invite men and women of today to the drama and beauty of a life of prayer, and to the conviction that prayer is essential for fullness of life in Christ."

—Fr. Richard Veras
Professor of Homiletics, Dunwoodie Seminary,
and author of Word Made Flesh

"*Personal Prayer* is a good sequel to the authors' previous book, *Spiritual Direction*. Prayer is a common topic of discussion in spiritual direction since it is the primary way we express and develop our relationship with God. The spiritual director often finds himself as a teacher of prayer. This would be a good book for him to have. It is not for beginners learning the first steps in prayer, but it would be helpful for those somewhat experienced in prayer who want to understand prayer and grow deeper in it. It will certainly prove helpful for those who are directing others in prayer. I believe this book will be helpful for all who pray and want to better understand the mystery of our relationship with God in prayer. And most importantly, it will inspire the growth that God so wills us to experience in the interior life."

—Fr. Thomas Nelson, O Praem
National Director of the Institute of Religious Life,
Canon of St. Michael's Abbey, Silverado, California

"Frs. Acklin and Hicks are sure guides to the deeper water of prayer where we move beyond mere external practices into the depth of relationship into which every living soul is called by God. I have no doubt that no matter who you are, or how much experience you have with prayer, this book will lead you deeper into prayer and into the heart of God."

—Dan Burke
President of the Avila Foundation for Spiritual Formation

"This treatise on prayer is a gem! It is a true and very encouraging guide for anyone traveling the spiritual journey and desiring to find his or her humble humanity in the loving heart of our Father. Fr. Acklin and Fr. Hicks have combined invaluable resources in its composition: sound study, years of experience in spiritual direction, and most important and certain of all, loving, personal communion with our dear Lord himself. Treasure this gift to the Church! You will be blessed in having done so!"

—MOTHER MARIA OF JESUS, OCD
Prioress, Monastery of the Holy Cross, Iron Mountain, MI

"Fr. Acklin and Fr. Hicks, both Catholic priests and Benedictine monks, offer the fruit of their extensive study and counseling experience to all of us who seek a deeper communion with God in prayer. The wisdom of *Personal Prayer* can open our minds and hearts to receive more completely the most precious divine-human gift of prayer through friendship with the Lord."

—RT. REV. DOUGLAS R. NOWICKI, OSB
Archabbot, Saint Vincent Archabbey, Latrobe, PA

"Too often books on prayer are so abstract in their description of the interior life that readers can fail to grasp the uniquely personal nature of relating to God in prayer. As a result, many fall into misconceptions and become discouraged in their prayer lives. In *Personal Prayer*, Frs. Acklin and Hicks offer the Church a brilliant description of contemplative prayer in its relational, personal, and human dimensions that will help any reader to grow in prayer. This book is filled with profound insights on the inner dynamics of personal prayer in which we receive God's transforming love and love him in return. I've been waiting for years for a book like this; I cannot recommend it enough!"

—FR. MATHIAS THELEN
President of Encounter Ministries, Pastor of St. Patrick Catholic Parish, Brighton, MI

"Mother Teresa accurately read the climate of humanity when she said 'The poverty of being unwanted, unloved, and uncared for is the greatest poverty.' In a world clamoring for love and validation, the authors offer a beautiful response with *Personal Prayer: A Guide for Receiving the Father's Love*. A tender, insightful, and straightforward work that takes an honest look at that which we all long for, whether we realize it or not, and which the Lord desires to draw us into—a loving relationship with Himself. It cracks open the vast subject of prayer in a poignantly simple way that will inspire and encourage both the beginner and experienced soul as they grow deeper in love and relationship with the Lord."

—MAGGIE ZBIEGIEN
Program and Relationship Coordinator,
Diocese of Cleveland Vocation Office

"*Personal Prayer* is a foundational work for anyone seeking to grow in his or her relationship with the Blessed Trinity. The authors are clearly men who pray deeply and have an intimate relationship with Jesus, and the words seep with authenticity. This is not simply another book about the theory or formula of prayer—it is a guide to prayer written by men who know the heart of the Father. *Personal Prayer* is intellectually enriching but easily accessible at the same time, filled with well-rounded and grounded sources such as Magisterial documents, sacred texts, and spiritual classics. Anyone who is serious about growing in his or her prayer life should read this book. It needs to be on the bookshelf of every Catholic disciple of Jesus Christ."

—ANNIE SARLO
Secretary for Catholic Life and Evangelization,
Diocese of Allentown, PA

"This book is for all who, like me, have counted the ways—on both hands!—why they will never be a good *pray-er*. It turns out that prayer actually is about humility and 'the answer is always Jesus.' When we feel too weak and impoverished to be good at prayer, it turns out that the path of prayer is right there facing us. This book gives us an opportunity to stop worrying about all our deficiencies in prayer and to start learning about Jesus' readiness for us—for our real selves—in prayer. At once a profound consolation and an invitation to the spiritual growth we need, this book points the way forward for the whole Church in our times."

—MATTHEW LEVERING
James N. and Mary D. Perry Jr.
Chair of Theology, Mundelein Seminary

"Whether you are a well-seasoned prayer warrior, a cloistered contemplative, an active missionary, or have recently entertained thoughts about possibly beginning to pray, you will benefit from the reflections and spiritual insights found in this book on prayer. If you want to know how it is possible to reach such a vast array of souls, you have only to *tolle lege*, take up and read. While the author's writing style is easy to grasp, the content is deeply penetrating and thought-provoking. It is a book to read slowly, allowing the Holy Spirit to open your heart as you move into a deeper encounter with the Living God, learning to foster the most important relationship of your life. You will be gently unmasked and begin to encounter the gifts of poverty and vulnerability in prayer. You will learn to rest in the arms of God and, like a little child, receive everything you need from Him. This book is a gift for the Church."

—MOTHER ILIANA LONCHYNA
Stavrophore nun, Christ the Bridegroom Monastery, Burton, OH

Personal Prayer

Personal Prayer

A Guide for Receiving the Father's Love

Fr. Thomas Acklin, OSB &
Fr. Boniface Hicks, OSB

EMMAUS
ROAD
PUBLISHING

Steubenville, Ohio
www.EmmausRoad.org

Emmaus Road Publishing
1468 Parkview Circle
Steubenville, Ohio 43952

Library of Congress Control Number: 2019957877
ISBN: 978-1-64585-023-6

Nihil Obstat:
The Reverend Monsignor Larry J. Kulick, JCL, VG
Censor Librorum

Imprimatur:
The Most Reverend Edward C. Malesic, JCL
Bishop of Greensburg
September 5, 2019

The nihil obstat and imprimatur are official declarations that a book or pamphlet is free of doctrinal or moral error. No implication is contained therein that those who have granted the nihil obstat and imprimatur agree with the contents, opinions or statements expressed.

Cover design and Layout by Emily Demary
Cover image: *Christ at the Sea of Galilee,* ca. 1740, Alessandro Magnasco, National Gallery of Art, Washington, DC, USA

Contents

Dedication

FOR A RENEWAL of personal prayer in the Church, that the Second Vatican Council's universal call to holiness might be fulfilled in our time and manifest in every heart the fruits of contemplation.

Foreword

WHEN THE TIME CAME to cobble together the fourth
and final section of the *Catechism of the Catholic Church*,
all previous parts having been assigned to various committees
of bishops, it fell to a single unprepossessing priest to provide
the concluding text, which was on prayer. Not surprisingly, it
proved to be the most moving of all. It was the fruit of a rich
and prolonged meditation by its author, Fr. Jean Corbon, who
set down in splendid detail the testimony of saints and martyrs,
whose resources reach far beyond the exertions of mere theologians, never mind cumbrous committees of bishops. What truly
astonishes, however, is the fact that the whole project was undertaken in a city then under siege (Beirut, Lebanon), the constant
bombardment of which drove poor Father Corbon underground
in order to finish the job.

One wonders if Fathers Acklin and Hicks faced comparable
dangers in putting together their text. Who knows, perhaps the
monastic setting amid the hills and the trees surrounding Latrobe,
Pennsylvania, is fraught with secret perils of which only they are
aware. If so, it certainly has not prevented the many excellences
of this book from reaching the reader, whose enrichment will be

considerably enhanced by close acquaintance with their work.

And what is its message? That if the life of faith, first given to us in baptism, is to remain fresh, vibrant and alive, then it must find its nourishment in the practice of prayer. Indeed, there is no other way to be fully human apart from the act and exercise of prayer. Why else were we made to stand upright if not to look upon the stars? And, like the Magi, to search out the one star whose trajectory will take us straight to Bethlehem? Isn't this why God came to us in the first place? "The good news," we are told early on by Fathers Acklin and Hicks, "is that God became man so that each one of us can have a deep, profound union with Him in prayer."

On no other source, therefore, does the maintenance of Catholic belief and behavior so depend—lacking which it soon falls away, blown apart, as it were, by the refusal to speak to God, to lay bare our vulnerability before Him. He Who has, amazingly, already placed His own infinite vulnerability before us. This is because there can be no real lasting love without first putting oneself at risk. "Be worthy," says Paul Claudel, "of the flame consuming you." Be like God, in other words, who, the authors tell us, "never hedges His bets or counts the cost. He gives without measure. This divine vulnerability was already revealed when God exposed His image by placing His 'fingerprints' all over His creation. Then He revealed His vulnerability more radically in making creatures with free will, in His image and likeness, who could relate to Him by sharing vulnerably with Him, but who could also choose to reject Him."

Think of it. That mere creatures, lacking any claim on being, may yet spit in God's eye, burning every last bridge to beatitude.

Even as God Himself, Lord of the Universe, seeks ever more ingenious ways to win us back. Surely this is the final wonder of the world. All because God wishes to be with us, to listen to and love us. "To enter into the presence of Him who awaits us," is how the Catechism puts it (2711). "God is thirsting for us that we may thirst for Him" (CCC 2560). Or, as the wise old peasant said confidingly to the saintly Cure de Ars: "I look at Him and He looks at me." Could the connection possibly be stated more simply? *I to my Beloved, my Beloved unto me.*

Nothing, therefore, so testifies to the deep longing of the human heart than the desire for God, for which the most necessary—and yes, natural—medium is prayer. Because, even in the order of nature, it is necessary and good that contact with God take place, that all of one's life be harnessed to the practice of raising the mind and heart to God. Even pagans pray, unlike post-moderns, who in their facile rejection of God evince an obtuseness entirely pre-human. When Tacitus, who chronicled the greatness of Rome, asked himself what makes it so, he did not cite the strength of its army, nor the nobility of its emperor but rather the temples of its gods. Why else would the blueprints for the Pantheon, that massive monument erected in honor of the household gods, require that its ceiling be thrown open to the sky if not to permit pagan man access to them? Prayer is an absolutely universal human vocation, a constitutive dimension no less of the life of *Everyman*. This is most especially true, of course, in the order of grace, introduced in that horizon-shattering event we call Incarnation, when Christ comes to redeem and sanctify all that pertains to man. If religion is the natural orientation of the creature bent on finding God, what then is Revelation but God's answering response in the gift of His Son?

There, as St. Teresa of Ávila reminds us, "a close sharing between friends" is made possible by the grace of Baptism. "That final mutation," as Pope Benedict daringly describes it, "in the evolution of the human species."

Prayer, then, is the lifeblood of the soul. Period. It is the connecting link between ourselves and God, who mysteriously empowers us to make it happen. It is His grace that provides the impetus, kick-starting the process by which we are drawn into ever greater intimacy with Him. And the coin of the realm which we are given to spend is, as always, love. It is for this alone that we are enjoined to pray. "The goal of Christian prayer is not found in extraordinary phenomena such as levitation or extraordinary states of consciousness such as ecstasy, but rather in the perfection of love."

To find out why, do read this book. It will deepen your understanding of prayer, even as it quickens the desire to grow in the practice of love.

Regis Martin, Professor of Theology,
Franciscan University of Steubenville

Acknowledgements

WE WOULD LIKE TO ACKNOWLEDGE a few of the countless people who have helped to form our own lives of prayer. Our relationship with God first developed in the community of our families, and then came to fuller fruition in the monastic community of Saint Vincent Archabbey in Latrobe, Pennsylvania. We want to acknowledge especially our mothers, may they rest in peace, for the way they formed our hearts to be more sensitive and contemplative, with a vulnerable openness to listening to others and to God. We are deeply grateful also for Archabbot Douglas and the monks of Saint Vincent Archabbey for fostering an environment in which prayer is highly valued. We thank the Saint Vincent Seminary faculty, staff, students, and alumni for all their love and support for our ministry throughout the years. We owe a special debt of gratitude to the Passionist Nuns of Our Lady of Sorrows Monastery in Pittsburgh, Pennsylvania as well as the Passionist Fathers of the House of Greater Solitude in Bedford, Pennsylvania. These dedicated contemplatives made a major contribution to our understanding and experience of prayer by opening their monasteries and their hearts to us. We are also very grateful to Scott Hahn and the editorial staff at Emmaus

Road for their excellence, professionalism, efficiency, faith, and friendliness in bringing this work to publication!

Introduction

CEASELESS INTERIOR PRAYER is a continuous aspiration and a yearning of the spirit of man toward God. To succeed in this sweet exercise it is necessary to ask God frequently that He teach you to pray continuously. Pray often and fervently and prayer itself will reveal this mystery to you, how it is possible for it to be continuous, but it takes time.[1]

Praying as Human Beings

"I went to pray but nothing happened. I just sat there. After a little while, I started to feel uncomfortable. I wasn't sure what to say. To be honest, I wasn't sure if anyone was listening anyway. I tried to talk to God, but I just heard the echo of my own thoughts. Then some random stuff started to fill my head. I remembered some past experiences, and then I got a little upset. I got out my Rosary to keep myself busy, but as I started through the prayers,

---

[1] Helen Bacovcin, trans., *The Way of a Pilgrim and The Pilgrim Continues His Way*, Reprint ed. (Garden City, NY: Image, 1992), 4–5.

I got distracted by someone who walked out of the chapel. Then I was alone. And I felt really alone. I started to get bored, and my eyes began to close. I started nodding off. Then suddenly I woke up, and I got really irritated. This is useless, I thought. I will never be able to pray. So I got up and left."

Such an experience is not uncommon, even for someone who has persevered in prayer for many years. Our images of saints in prayer give us the misimpression that those who pray well somehow transcend these experiences. We imagine that experts at prayer look more like angels, sitting enraptured without any distractions, focused intently on the Lord while carrying out deep, meaningful conversations with Him. That is so distant from our own experience that it seems there must be a secret technique or that some people must have a special gene that makes them different from everyone else. The bad news is that it is not so easy as finding a secret technique or a magical formula. The good news is that God became man so that each one of us can have a deep, profound union with Him in prayer and throughout the rest of our lives as well as into eternity.

We pray as human beings. This statement appears obvious, but it points to what can be a stumbling block for us when we try to pray. It seems that part of being human is to be unable to reach a transcendent, infinite God. Thus, because prayer is communicating with God, we think we must somehow rise above being human in order to pray and reach God. We feel that our humanity is inadequate to get God's attention. In fact, we are often disturbed by our humanity. We use it as an excuse when we say, "I'm only human." We feel weighed down by it. We are embarrassed by who we are.

Much of the time, we are disturbed by distractions, temptations, tiredness, sadness, irritation, and other foul moods! These seem to get in the way of prayer, and we get discouraged. Fortunately, these are not actually obstacles to our prayer—they are simply a part of our humanity, and we must learn to incorporate them into our prayer. The actual obstacle to our prayer is when we try to be angels by rejecting these aspects of our humanity as if there were something wrong with us. Rather than His being displeased with these aspects of our frail humanity, God intends them as part and parcel of our relationship with Him and as the very way by which this relationship deepens in prayer.

Besides our weaknesses, we also are sinners. Sometimes our guilt and sense of unworthiness can present an obstacle to our even daring to approach the Lord in prayer. We may feel that the burden of our sin will prevent us from being able to communicate with God. We may actually think that He is not open to us! To the contrary, our fallen condition intensifies our need for prayer, and when we properly understand our sense of unworthiness, it can enhance our disposition toward prayer. When we truly know how desperate our fallen condition is, we know how much we need to pray, and we know how much we need God! As St. Paul reminded us, "we have this treasure in earthen vessels" (2 Cor 4:7). God created us as human beings, and He enters into a relationship with us as human beings, and so we grow in prayer as human beings. If God wanted us to pray like angels, He would have created us as angels.

In some ways we are like the angels, but in some ways we are like the animals because we are made as a unity of soul and body. Like the animals, we have a bodily life consisting of the five external senses along with the internal senses of imagination and sensible memory. We are also moved by passions in our sensitive appetite, which we normally refer to as emotions or feelings. These are designed to move us in response to what is good or bad for us. The evaluation of good and bad is purely practical in the animal (fire is bad, treats are good), but unlike the animals, human beings also have an intellect and free will and are able to make moral judgments to determine what is morally good (an act of kindness, for example) and morally evil (causing unnecessary suffering to an innocent, for example). In our intellect and free will, we are like the angels, but unlike the angels, our intellect still depends on the senses in this life to receive the initial data of our thinking. The body is not a prison for the soul, as Plato thought, nor a necessary evil, but rather an intentional part of God's design. Even in heaven, our soul will be united with a glorified body. So when we pray, we always pray as a spiritual, embodied creature, and our emotions, imagination, memory, intellectual concepts, moral judgments, and free choices are all taken up in our prayer to be part of our relationship with God.

When we think of the messiness of our humanity, with feelings and thoughts that can go in embarrassing directions, we not only feel inadequate to enter into a relationship with God but also perhaps even feel inadequate to enter into a relationship with a highly regarded human being; how much more then must God be far beyond our reach! Nonetheless, we are all called by God into relationship with Him! Our embarrassment of ourselves and sense of awe before God give us a chance to be humble, even to lower ourselves, to be like little children, to recognize ourselves as the least, the lowest, and the last. These are precisely the human qualities that Jesus identifies as prerequisites for our relationship with God. He required that we be like children when He said, "Unless you turn and become like children, you will never enter the kingdom of heaven" (Matt 18:3). He wants us to admit that we need a father, and indeed that we *have* a father, when He teaches us, "When you pray say, 'Father'" (Luke 11:1). He reminds us that we are the least and deserve the lowest place, but He will raise us up: "When you are invited, go and sit in the lowest place, so that when your host comes he may say to you, 'Friend, go up higher'" (Luke 14:10). Jesus does not expect to find us in the place of the angels. He looks for us in the lowest place, at the children's table, and He comes to sit with us and then to take us to sit next to Him and our Heavenly Father.

Our humanity, which seems to be the primary stumbling block to prayer, is in fact what makes prayer possible and even makes prayer such an amazing gift. God condescends to enter into the very depths of our humanity. In doing so, He also divinizes us and makes us one with Himself, insofar as we let Him. This process of divinization does not destroy our humanity or replace it. Grace builds on nature;[2] it "purifies, strengthens, elevates and ennobles" all that is authentically human.[3]

Reflecting on the fact that we can only pray as human beings, many questions arise that we hope to address in this book. Given that we are weak and even sinful human beings, how can it be that God has anything to do with us? What does it mean to have a relationship with God? Why is God so silent and hidden? How can we pray in the light of our weakness? How do we grow

---

[2] Thomas Aquinas, *Summa Theologiae*, I, q. 1, a. 8, ad 2: "*cum enim gratia non tollat naturam sed perficiat.*"

[3] Second Vatican Council, *Lumen Gentium* (1964), §13.

in prayer? Does the poverty of our humanity place limits on our union with God?

Because we focus on the humanity of the one who prays, we do not want to discuss prayer only from the heights of abstraction but rather also from the depths of the human experience of being in relationship with God. As Catholic priests and Benedictine monks, we discuss prayer from the biblical tradition, our Christian faith, and our experience of offering spiritual direction, helping people of many backgrounds. We are careful to substantiate our claims with sound Catholic theology, but we also seek to explore the human experience of prayer. The descriptions of prayer experience that we offer are derived not only from our own prayer lives but also from the personal experience shared with us by a significant number and wide variety of spiritual directees. As spiritual directors, we have been richly blessed to gaze into the interior lives of many people, and we share our discoveries through this book in hopes of helping even more people grow in the precious gift of a relationship with God in prayer.

Each human being is in relationship with God the Creator by the very fact of being a creature. Unlike other creatures, however, human beings are persons capable of personal relationships with other human beings, and moreover are capable of knowing God and entering into a mutual and personal relationship with God as well. The more that we can allow our relationship with God to be personal and the more we can intentionally bring our whole lives with all our human messiness into that relationship, the more we participate in Him and become like Him; that is, the more we are divinized.

Vulnerability

When we bring our whole human lives before God, this opens in us a radical human vulnerability. Rather than hiding behind the facade of what we wish we were or what we someday hope to be, we must learn to come before Him as we are. When we open up the depths of our hearts to Him and expose our littleness, our weakness, our uncertainties, our failures, our sins, our big dreams, and our playful plans, we make ourselves very vulnerable before God. This is the key to the most fruitful prayer. This is what makes the messiness of our humanity a path to prayer rather than an obstacle to overcome. In our frailty we have many misleading feelings and sometimes dreams of grandeur; we also have tender expressions of love for our Abba, our Daddy, that can be expressed with the innocence of a little child. We admit that we do not know what we are doing, and we sometimes cry out in the suffering of darkness. We feel our inadequacy, our poverty; we experience the weight of silence and sometimes project our fears onto it. None of this is pretty or impressive, and we fear rejection; but when we can be vulnerable enough to show it all to God, to let Him into it and let ourselves be loved in the midst of it, we experience the transforming power of His love.

Human vulnerability is the unifying thread that passes through all of our prayer. It is the meeting point of God and man. This is because God is vulnerable too: infinitely vulnerable! This is a key to the way in which we are like Him (see Gen 1:27). God's vulnerability is eternally present in the self-emptying filiation of the Son and the spiration of love between Father and Son in the Holy Spirit. There is no love without vulnerability, and God's infinite love is infinitely vulnerable. God never hedges His bets or counts the cost; He gives without measure. This divine vulnerability was already revealed when God exposed His image by placing His "fingerprints" all over His creation. Then He revealed His vulnerability more radically in making creatures with free will, in His image and likeness, who could relate to Him by sharing vulnerably with Him, but who could also choose to reject Him. He fully shared His image with human beings, knowing that they could mar that image so that His beauty would no longer shine so brightly in them or in His creation. After Adam and Eve fled from the vulnerability of being humans in relationship with God and strove to become no longer human but divine—as promised by Satan—God redeemed our sin through extending His vulnerability to us again. He united Himself with human vulnerability through the vulnerability of the Incarnation and became one of us. Ultimately, He revealed His divine power most fully by consummating the Incarnation through the infinite vulnerability of the Passion of Christ His Son on the Cross.

The mystery of the Incarnation united divine vulnerability with human vulnerability and consequently, vulnerability always remains our meeting place with God and facilitates the deepest human and divine encounter in prayer. Throughout this book, we will see how it is vulnerability that draws us and also vulnerability that we often run from; but the more we give ourselves to God through a Godlike vulnerability, the more deeply we will be imbued and sustained by the divine love that God revealed and poured out for us in the vulnerability of Christ crucified.

Contemplation

A traditional approach to teaching about prayer follows the normal chronological stages and development of the average person who prays. It would highlight first the simple vocal prayers of beginners, such as the Hail Mary, Our Father, Daily Offering, and liturgical prayers. The beginner's prayer then generally expands through more sophisticated forms of meditation with their starting points in Scripture and the mysteries of faith. Meditations on the Mass can accompany liturgical prayer and devotions such as the way in which the Rosary and the Stations of the Cross combine vocal prayer with a more meditative approach. As the faith of the one praying grows and personal effort gives way to God's initiatives, prayer moves into a more simple, contemplative form, which leaves behind merely discursive meditation. This fuller stage of contemplative prayer generally begins with some purifications that come in the form of darkness or "nights," to use the language of St. John of the Cross.

Much has been written on all these aspects of prayer. Books have been written with collections of vocal prayers and countless, eloquent meditations. Many classic works have also described in detail the stages of prayer, particularly focusing on the purifications—both why they are necessary and in what they consist, and how they eventuate in illumination or even union or mystical marriage. Fewer books have described the *experience* of prayer as these stages unfold and as a person develops a more contemplative prayer life. All of these other books have their own role to play in guiding the faithful to a deeper life of prayer, but they also have their limitations. The most significant limitation is their potential for fostering some misconceptions about prayer. From reading them, one might fall into the illusion of thinking that prayer is something esoteric or foreign to us for which we need to use special words that can seem more like magical formulae, or that we have to pray in a particular way or follow a particular method in order to pray the best or truest way. A further misconception would be that the development of the life of prayer is strictly linear and that one could measure one's progress in prayer analogously to identifying what grade one is in in school. Another misconception would be that one must be learned enough to read such books in order to become a master in prayer.

Our approach is different. We prefer to describe prayer in a way that is more familiar to our human experience by using the language of personal relationships. Furthermore, instead of seeing contemplation merely as a rarified height of the most advanced students of prayer, we focus more attention on how the contemplative dimension of prayer is foundational and permeates the entire experience of prayer and indeed the whole of the Christian life. It is a real and a universal aspect of all Christian prayer, that is to say, all prayer that is lived as a relationship between finite human beings and our infinite, tri-Personal God. We do not believe that contemplative prayer is a stage of prayer so much as it is a fundamental aspect of all Christian prayer, both individual and communal, and that it grows steadily in the life of everyone. It becomes progressively more and more dominant as the life of prayer grows. It is not an achievement that is reached after strenuous effort so much as it is a consequence of Baptism and the gifts received there in seed form. It is recognized more and more as a gift as it is persistently nourished through perseverance until it grows increasingly into an all-encompassing union of love. As the Catechism of the Catholic Church teaches in the section on contemplative prayer: "One cannot always meditate, but one can always enter into inner prayer, independently of the conditions of health, work or emotional state. The heart is the place of this quest and encounter, in poverty and in faith."[4]

In this view, contemplation can even be part of the prayer of individuals without a developed power of reason or of those who have lost their reason. This is because contemplation is not so much an elite stage of prayer development as it is an aspect of a personal relationship. When we think of prayer in relational terms, we understand how a relationship between a mother and child can be very deep and intense even before words are possible. That relationship continues to grow and deepen through words (from simple sentences to complex conversations) until it may reach another stage of wordlessness in which the mother herself is incapable of speech. The significant dimension of vulnerable, attentive, loving presence persists throughout the whole relationship. That kind of presence and relationship between a mother and her infant is already contemplative and is the best example we can give of "contemplation." Indeed, it is harmonious with the description provided by the Catechism of the Catholic Church.[5]

While it is clear that infused contemplation is a grace that cannot be earned or deserved, we agree with theologians such as Fr. Reginald Garrigou-Lagrange that it is intended for everyone as a normal part of the path of sanctity.[6] When we speak of

---

[4] CCC 2710.

[5] CCC 2709–19.

[6] This is precisely the thesis of his comprehensive two-volume work *The Three Ages of the Interior Life* as stated in the Preface: "We conclude that infused con-

contemplation, we follow the kinds of descriptions found in the Catechism of the Catholic Church and expressed by Doctors of the Church such as St. Francis de Sales, who wrote, "Contemplation is nothing else than a mental attitude of loving, simple, persistent attention to holy things."[7] Further, he explained, "prayer is called meditation until it has produced the honey of devotion; after that it changes into contemplation. . . . Thus, as bees draw nectar from the flowers, we meditate to gather the love of God, but, having gathered it, we contemplate God and are attentive to His goodness because of the sweetness that love makes us find in it."[8] This contemplation is fundamentally a simple gaze of love: "Meditation considers in minute detail and, as it were, item by item the objects that are suitable to excite our love; but contemplation gazes with simplicity and concentration on the object that it loves."[9]

With this in mind, our focus in this book is on the contemplative dimension of prayer, understood as vulnerable, attentive, loving presence in the relationship between God and man. At the same time, we recognize that no Christian is an island—we always relate to God both as "I" and as "We."[10] Our personal relationship with God takes place in a whole context of corporate prayer. We are each an *alter Christus*, another Christ, but we are

templation is, in principle or in theory, in the normal way of sanctity, although there are exceptions arising from the individual temperament or from absorbing occupations or from less favorable surroundings, and so on." Reginald Garrigou-Lagrange, OP, *The Three Ages of the Interior Life: Prelude of Eternal Life*, trans. Sr. M. Timothea Doyle, OP, vol. 1, (St. Louis, MO: B. Herder Book Co., 1947), x.

[7]   St. Francis de Sales, *Treatise on the Love of God* (Blacksburg, VA: Wilder Publications, 2011), Bk. VI, chap. 3.

[8]   de Sales, *Treatise on the Love of God*, Bk. VI, chap. 3.

[9]   de Sales, *Treatise on the Love of God*, Bk. VI, chap. 5.

[10] CCC 26.

also simply members of the great mystical Body of Christ. Thus, our personal prayer is always located within the tension of "the great, unfailing prayer of the Church and the hesitant, groping prayer of the individual ... the millions of the people in the world who pray . . . all their isolated prayers gathered up into one, the all-inclusive prayer of the Church."[11]

In the first part of this book, we explore the foundations and characteristics of the contemplative dimension of prayer. Then from that perspective, and using the concepts developed in the first part, we discuss the various forms of Christian prayer (including vocal prayer and meditation, liturgical prayer, and extraordinary graces) and we show how these can be understood and approached in a more contemplative way. In this way we believe we will best assist those who are earlier in their life of prayer to engage prayer in a way that will most quickly develop its contemplative dimension.

Relationship to Other Works on Prayer

In this book, we hold to all the traditional teachings on ascetical and mystical theology as found in the teachings of the great saints, such as those of St. Thomas Aquinas, O.P. or in the Carmelite Doctors of the Church and synthesized in an excellent way in such treatises as the *Three Ages of the Interior Life* by Fr. Reginald Garrigou-Lagrange, O.P.[12] or in *The Spiritual Life* by Adolphe Tanquerey, S.S.[13] The description of the progression of personal

---

[11] Hans Urs von Balthasar, *Prayer* (San Francisco: Ignatius Press, 1986), 82.

[12] Garrigou-Lagrange, *The Three Ages of the Interior Life.*

[13] Adolphe Tanquerey, *The Spiritual Life: A Treatise on Ascetical and Mystical*

sanctification as passing through stages of purgation and illumination to arrive at union is ancient and well attested throughout the ages. In that development, there is technical vocabulary describing stages of prayer and experiences of prayer that is important for gathering up the wisdom of saints throughout the centuries. We will try to point to those works and reference that vocabulary throughout our book. At the same time, our focus in this work is more psychological and experiential as we focus on the internal experience of the one praying and the way that prayer grows relationally. We are also interested not so much in categorizing and describing universal prayer stages as we are in inspiring our readers to take concrete steps to enter into a deeper relationship with God in prayer. In describing the subjective experience, we hope that we can also give courage to those who are struggling to persevere that they may go deeper into union with God in prayer.

The Greatest of These Is Love

"Being Christian is not the result of an ethical choice or a lofty idea, but the encounter with an event, a person, which gives life a new horizon and a decisive direction."[14] God's love for us and our response of love for Him in return is the beginning and the end of the Christian life. This is not merely a basis for Christian morality but also describes the consummation of our life of prayer. The goal of Christian prayer is not found in extraordinary phenomena such as levitation or extraordinary states of

---

Theology, trans. Herman Branderis, 2nd ed. (Rockford, IL: Tan Books & Pub, 2001).

[14] Pope Benedict XVI, *Deus Caritas Est* (2005), §1.

consciousness such as ecstasy, but rather in the perfection of love. In Christianity, holiness and love are synonymous. St. Paul stated it simply: "Earnestly desire the higher gifts. And I will show you a still more excellent way" (1 Cor 12:31). And he concluded his great chapter on love, "So faith, hope, love abide, these three; but the greatest of these is love" (1 Cor 13:13). Everything in Christianity finds its fulfillment in love, from morality— "he who loves his neighbor has fulfilled the law" (Rom 13:8)—to divine union—"As the Father has loved me, so have I loved you; abide in my love" (John 15:9).

God's love is perfect and has been fully revealed and given to us in Christ. His love is infinite and never changes. The change, rather, must take place in us. The journey of the Christian life involves the gradual transformation of the one who comes to believe in the love that God has for us and steadily opens to that love. As the love of God slowly and steadily permeates the life of the believer, he becomes more like God. This is a journey that requires our active participation in the moral life and also our steady adherence to God's love in our lives of prayer. This journey is the beginning of eternal life (John 17:3) but is only completed when we stand before God and behold Him face-to-Face. That is the perfection of the life of prayer and that is the conclusion of our book. Be sure not to rush to the conclusion, however, because the journey to reach that consummation is essential. We must learn to become more human, and as we persevere in our relationship with God, He will divinize our humanity until we realize and become "what no eye has seen, nor ear heard, nor the heart of man conceived, what God has prepared for those who love him" (1 Cor 2:9). Namely, "We shall be like Him" (1 John 3:2).

Let Us Pray

Not surprisingly, we understand prayer and we grow in prayer best through praying. We hope this book will not simply teach the reader how to pray, but that the reading of this book would be accompanied by prayer. The reader will derive more from praying than from reading, but we hope that reading this book will help to remove some obstacles and open up the reader's life of prayer into an ever-deepening communion with God.

1

Human and Divine Relationship

EACH OF US can experience that in [Jesus's] eyes we are loved, chosen by God, in an extremely personal way. We often have a feeling that God loves in a general way: he loves all men. But being loved in a "global" way cannot satisfy us. And it is absolutely different from the reality of the particular, unique love that God the Father has for each of his children. God's love is personal and individual. God does not love two people in the same way because it is actually his love that creates our personality, a different personality for each. There is a much greater difference between people's souls than between their faces, says St. Teresa of Avila.[1]

As human beings, we are persons, and we are capable of having personal relationships. We are made in the image and likeness of God, who is relationship Himself: an interrelation among three Persons whose love for each other is so perfect that these three

---

[1] Jacques Phillippe, *Thirsting for Prayer* (New Rochelle, NY: Scepter Publishers, 2014), 22–23.

Persons are truly one God. When we were created in His image and likeness, we were created in relationship with each other, male and female, and even more fundamentally, in relationship with Him. From the beginning, God walked with man in the garden. Pope St. John Paul II called this "original solitude" and taught that each one of us is "set into a unique, exclusive, and unrepeatable relationship with God himself."[2]

The most fundamental relationship we have as human beings is with God. Even before our conception, we each are eternally known and loved by God. This relationship with God is the ground and possibility of every other human relationship. Other things will fade away in death, but our relationship with God will remain eternally and will forever be the ground of all our human loves and even our relationship with all creation. When, as has been revealed, creation is renewed and transformed into a new creation, how much more will our deepest loves and human relationships be transformed, individually and communally, in the interpersonal Communion of Love in the Holy Trinity. We do not know exactly what this will be like: "What no eye has seen, nor ear heard, nor the heart of man conceived, what God has prepared for those who love him" (1 Cor 2:9), and yet we know that "this is eternal life, that they know you the only true God" (John 17:3). Eternal life is to know a Personal God. It is a relationship. For all eternity we are called to live in a relationship of perfect Love.

So, the foundational way that we, in our humanity, can begin to enter into prayer is by entering into relationship. The only way

---

2   Pope St. John Paul II, Audience of October 24, 1979, no. 2, in *Man and Woman He Created Them: A Theology of the Body*, ed. Michael Waldstein (Boston, MA: Pauline Books & Media, 2006), 151.

to enter into a relationship with someone is to pay attention to him, to be attentive by focusing on him, but also by remaining in the relationship even when we are not attentive to it. Prayer is focusing on God, turning towards God as another Person, in fact, three Persons. When we are actually living in relationship with someone, we move in and out of attention to that person, refocusing each time we relate actively within the relationship. Fundamentally, prayer is a matter of turning to God over and over again. We turn to Him when we begin to pray, and we renew our prayer by refocusing on Him many times during our prayer time, both in personal prayer and in common prayer. However, this is not something we can only do during our time of intentional prayer, but we extend it throughout our day, in the midst of our daily lives.

While the goal is to turn our hearts repeatedly and continually to the Lord even to the point of an habitual state of recollection, this only happens by also setting aside and dedicating an exclusive, extended, and focused time to cultivate our relationship with the Lord.[3] In that exclusive prayer time, we may do many different things, but the most important thing is just to return our focus to God as an act of prayer and ultimately as an act of love. We do it as an act of prayer by recognizing that we have a relationship with Him as a real other Person, and then by actually entering ever more deeply into that relationship. Unlike many other human relationships, because He is God, we have confidence that even before we turn to Him, He has already turned to us.

---

[3] "We cannot pray 'at all times' if we do not pray at specific times, consciously willing it. These are the special times of Christian prayer, both in intensity and duration" (CCC 2697).

The ongoing experience of prayer is finding out, enjoying, and uncovering all that it means to have and actually enter into a real relationship with God. It is much like a relationship with any other person. Again, we can refer to our humanity as a starting point for understanding prayer. What are some aspects of my human relationships? How can I learn from them to deepen my relationship with God? As prayer deepens, we can learn from our relationship with God how to deepen our human relationships. One key point, as mentioned earlier, is the importance of vulnerability. Relationships only deepen when each person takes the risk to open up more interior and vulnerable areas of the heart to the other and to receive the other's vulnerability with loving attention.

In a loving relationship with a human person, we want to be in that relationship, to be with that person. We want to enjoy, get to know, and love that other person. We enjoy doing things together so that, in deeper relationships like marriage, we do not want to take separate vacations or be away from each other. We realize we are never really apart from each other, because one who is beloved is always in our hearts and on our minds, always a point of reference for us. When we experience something, we might think, "I wonder what my spouse would think of this. I bet she would really enjoy it." In another situation we might ask ourselves the question, "What would my friend do if he were here?" This is not codependence because it is free.

This is how our relationship with God can be and how we can fulfill the command of St. Paul to "pray constantly" (1 Thess 5:17) or the teaching of Jesus, "that they ought always to pray and not lose heart" (Luke 18:1). Love never wearies us (see 1 Cor

13:7). When we deepen our love relationship with God, we start to do more and more with Him, so much so that we freely start to "live and move and have our being" in Him (Acts 17:28). We start to share everything with Him, as with a best friend or like spouses who are deeply united in love with each other.

How to Relate to God

The key is that we need to be sure we do not let God be or remain abstract when we pray. Sometimes we mistakenly think of Him as far away, off in the heavens somewhere. Sometimes He seems like a force or a principle, or as pure energy which we try to incite in some impersonal way. It is impossible to have a relationship with a force or a principle. As Christians, we know that He is personal and not merely an abstract principle, and as we profess, we know that He loves us. Many Christians, however, merely imagine He is around somewhere, that He cares in some way, and that He loves us somehow; but then God remains implicit in our lives and never really becomes explicitly, concretely personal to us. He never actually becomes *real* to us.

Our human relationships provide helpful starting points for us in making our relationship with God concrete. Can we really talk to God? Yes, we can! At first it might seem awkward, but we can begin by talking to Him in the same way we talk to a human being. We use our own language. The way we approach Him or choose to speak with Him will determine the depth of the relationship, just as it does in human relationships. If we treat Him like a stranger, He will remain a stranger to us. If we only share ourselves with Him at a superficial level, the relationship will remain superficial. If we only spend time with Him sporadically, the relationship will remain at the level of acquaintances. If we bring our whole lives to Him and share our fears, our hopes, our wounds, our failures, and our love, then we will see that the relationship opens up more and, because He is God, becomes infinitely deep. In fact, there is no limit to how deep our relationship can be with Him; it is limited only by our own willingness to trust Him and be vulnerable with Him.

When we speak to God, we can start with the kind of words we would speak to a close friend, a parent, or a spouse. One young college student named John, shortly after his conversion and baptism into the Catholic Church, began to attend Eucharistic adoration weekly. Throughout the week he saved his questions and frustrations until he could come before Jesus in the Eucharist. Then he simply spoke his concerns. In some cases, when the chapel was empty, he even spoke out loud. He spoke to Jesus as a friend or as an older brother. He spoke with confidence that Jesus would understand his problems and could answer his questions. After speaking from the heart, he also stopped, waited, and listened. He knew that Jesus would respond in the silence. Jesus did not respond to him in an audible way, but in the silence of his heart he could recognize a truth. Some clarity emerged. He developed a conviction for how to proceed in the various situations in his life. This was an initial form of prayer that developed over the years, but the key was that it was explicit and concrete. Jesus was not merely an idea or an abstract concept, but a real person with Whom he knew he could have a real relationship.

How should we relate with God? How does He speak to us? In our example, we see how John related to Jesus as a wise friend.

Was he merely projecting his needs onto ideas he had of Jesus? John also used his imagination to picture how Jesus would be present to him, listening attentively. John was not afraid that Jesus would get bored with him or interrupt him or walk away because he had learned through Scripture and the Catechism how Jesus wants us to approach Him. Were these merely examples of John's wishful thinking? We are right to be concerned that we not turn God into an imaginary friend or project human qualities onto Him like we would a pet rock!

Such concerns would be valid if God did not exist as a real person, if God were only a figment of our imagination. God is not a blank screen onto which we can project whatever we want, though surely our imagination does project some desirable qualities onto Him in the way in which we understand them and need them. And, truth be told, we actually project imaginatively into every relationship we have, including onto other human persons! We do it all the time, and we project into our relationship with God as much as with any other person. But the reality of who each person really is conflicts with and modifies our projections and preconceptions over time, if we are open in the relationship. God is more real than any other person, and the reality of who He is and how He relates to us leads us deeper into a real relationship with Him. Besides, we believe that God really is Who He says He is, and that He is much, much more than we could ever imagine Him to be.

Indeed, it is impossible for us to know or even imagine Him in His totality. For example, we cannot imagine Him being a better friend than He actually is, or a better brother or a better spouse; because He is infinite, He is the best spouse, friend, brother, and father, far beyond our imagination. We cannot imagine God being more loving than He actually is. He exceeds all our hopes and expectations. So, when John imagined that Jesus was really attentive, and listening and interested in what he had to say, he was perfectly right. In fact, God was attentive and listening and interested in him beyond his wildest desires and imagination, long before he entered the chapel and long after he left.

Because we are partners in a personal relationship, we each bring ourselves into it, including our mind and heart, and so naturally also our imagination, sentiments, and free will! To make our relationship with God as concrete as possible, we use our own language and our imagination. When we use our imagination, this is not make-believe since imagination is an essential part of our human way of entering into every relationship. This process becomes all the more evident when we are relating to realities that are not visible and perceptible in the usual ways. Then our interior senses take over what our exterior senses are no longer able to provide. In this sense, we perceive invisible realities with the interior senses. But the interior senses are always active, even when we are dealing with persons who are visible and who speak back to us in audible ways. God is beyond our sight, but He is still imaginable. Our imagination falls short of the reality of all things, including human persons, and falls radically short of the ultimate reality of God, but at least it moves us in the right direction.

Speaking with God is thus both like and unlike speaking with another human being, but imagining what it is like to speak to another human being is a helpful starting point. We can imagine God looking at us, gazing into our eyes, seeing deep into our hearts. This is not the same as when another human person looks at us, though it is closer to what it is like when a person who really knows us looks into our eyes. If we use our imagination to visualize God giving us a penetrating look filled with love, that will engage our humanity in the right way to help us enter into a concrete encounter with the real and living God.

Placing ourselves in God's loving presence is the starting point that St. Francis de Sales recommended for all of our prayer: "Begin all prayer, whether mental or vocal, by an act of the Presence of God. If you observe this rule strictly, you will soon see how useful it is."[4] He then elaborated on several ways that we can think of the Presence of God: First, that He is universally present; then, that He is profoundly present in our own heart and mind; that we can remember Him in His constant thought about us; and that we can also picture Him next to us like a dear friend. The more concretely we envision our relationship with God, the better our prayer will be.[5]

Infinite Personal Love

Of course, as we speak to God and as we imagine Him, we want to make sure that our imagination is always formed by God's definitive self-revelation found in Sacred Scripture and Tradition. This is where we find the importance of the Word of God, as well as theology and spiritual reading in the formation of our prayer. As Catholic theology teaches us in its synthesis of divine

---

[4] St. Francis de Sales, *An Introduction to the Devout Life* (Dublin: M. H. Gill and Son, 1885), 47.

[5] de Sales, *An Introduction to the Devout Life*, 49–51.

revelation, God has revealed that He is love, and indeed that He is a Trinitarian, relational communion of love so perfect that He is one God. God has revealed through Jesus Christ that He is a loving Father whose love is infinite in His mercy for sinners. He has revealed that He is sovereign, and yet He reverences and sustains our freedom. He has a definite plan for our eternal lives which He realizes by providing for us and drawing us in a way which potentiates our free will. He pursues us like the Good Shepherd (Luke 15:3) and yet gives us space and patiently waits for us like the father of the Prodigal Son (Luke 15:20). Most times our ideas of God are formed too much from our limited human relationships, and we have to allow God to be bigger than those human examples: "The purification of our hearts has to do with paternal or maternal images, stemming from our personal and cultural history, and influencing our relationship with God. God our Father transcends the categories of the created world."[6] Human beings grow impatient, tired, or distracted, and we project those qualities onto God, thinking God is angry, distant, sick of us, or too busy for us. Perhaps our own father had a short temper, but we have to allow God to be greater than the limitations of our human experience. God's patience, focus, endless love, and cease-less pursuit of us are unlike anything we have ever experienced in mere human relationships.

To put this unique relationship with God in perspective, let us begin by realizing that His love for each one of us is infinite. He loves me infinitely. He loves you infinitely. Pray in the face of this unfathomable mystery! Actually, God *only* loves infinitely. He also loves each creature uniquely, as He has created each in

---

[6] CCC 2779.

relationship to Himself. He loves each human being in an absolutely uniquely personal way, in His Heart eternally. So uniquely personal is His love that He loves each one as if each were the only person in the world! Furthermore, He has created human persons with the capacity to be in relationship with Him, participating as a self-gift in His infinite, self-giving love. Our ability to comprehend or imagine this infinite, intimately personal love is limited, but His love is not. He has created us with the dizzying freedom to enter more deeply into His Love, or to deny it and ignore it.

Even more mysteriously beautiful, God's infinite love also makes Him infinitely vulnerable. Love makes the lover vulnerable. He is moved by the Beloved. She brings Him out of Himself. He gives all He is to each one without ever becoming less because He is infinite. He pours Himself out in creating us *in His Image*. He pours out His image and shares His very self with us. He pours Himself out in infinite vulnerability, emptying His divine self to become human (Phil 2:6–8), and becomes one with us in the Incarnation. He pours Himself out totally for us on the Cross as He suffers anything and everything that has ever been suffered for the sake of His Beloved. God becomes radically vulnerable, using all His divine power not to protect Himself but to love more deeply and become more vulnerable to us. And He does this for all, and for each and every one as if each were the only one.

The Incarnation

The Incarnation of Christ and His self-revelation by becoming human incites a deeper awareness of the infinite love God has for us, which might otherwise remain unrecognized in the depths of ourselves. Because of the mystery of the Incarnation, Christian prayer is absolutely unique.[7] We might find some similarities with other religions in technique and experience, but the Christian understanding of prayer is necessarily and essentially different as a result of God becoming flesh in the Incarnation. In other words, prayer is not Christian unless it is incarnational. Anything else is from the anti-Christ, as St. John taught us (see 1 John 4:3). When God became man, He opened up an entirely new kind of relationship with us. In Christ, God and humanity have been joined into the type of union that persons in love long for: as one person! Here we learn the true meaning of God's infinitely personal love for us and our capacity to receive and return this love. The fundamental dynamic in Christian prayer is self-gift, which is the heart of divine love and the height of human love. Furthermore, in the Incarnation, God reveals the intimate communion between Himself and every human person that is possible through the mysterious yet intimate union of the human and divine in Jesus Christ.

Jesus described the height of prayer possible through the Incarnation: "Abide in me, and I in you" (John 15:4). This supreme union is opened up in a person who has been baptized, and is fortified through the sacraments and prayer: "even as you, Father, are in me, and I in you, that they also may be in us, so that the world may believe that you have sent me" (John 17:21). The Incarnation makes this intimate union between God and man possible by forming it first in Jesus Himself who is true God

---

[7] Joseph Ratzinger, *Orationis formas*, October 15, 1989, §11, (at http://www.vatican.va/roman_curia/congregations/cfaith/documents/rc_con_cfaith_doc_19891015_meditazione-cristiana_en.html).

and true man. The union of God and man in Jesus Christ is more intimate than any previous divine initiative toward communion, covenant, or conversation with any patriarch, prophet, or king.

The Incarnation redefines the moral life of the Christian as well as the prayer life of the Christian. The intimate union with the Persons in the Trinity[8] first becomes accessible to every human being through the Sacrament of Baptism and then is renewed and deepened through every celebration of Mass and reception of Holy Communion. This intimate union establishes the moral life of the Christian and redefines our relationships with each other. It is also the heart of the one mystical Body of Christ incarnate, of which we are all members. As members of the same body, we learn not to hate or hurt each other, and even to reverence and love each other. Because we are all incorporated into Christ and thereby into the Trinity by grace not by right, we rely on and help each other rather than striving to overcome one another. We are interconnected in such a way that even though we may feel distant from each other, we are actually interconnected through a circulatory system and a nervous system of grace and love, under the direction of our Head, who is Christ. This interrelationship among us is made possible by the mystery of interrelationships within our Triune God, into which we are drawn by the mystery of the Incarnation. Prayer is the love that flows in our relationship with God, and which flows out into all our interrelationships with the members of Christ's body.

The Incarnation also redefines Christian prayer, in particular through our use of created things in prayer. Far from forbidding

---

[8]   See Adrienne Von Speyr, *The World of Prayer* (San Francisco: Ignatius Press, 1985).

images as He did in the Old Law, in the New Law of Christ God has made Himself the ultimate image by uniting Himself with a visible, tangible human nature in Christ. This invites us to use our imagination to visualize Him, speak to Him, and draw close to Him. At the same time, we do not want to stop at what is imaginable but proceed forth into the transcendent dimensions that surpass our imagination. We already do this, in part, in our human relationships. We know the profound difference between hugging a living person and hugging a dead body. The intangible, invisible reality of the living soul makes an essential difference in how we relate with a human body. In fact, we could say we are really more interested in hugging the soul than hugging the body, but of course we cannot hug the soul without hugging the body. Likewise, with our use of imagination in prayer and even the Sacramental realities in the Church, we want to go beyond what we can imagine and rise up to the transcendent dimension of encounter with the living God. If we stop at the material realities, we make our images into idols. If we pass through the images to the transcendent realities, we allow the images to be icons that bring us into contact with God.

To illustrate the impact of the Incarnation, consider the number of young people whose lives have been radically changed through movements like the Franciscan University Summer Youth Conferences or by movements such as Youth 2000, or the Emmanuel Community's outreach called Nightfever, or many others. The basic structure involves creating a time of praise and worship together in a large group centered on the Exposition and adoration of the Most Blessed Sacrament. We see both aspects of the Incarnation at work in these settings. Firstly, in praying together, those gathered have a profound experience of unity as their unified prayer helps them experience the presence of the mystical Body of Christ. Secondly, the incense, prayers, and other liturgical rites make a tangible impact on the participant as he or she is led by the priest who is in the person of Christ as head of the body, in adoring the Word-Made-Flesh who is substantially present in the Sacrament of the Eucharist. This same model was taken up by Pope St. John Paul II and his successors as a regular part of the final stage of World Youth Days.

One young woman was adoring the Blessed Sacrament at a Festival of Praise and it facilitated a life-changing encounter with Jesus. She had suffered from her father's absence growing up and men had caused much suffering in her life. She was a faithful Catholic, frequenting the Sacraments, but there was a kind of artificial ceiling on her prayer life. Her heart struggled to open up in trust. She met the standards and she continued showing up to everything, but she could not access a deeper ardor in her heart and abandon herself more radically to the Lord. During a time of adoration, surrounded by a fervent worshipping community, after several praise songs directed to Jesus in the Blessed Sacrament, she entered into imaginative prayer in silence. She perceived a glass barrier between her and Jesus. She experienced desire welling up in her heart and a deep longing to break through that glass barrier. It was a barrier of fear caused by past hurts from men in her life. It was a barrier of self-protection and excessive caution that she had needed to keep herself safe. She had grown up too fast because of the suffering she had experienced. But there was a little girl whose heart cried out for a father and in the context of that time of worship, she was able to empower that girl to run into the arms of God. She imagined herself breaking through that barrier and running to Jesus who was on the altar. As the barrier fell, she broke down in tears and experienced a profound healing. She was never the same after that.

The Trinity: Three Persons Drawing Us into Their Union in Relationship

The disciples asked the Lord to teach them to pray. In fact, it is the Lord who leads the way every time we pray, and He teaches us how to pray. Without Him prayer is not possible and without Him we would be simply talking to ourselves or talking to nothing. Jesus becomes transparent and introduces us to our Father in the Holy Spirit, revealing that God is three Persons in one God. In prayer we are taken up into the intimate relationships among the persons of the Trinity. This is the reason why we always begin our prayer with the sign of the cross, making our prayer in the name of the Father, and of the Son, and of the Holy Spirit. Anthony Lilles writes:

> The story of the Trinity at the heart of Christian mystical wisdom has the form of a thanksgiving. An offering of joyful thanks for the glory of the Father by the Son in the unity of the Holy Spirit, this exchange of love in the heart of God is the very source from which proceeds every blessing here below and in the heavens above. Christian contemplation beholds this Eucharistic sacrifice in the heart of God and in this vision is baptized in a meaningfulness and fullness of

life this world cannot contain but yearns to know.[9]

The relationship among each of the divine persons is spousal, each one infinitely pouring out his divine self to each of the other divine persons. This infinite spousal love is so perfect that these three persons are one. The more they are one, the more they infinitely pour out divine love. Thus their spousal love is at once unitive and generative, as is the spousal love of a man and a woman. Our creation was not necessary, but is the generative fruit of the unitive spousal love of each of the persons of the Trinity and of their unity. The more we enter into this spousal love by a finite, total offering of self, the more we become like God, because our finite love participates in infinite love and makes our love more like His, makes us more like God. This prayer is contemplative because it is taken up, beyond appearances, into the very heart of God, into the love of God. For this reason, it is love that makes us like Him.

The Holy Spirit, who is Himself the Love of God,[10] has a special role in prayer. "Through pure grace, the Holy Spirit freely communicates to the soul that humbly welcomes Him what He has received in the depths of God: the blessing of the Father and the thanksgiving of the Son in a transforming harmony of love and knowledge." [11] In this way, the Holy Spirit moves us into greater freedom. The freer our will becomes, the more our will actually becomes conformed to the will of God. This freedom is beyond mere human freedom; it is the freedom of the adopted

---

[9] Anthony Lilles, *Fire from Above: Christian Contemplation and Mystical Wisdom* (Manchester, NH: Sophia Institute Press, 2016), 39.

[10] Rom 5:5; CCC 733.

[11] Lilles, *Fire from Above*, 43.

children of God. Then we experience the Holy Spirit not only leading us in prayer, but praying in us. "The Spirit too comes to the aid of our weakness, for we do not know how to pray as we ought, but the Spirit himself intercedes with inexpressible groanings" (Rom 8:26). One of the authors actually had the privilege of witnessing St. John Paul praying privately. He began with eyes closed praying silently, and then slowly his head would begin to drop. About the time his chin touched his chest he would begin groaning in a low deep way. Then he would fall silent as his head rose and then began to drop again. He seemed to be wrapped in prayer and to have surrendered to the Spirit.

Jesus and the Father

The Bible teaches us much about prayer but nowhere as forcefully as in the prayer of Jesus. The Compendium of the Catechism of the Catholic Church says that "prayer is fully revealed and realized in Jesus."[12] This is because we are fully revealed and fully realized in prayer. The Scriptures present Jesus early on as one who gets lost while praying in the temple (Luke 2:46). Prayer seems to precede His approaching John for Baptism (see Luke 3:21–22), and after the Spirit comes upon Him, the same Spirit then drives Him out into the desert where He is tempted (see Mark 1:12). Jesus cries out in prayer when He is teaching and preaching, such as in His cry of exultation (Matt 11:25–30; Luke 10:21–22), but He also withdraws in prayer, often spending the whole night hidden in communion with His Father (Luke 4:42).

---

[12] *Compendium of the Catechism of the Catholic Church*, Section title for paragraphs 541–547.

He does this especially when He is about to teach or do important things like choosing the twelve or sending them out on mission (Luke 6:12). He also prays when He heals (John 11:41).

What is common to all this prayer is Jesus's total surrender to His Father's will, "His Father's business" (Luke 2:49, NKJV). To do this most fully is to surrender everything. We see this especially in Gethsemane at the moment of greatest anguish in offering the Father everything, though He takes His disciples with Him into the garden to watch with Him, and takes Peter, James, and John to be closer to Him than the others. He still goes off by Himself alone to pray, in the greatest agony and the greatest aloneness anyone has ever known. Anyone who prays in the name of Jesus and in the Holy Spirit, seeking to offer all to the Father, quickly discovers the power in imitating Jesus in going to a hidden place, indeed to the *most* hidden place in ourselves, in order to enter more deeply and intimately into a loving relationship with Him. And anyone who does this discovers the deepest possible communion, in an aloneness like no other and in a oneness with Jesus. This oneness with Jesus is also the deepest intimacy with His suffering and the deepest love.

Yet in the aloneness of Jesus, and in aloneness with Jesus, there is also always the Father, for Jesus and the Father are one (see John 10:30). Actually, all that is brought to Jesus and shared with Jesus is always already shared with the Father (see John 16:15). Properly speaking, we pray to the Father in the name of Jesus, through the power of the Holy Spirit. While we do not have to explicitly mention all the Divine Persons, and while we each usually have a particular one of the three persons to whom we address our prayer, we are really praying in union with all of them in their communion of love. "It is a mystery of mutual, tender selfless love."[13] There is nothing freer than this love. In subordinating our will to the will of God as we pray, we are imitating the spousal love among the persons of the Trinity by which each subordinates Himself to the others.

Dying to Self in Relationship with God

Because of the infinite depths of God, prayer can go deeper beyond what is possible in any other relationship. Indeed, the infinite depths of God can take in our own depth which reaches out into the infinite as deep calls out to deep (see Ps 42:7). To reach these infinite depths, however, it is necessary to die to ourselves and pour ourselves out into God.

All our prayer should always focus on the Lord. This will not cause us to become blind or deaf to what is going on around us or keep us from knowing ourselves. Indeed, by focusing on God, these will be deepened. By focusing on the Lord, we allow Him to shed His light upon us. Rather than looking directly at ourselves, we actually pursue self-forgetfulness. Nonetheless, the light the Lord shines on us as we focus on Him lets us see ourselves indirectly. Indirect self-knowledge is truer than the knowledge we get by navel-gazing or by focusing directly upon ourselves. By concentrating on the Lord, His Presence flows over us, thereby shedding His divine light upon us. In some stages of prayer this can seem confusing because our intellect, our memory, our imagination, and our feelings seem dormant. In

---

[13] Lilles, *Fire from Above*, 44.

those times, this light is mostly experienced as darkness. Deeper recollection means that all of these faculties are drawn together, re-collected. Sometimes God even gives us the grace of infused recollection, by which we enter into a profound quiet which is effortless and obviously has not been produced by us but given by God. But more often, the faculties and even the very self seem to be dying or dead.

When we go deeper into prayer, we discover an enormous depth to ourselves which at some point is discovered to be like a great abyss or void. But, as Romano Guardini writes in his classic work, *The Lord*:

> There are different kinds of voids. There is the void which is caused by the lack of something—the void of non-existence. But there is another void, a void which is vibrant with being . . . Into this void of not seeing, not hearing and not experiencing, there may at times enter something, something inexpressible, yet significant—a hint of meaning amidst apparent nothingness which pre-vails over the nothingness. It happens more frequently than one would expect and one should pay attention to it. This breath, this vibration is the manifestation of God; faint and intangible though it is, it can support faith, so that we may persevere.[14]

Yet it is the avoidance of darkness, dryness, and this abyss that keeps most people from entering into deeper prayer, or into prayer at all. In the depths of ourselves we often encounter great pain and sorrow, and often experience our own negativity and

---

[14] Romano Guardini, *The Lord* (Washington, DC: Regnery, 1954), 37.

depression. Sometimes we have wounds and painful memories. Sometimes we are deeply aware of what we have done and what we have failed to do. Mostly we experience our poverty and weakness. Worst of all, we feel the weight of self, of being who we are. Sometimes we seem complete strangers to ourselves. In all of this, God can seem to be completely absent.

In fact, this deepening entrance into the darkness of ourselves is taking us into the depths of the heart of God. At first the heart of God seems like His complete absence. It takes perseverance in prayer in order to be able to begin to know the Lord in ways that are very unfamiliar to us, ways in which He wants us to come to know Him. These are ways of faith, hope, and love. It is disturbing to us that we cannot figure out what God is doing, and that we seem to be doing nothing. All of reality can seem to us to be without God. This is because we are coming to see God in a new way, in the depths of our darkness which is in the depths of the heart of God, revealed as the Cross of the Son. An infallibly effective way to pray is simply to cry out with all one's heart, begging the Father to hear, as Jesus cried out from the Cross (see Matt 27:46).

All of this requires great surrender and great faith. Self-analysis has to give way, as does self-absorption and all self-preoccupation. Perhaps the deepest fear of all is the suspicion that God is not really here for *me*! But we are not alone in this darkness of the void we find in ourselves, in the emptiness we find in reality. In becoming keenly aware of not only our *own* suffering which we actually begin to forget, but of the suffering of all people, of all life, and of the whole of creation, we realize that the Lord suffers in all of this too. He took all of this into His suffering on the

Cross. He took it into His Sacred Heart which was pierced with our suffering as He hung on the Cross. In this, God's greatest demonstration of weakness, the infinite power of his love, leading even into resurrection, is revealed. So also it is revealed in us and through us in prayer.

When we know the night where what should not be, is, the night of the passion begins.[15] It is the night when the purification and redemption of the human race begins. But, as we have said, there is no place we can be where Jesus is not already present, that Jesus does not already know. At His death He descended even into hell, and more importantly, brought back with Him a redeemed human race. This happens for the individual soul in the purification of prayer. We can never feel that we are entering into a suffering where His Love is not to be found, because in Christ, God entered into all suffering.

"Whoever does the will of God is my brother, and sister, and mother" (Mark 3:35). Mary is the model for this type of prayer, for this type of accepting obedience. She always leads to Jesus, and Jesus invites us to open our hearts to disclose the deepest places in us which reveal His Heart pierced after His crucifixion, in the presence of His Mother whose heart was also pierced. Mary witnessed this as did His beloved disciple, seeing all that remained in Him being poured out. Therefore, we can begin prayer with their witness, for each of us is called to be that beloved disciple, to have her as our mother and Christ as our brother. If our images of God or even of Mary or Jesus are troubled by painful experiences we have had with people in our own lives, the Lord will heal these as we turn to Him and will correct our distortions.

---

[15] Iain Matthew, *The Impact of God* (London: Hodder & Stoughton, 1995), 130.

A good way to facilitate this is to just reach behind and beneath our wounds and to simply press ourselves and our wounds against His wounds. Our ideas of God that are not God will melt away in the fire of His love. He will never expect anything of us that he does not give us the grace and strength to accomplish for He has poured out everything and invites us to do the same *in His* self-outpouring.

How is this possible? Only in Him. What does it look like? Remember, only in trusting like a little child can we do it. It looks like a growing eagerness to accept my life, my death, and what lies beyond my death, *on God's terms.* This gives great peace. Jesus disarmed Peter of his sword in the Garden of Gethsemane so that Peter could truly set aside his will as Jesus, setting aside His own will to obey the will of the Father, suffered in His humanity His infinite self-emptying. Jesus invited Peter to a fuller participation in what He was doing, but out of fear that he would die a miserable death, Peter denied Jesus (see Luke 22:54–60). By meeting Peter's eyes, Jesus disarmed him of his fear (Luke 22:61). Earlier, Peter did not want to let Jesus suffer or die (see Matt 16:22). We must allow Jesus to die on the Cross and allow ourselves to die a spiritual death with Him in order to be able to rise with Him.

This is a death of self, a death that is extremely deep. It begins with the death of selfishness, and it ends with the death of self. The death of the self has its most painful moments in the death of the ego. For our purposes, we can define the ego as the self as we present ourselves or objectify ourselves to ourselves. We discover the ego in how we are always preoccupied with how we come across. Sigmund Freud commented that the ego has ego ideals which project how I must be and appear if I am to be lovable. It is a constant and frustrating struggle for most people to live up to these ego ideals, unless I am so narcissistic as to manage to convince myself that I am already and always the object of everybody's desire. But, in fact, such a narcissistic ego is very fragile. The ego relies on a lot of self-preoccupation, which can lead to pride or selfishness. This can alternate with self-hatred and shame, and some people fundamentally live in fear of or wallow in self-hatred and shame. The ego dies hard, and has a very long and bad death. But freedom from self-absorption is the great gain from this death to self.

As I die to myself more and more, then "it is no longer I who live but Christ who lives in me" (Gal 2:20). Then I want only to do whatever He tells me (see John 2:5). I only want what He wants. We need to take back all the crosses we've given to others, even the crosses that we've given ourselves, and carry the Cross of dying to self. We must deny ourselves, take up our cross and follow *Him*! Instead of imagining we are carrying our Cross alone, we should see Him coming to help us carry it, leading the way to resurrection. This means taking up our cross and not focusing on our cross or on ourselves, but on Him. This means taking up our cross and not feeling sorry for ourselves but rather focusing on Him and letting Him help us.

Entering into the hour of the passion, we encounter Christ sharing His glory with us, letting us share in the love flowing between Him and the Father, into their loving dialogue which is the Holy Spirit (see John 17:24). "If what you heard from the beginning abides in you, then you will abide in the Son and in the Father. And this is what he has promised us, eternal life" (1 John 2:25). This communication of infinite love among the Persons of the Trinity and with us in prayer is not usually expressed in words but rather in the total, infinite outpouring of divine love of the Persons of the Trinity, a love which reveals them as one God. It is in dying to ourselves that we participate in the self-emptying love of Christ in His passion, death, and resurrection, and in so doing, we participate in the life of the Trinity.

The mystery of the finite meeting the infinite is felt nowhere more poignantly than in the infinite longing we encounter in our deepest poverty where we see into the bottomlessness of our desire and find it to be trumped by the infinite immensity of Divine love. As an anonymous Benedictine monk once journaled: "The plenitude of emptiness: the infinitely great and infinitesimal seek and harmonize with each other. The human soul is, in the sense of emptiness and poverty, what infinite perfection is in the sense of opulence. Extremes meet. Scandal and madness, on account of our ignorance, is the contact point where the secret of the Triune God lies, with the weakness of the flesh, with obedience in the face of death, and the silence of the Eucharist. It is through this that infinite life is poured out upon our wretchedness. Oh the happiness of being thus destitute! If I had much, God would be little in me. If I had less God would be more in me. If I had little, God would be much in me. If I have nothing, God is all in me."[16]

---

[16] Jean Petit, *Descending Fire: The Journal of a Soul Aflame* (Manchester, NH: Sophia Institute Press, 2001), 77.

2

Experiencing Prayer as a Relationship

"**P**RAYER IS nothing else but union with God. When one has a heart that is pure and united with God, he is given the kind of serenity and sweetness that makes him ecstatic, a light that surrounds him with marvelous brightness. In this intimate union, God and the soul are fused together like two bits of wax that no one can ever pull apart. This union of God with a tiny creature is a lovely thing. It is happiness beyond understanding." [1]

How to Enter into Prayer

In light of these reflections on prayer as a relationship with God, we can look in more detail at how to enter into prayer. We cannot be overly prescriptive because every relationship has many different moments that call for different initiatives or responses. In our prayer, we are aware of our personal characteristics, such

---

[1] St. John Vianney, *Catechetical Instructions*, "Catechism on Prayer."

as childlikeness, distractedness, self-centeredness, simplistic concreteness, or an abstract analytical approach. We do all these
things in human relationships, and so we bring them into prayer
as well—wherever you go, there you are! We always bring ourselves. Sometimes we are painfully aware of the terrible burden
of ourselves. All of these moments can be experienced in a deeper
way in prayer because the other partner is God.

Having said all that, there are some steps that we can take in
prayer. When we pray, we usually have a starting point. We may
have just read something or pondered some Scripture. We might
start with a particular prayer. We each have our own ways of
starting out. We can think again of the analogy here with human
relationships. When we meet up with someone, we usually have
some initial gesture or greeting, question or introduction. Similarly, we want to make the beginning of our prayer concrete in
our relationship with God. It is not that we have to follow a
certain ritual in order to invoke or summon God to us. This is
not a magical formula or incantation, but is simply the way of
connecting or reconnecting which is a regular part of any relationship. Consequently, it need not be ritual or formulaic, but an
organic human expression.

At the same time, we do not want to underestimate the value
of habits and rituals. Our souls move our bodies, and our bodies
also move our souls. In fact, we could say that a good way to
enter into personal prayer is simply to act as if we are praying. In
that sense, it is like falling asleep. When we want to fall asleep,
we darken the room, lie down, and act as if we are already sleeping, and soon we are! When we want to pray, we enter a chapel,
kneel down, fold our hands, close our eyes, and put ourselves

into a disposition of praying. And soon we are!

In addition to arranging our bodies and our external circumstances, we can also start to arrange our minds and hearts. As we begin to pray, we can use a phrase of Scripture or slowly repeat the name of Jesus. As we settle into prayer it can also be helpful to become aware of our breathing and our thoughts and feelings, since our bodies and minds can tend to be highly stimulated. Depending on how keyed up we are, it can be helpful to slow our minds and bodies down, though we do not have complete control over those parts of our interior. It is more like letting the dust settle or letting the little flakes of snow in a snow globe come to rest. In the Eastern Christian tradition, the slow, quiet repetition of the Jesus prayer facilitates this practice of shifting our attention to the Lord. This consists of repeating the phrase "Lord Jesus Christ, Son of the Living God, have mercy on me, a sinner." We discuss this practice in more length in Chapter 9.

In the monastic tradition, the first verse of Psalm 70 was used: "God, come to my assistance. Lord, make haste to help me."[2] We can also simply use the name of Jesus, or some other way of glorifying God as we call upon Him. While this can be seen as a technique for slowing down our minds, it is important that it not merely be a technique. After all, we pray in order to enter into a relationship with God. Our use of a repetitious mantra like this is distinguished from eastern prayer techniques by our intention. Eastern practices of meditation seek annihilation of self or some vague higher or inner consciousness[3] while Christian prayer is always relational. The use of a mantra can achieve inattention to

[2] See Conference 1.10.10 in Boniface Ramsey, trans. and ed., *John Cassian: The Conferences*, Ancient Christian Writers, vol. 57 (New York: Paulist Press, 1997).

[3] For example, see Ratzinger, *Orationis Formas*, nos. 12, 19.

passing thoughts, but it is not used merely for the sake of having an empty mind. Rather, our purpose in letting go of particular thoughts or words is to make room for the Divine Presence and focus our attention on Him who is greater than every word and every idea. This is also something that can happen through praying the Rosary or other repetitious prayers such as litanies.[4]

In his Catholicism series, Bishop Robert Barron referenced the Buddhist tradition that describes these practices as "calming the monkey mind. The mind is always leaping around from tree to tree, from branch to branch, thinking about this and about that. The mind's always rolling. Well, that mind is not ready for communion with God. It needs to be calmed. That's why the praying of the Rosary can be this calming of your consciousness to prepare you for union with God."[5]

Becoming Vulnerable

Though we have just described some particular practices for entering into prayer, these are not enough in themselves. To develop a deep relationship with God, we must become vulnerable. The best way to open up to vulnerable intimacy with Him is to make a profound act of humility and to open our hearts wide to Him. As explicitly as possible, we should offer our entire selves to Him, every part of us, especially the parts we consider poorest and ugliest. To Him it is all precious. We do this with our mind

---

[4] Fr. Donald Haggerty, *Contemplative Provocations* (San Francisco: Ignatius Press, 2013), 100.

[5] Fr. Robert Barron, "The Fire of His Love," *CATHOLICISM*, episode 9, directed by Matt Leonard (Des Plaines, IL: Word on Fire, 2011), DVD.

and heart, and we also do this with our bodies by our posture. We can enter into prayer with a prostration or spend time on our knees. We can open our arms to signify the openness of our hearts or simply open our hands to express our receptivity. We can bow our heads or cover our heads in humility, or we can even remain prostrate before the Lord.

In fact, there are many ways to open up vulnerably in our relationship with God. In fact, as we persevere, we discover that God is actively trying to open our hearts and draw us into a deeper, vulnerable intimacy with Him. He does that through Scripture, through silence, through receiving our feelings and patiently loving us in our distractions. He loves us in our secret desires and in embarrassing or even painful memories. In this way, our relationship with Him is like any other deep, personal, intimate relationship. We will explore all these dimensions in greater depth throughout the remainder of the book, but we touch on each of them here to see how vulnerability plays a key role in our relationship with God in prayer.

God's word opens our hearts in vulnerability

"He is present in His word, since it is He Himself who speaks when the holy scriptures are read in the Church."[6] This proclamation is true above all in the Liturgy, but it tells us also how powerful the Scripture can be for us in prayer. St. Augustine said simply, "When you read the Bible, God speaks to you." The presence of God and the speech of God open our hearts. We do well to begin prayer by meditating on the words and images drawn from Sacred Scripture. In Chapter 8, we will explore techniques

---

[6] Second Vatican Council, *Sacrosanctum Concilium* (1963), §7.

that help us enter into and apply the images and words of Sacred
Scripture. This meditation mediates a relationship with the Lord
Whom we believe is speaking to us and is actively present to us.
The intellectual, imaginative, and other faculties are at work on
our end to connect as best as possible with the Lord. We experience God speaking through our meditation by showing us how it
applies to us, by giving us a word or working with our imagination, making it an extremely rich and fruitful prayer. As noted in
the Introduction, this meditative prayer may already have a contemplative dimension as God begins to manifest His Presence
and infuse His grace and knowledge in us as we reflect on the
words and images He provides. In response, we may now want to
talk to God in our own words, and to encounter Him even more
directly. This is what St. Ignatius called a "colloquy," and he considered it a necessary part of the spiritual exercises. [7]

Silence opens our hearts in vulnerability

As we try to speak to God, it can seem that no one is there. Sometimes we feel silly talking to someone we can't see and wonder if
anyone is there. In these times, if we simply talk as if someone
were there, as if there were someone listening, soon we will know
that someone *is* listening. As we open our hearts, we begin to
feel we *are* being heard. We start to be aware that we are sharing
more than we knew we had to share, that our very thoughts are

---

[7] *Spiritual Exercises* no. 54 explains the colloquy, and it is prescribed for the daily
exercises thereafter for the duration of the 30-day retreat: "The colloquy is
made by speaking exactly as one friend speaks to another, or as a servant speaks
to a master, now asking him for a favor, now blaming himself for some misdeed,
now making known his affairs to him, and seeking advice in them." St. Ignatius
of Loyola, *Spiritual Exercises*, trans. Louis J. Puhl (Westminster, MD: Newman
Press, 1960), no. 54.

being shaped by someone else, that the sense of a response we have is clearly coming from someone else. As we will discuss at greater length in the next chapter, the language of God is most often silence, the silence of the Word in Whom all words have their meaning. Most often we hear the words as if they are our own thoughts, words, or images, though we know they are much more than our own. We find the lack of words on His part not as evasive or remote, but as clearer and more explicit than any conversation. We know Him in a deeper way than if He were with us bodily and if we could see His face because we know and see from within. We know without knowing how we know.

We also find that God uses silence in the same way that a good spiritual director uses silence. In His patient listening, without interrupting, the speaker finds more being drawn out of his heart. Sometimes we pose important questions, and they are only met with silence. If we do not run from the silence, we slowly start to realize He is not refusing to answer but is going beneath our question and often making it irrelevant because He moves us beyond it. As we wait in silence, savoring what we have received or waiting to receive, we suddenly recognize we are surrounded by supernatural light which is transforming us from within and from without. We realize, in fact that *He* is within and without.

Feelings open up our vulnerability

Ultimately, we want to open up every faculty to Him, every power of our soul: our memory, our reason, our imagination, our emotions, our interior and exterior senses. In other words, our hearts, minds, and souls (see Matt 22:37). We can express sorrow for our sin and make acts of love. We can talk to God in our own words and we should prolong our communication to express everything we want to say. We should make the thoughts and sentiments of our hearts as explicit as possible. There may be some feelings that rise up, such as fear or sadness. Whether or not we know the reason for it, the best thing is to open it to God and show all this to Him. By talking with Him like we talk to an intimate friend, we will begin to process the feeling and work through it as it unfolds the more we talk about it. We are not merely engaging in introverted introspection as long as we hold it out to Him. Include God in the conversation. I am praying whenever I bring God into my interior conversation or inner life, and whenever I look at what is happening in me *together with God.*

Distractions can open up our vulnerability

Here again we can draw insight from human relationships. Sometimes we ramble on about ourselves as if it does not matter whether anyone were listening, let alone the particular person that is in front of us. Such self-absorbed prattling is neither helpful for human relationships nor for prayer! In true, intimate communication, we are aware of ourselves and what we are sharing at the same time as we are aware of the other person with whom we are talking. Indeed, it is even better when we can start to focus more on God than on what we are sharing. In this way, we may even start to lose track of ourselves and lose ourselves in Him. In fact, that is the ideal! The deepest forms of prayer move into silent communion in which I look at Him and He looks at me.

But we all know how easily we can get distracted or have difficulties focusing our minds on God. Often this is just a natural movement of the mind which does not want to be settled or to focus on what seems to be nothing, but to move on to roam and find something more interesting and entertaining. There is something in the mind and imagination that abhors a vacuum! The desert fathers described the mind as being like the great spinning grindstones in a flour mill.[8] Those stones are mighty wheels that keep turning to grind up whatever is put into them. If they go dry, the stones can be damaged, so the miller feeds them constantly with wheat. The mind behaves likewise, drawing more grist for the mill from the memory and imagination. By sprinkling in a few wheatberries, like in the Jesus prayer or a gentle repetition of Scripture or refreshing of an image from prayer, we can prevent our subconscious processes, and also the demons, from throwing weeds in amongst the wheat.

Even with a little grist for the mill, however, we find ourselves weighed down by our human frailties. We try to sit quietly and focus on the Lord, but we find ourselves fidgeting—aware of the tightness of our back—or we end up squirming uncomfortably in a chair that never seems comfortable enough. What are we afraid will happen if we stop fidgeting? The best thing to do is just invite God into that, into the fidgeting, into the squirming, and lift it all up into Him. It might help to envision ourselves as a squirmy three-year old-child who is totally focused on himself but who suddenly realizes someone is watching him, and he becomes sheepish and vulnerable. This can be a moment of intimacy in childlike vulnerability before God. We can realize Christ is watching and loving us with delight and attention. We can realize we are seen and loved.

A man named Bill was struggling with a sense of urgency to

---

[8] See Conference 1.1.18 in Ramsey, *John Cassian: The Conferences.*

get up and leave. He continually looked at the clock to make sure he would leave in time for an appointment. He even thought, "Maybe I should leave early so I don't lose track of the time and arrive late." Then he became aware of this inner struggle and decided to bring this anxiety to the Lord. When he did, he gained a deeper insight into the urgency he had felt. He remembered an experience from his childhood and realized he had a residual fear of being left behind or a fear of being forgotten. Then, instead of leaving, he held out this longstanding fear to God and experienced tender love, understanding, and healing. If he had left early, he would have missed this opportunity. Instead, by offering this fear to the Lord, he could feel that God was somehow speaking into his heart saying, "I will never leave you behind. I will never forget you!" Having found God already in the place where that deep fear lies, he could rest there and be healed, and he learned to relate to God in a deeper way.

Our deepest desires open up our vulnerability

Another deep place within us is the place of our secret desires, our hidden dreams or our disappointments. We might spend more time than we are aware of dreaming of being a hero, a superior, or a powerful official who is loved or desired by everyone. Even though we have long dwelt in these places, sometimes we have never shared them with the Lord or anyone else. Sometimes this is because we have been taught that those desires are forbidden or intolerable and will make us unlovable. We may have hidden all this so deeply that we never realized the anxiety and defensiveness that came from it. That leads us in turn to be afraid to enter more deeply into prayer because we do not want to bring this desire or aspect of ourselves to God, because we are ashamed of it. When we are hiding or burying shame, we become anxious and resistant to prayer, especially to listening in prayer, because such prayer can expose all of this. But as we come to believe in God's unconditional love for us and as we let Him see these desires, we will also come to see how He forgives and heals, how He accepts us and helps us accept ourselves. A Benedictine monk and priest recounts from his private prayer how Jesus said to him, "You do well to give Me everything . . . I have set My Heart upon you. Love Me, and show that you love Me by giving Me all things. Nothing is too small for Me and nothing is too great."[9]

Deep memories and sins open up our vulnerability

Our memories can also have places where we do not want to go. Behind the defensive wall of his achievements and self-sufficiency, a man may find a little boy who was told by his father that he was "useless" or who never felt successful enough to capture the attention of the more popular kids in class. Behind her defensive wall of vanity or talkative sociability, a woman may find a little girl who never felt pretty enough or felt she was too boring or uninteresting. These hurt memories and experiences are hidden, and our avoidance of them in prayer as well as anxiety over entering into deeper human relationships often is a fear of exposure. Often the pain is sealed in an embarrassment which feels like unspeakable shame. But in those hidden places God is already present, and if we find Him there, an intimacy ensues that goes even deeper than between friends who share their deepest,

---

[9] A Benedictine Monk, *In Sinu Jesu: When Heart Speaks to Heart—The Journal of a Priest at Prayer* (Kettering, OH: Angelico Press, 2016), 77.

darkest secrets. Our God loves us in these places. In fact, it will seem to us that He loves us there most of all.

Another hidden place in us is the unacknowledged sins which we may not want to remember or take credit for. Maybe we feel they are unforgivable. Maybe we have been told they are unforgivable. In our wretchedness, we bury our sin, but Jesus has told us that the friend hides nothing (John 15:15). God hides nothing from us and wants us to hide nothing from Him. These places or tendencies, so abhorrent to us, seem to be the places where we can potentially know God loves us more than we could have ever realized before. As we prayerfully dwell in those places with Him, we realize we are loved infinitely more than we knew, and that He truly loves us there where we have been most ashamed, and that He forgives. Vulnerable interior prayer now develops in us in a deeper and more personal place than ever.

All of these pathways to deeper vulnerability in prayer are related to similar pathways in human relationships. Overall, we see that the key is simply to share our entire lives with God. Love always seeks totality, and by sharing the most vulnerable parts of ourselves with Him, we start to see how prayer gradually flows out into every aspect of our lives.

Growth in Vulnerability and Trust: Transformational Prayer

Continuing our reflection on the similarities between human relationships and the human-divine relationship of prayer, we can gain insight by looking at the dynamics of human conversations. In her book *Conversational Intelligence*, Judith Glaser reported the results of years of research in the neuroscience of human interactions. She identified three levels of conversation and distinguished them based on the way they impact our brains. These levels of human conversation are not only helpful for understanding the quality of our human-divine conversation in prayer, but analogously also for understanding the levels of relating and vulnerability. The basic metric that distinguishes each level of conversation is the level of trust between the conversation partners. In prayer, that boils down to the level of trust that we have in God, since His trust in us is already infinite.

> **Level I: Transactional Conversations** often can be categorized as "Tell and Ask" interaction dynamics. People are exchanging information, updates, and facts that help us align our realities or confirm we are on the same page. There is not a lot of trust, and people are focusing more on what they need to get from each other to validate and confirm their view of reality. [10]

This describes the most basic form of prayer. We ask God for things. We ask Him for answers. We try to use Him to achieve our own ends. We view God as being very foreign, and we have a low level of trust because we do not really know whether He loves us. Because of our lack of trust, we often only ask God for things that are general or which we do not desperately need, or we go to Him only after all our own efforts have failed. We basically treat God as an oracle, seeking information or favors from Him that would give us an advantage in life, but we are unwilling to take

---

[10] Judith Glaser, *Conversational Intelligence: How Great Leaders Build Trust and Get Extraordinary Results* (New York: Routledge, 2016), 69.

any risks with Him. At its worst, we try to manipulate God into serving our agenda rather than placing all our agendas in service of Him.

To be sure, there is a place for Level I conversations between humans as there is a place for Level I conversations with God. Just as human conversations start with sharing simple facts and validating personal understanding, God also invites us to ask Him things and tell Him things. When a human conversation remains at this level, however, it starts to be more like an interrogation or like a dictatorship where there is no freedom and no mutuality. This leads to the release of stress hormones and creates an increasingly uncomfortable defensiveness. We don't want to stay in Level I conversations for an extended period of time.

> **Level II: Positional** These conversations are characterized by "Advocate and Inquire" interaction dynamics. In a Level II conversation, I am advocating for what I want (not just telling you) and I am inquiring about your beliefs so I can influence you to my point of view. Trust is conditional. If I feel you have my back and will not try to steamroll me or win at all costs, I will move into higher levels of trust. However, if I feel that you are not going to be fair or are lobbying at my expense, I will retreat into protective behaviors. Conditional trust raises the levels of uncertainty, which can also trigger the fear networks (Can I open up or not? Can I trust or not?). [11]

At this level of prayer, we are entering into more of a relationship with God. We still want to further our own agenda, our

---

[11] Glaser, *Conversational Intelligence*, 69.

own will, but we feel that God at least listens to us. We might be able to convince Him that our idea is good and that He should help us. We are approaching Him like a boss or a benevolent master. We are trying to get what we want, but we are willing to express it in terms that we think would be acceptable to Him. We believe that He will listen to our arguments, and if we can clothe it in Christian language, He might be willing to do our will. There are memorable accounts of prayer in the Scriptures that are Level 2 conversations. Think of Abraham trying to convince God to save Sodom and Gomorrah (see Gen 18:16–33) or Moses bargaining for his people (e.g., Num 14:11–25) or many of the Psalms which try to leverage God's covenant with His people (e.g., Ps 74:20–23).

At this level we are also willing to listen to God, but in a limited way. We are looking for answers or looking for results. We want to know if we should take a certain course of action or handle a situation in a particular way. We are not looking into the Heart of God, and we limit the way that He could give Himself to us. This is not "bad" prayer, and it is an important part of human conversations as well. It helps us to get on the same page with each other. It even seems to be the kind of prayer that was lauded by Jesus when He spoke of the persistent widow as an encouragement not to give up in our prayer. He summarized that parable saying, "'And will not God vindicate his elect, who cry to him day and night? Will he delay long over them? I tell you, he will vindicate them speedily." But then he added, "'Nevertheless, when the Son of man comes, will he find faith on earth?'" (Luke 18:7–8). It takes faith to persist in our cries for justice. It takes greater faith to surrender everything to the will of God. Jesus

Himself gives the example of a Level II conversation with the Father in His Agony in the Garden when He sweats Blood as He begs the Father, "Father, if you are willing, remove this cup from me" (Luke 22:42a). He then opens that to a Level III conversation with a deeper trust and surrender, "Nevertheless, not my will, but thine be done" (Luke 22:42b).

> **Level III: Transformational** conversations are marked by "Share and Discover" interaction dynamics. When I share first, my brain receives a cue that I will be vulnerable with you and that I will open up my inner thoughts, ideas, and feelings. Others in the conversation receive the signal that you are willing to be influenced, that you care about them, and that they can trust you to experiment and innovate with them. As we share and discover, we become "mentors of the experiment," and we will be able to co-create with one another to achieve greater shared success—far beyond what we ever imagined.[12]

The highest level of conversation and the highest level of prayer are characterized by the highest level of trust. At this level, we actually believe that everything about us is valuable to the person with whom we are speaking, especially the most interior parts of us. Our conversation partner wants to know our thoughts and our feelings, even things that might seem trivial. We can share in a way that we are not afraid of being judged for saying the "wrong" thing or feeling the "wrong" thing. We can open up our dreams, our desires, our fears. Anything can be shared, and it will be received with reverence and genuine appreciation. It

---

[12] Glaser, *Conversational Intelligence*, 69.

is even better when we can enter into a conversation in which that experience is mutual. That is the deepest form of friendship. "No longer do I call you servants, for the servant does not know what his master is doing; but I have called you friends, for all that I have heard from my Father I have made known to you" (John 15:15). Jesus wants us to share *everything* with Him, and He shares *everything* with us if we let Him. In order for this to happen, however, it is important that we let down our guard, set aside our agenda, and open our hearts in love.

A consecrated man named Bernard discovered this transition after many years of consecrated life. He certainly had many transformational moments in prayer during his life, but after a meeting with his spiritual director, he had a moment of understanding and made a more fundamental shift in his approach to prayer. At the next spiritual direction meeting he declared joyfully to his spiritual director that he was taking a completely different approach to prayer. His prayer had consisted largely of Level I and Level II conversation. He was saying rote prayers very faithfully, and in his times of meditation he focused on particular difficult situations. There were troubles in the community and difficulties in his own friendships. He was discerning how to proceed and looked to God for help in handling the struggles. But then he made a shift, and instead of looking for something in particular from Jesus, he opened his heart and shared himself. He simply extended his aching heart to Jesus without looking for answers. He let himself feel the disappointment that his community was missing some elements and his own friendships were not as deep as he had wished. As he remained in the Lord's presence with all that on his heart, he began to feel some peace. He did not get answers to his questions or solutions to his problems, but in the end they all seemed less pressing and he was able to trust in God more deeply. He discovered that the answer is always Jesus. Jesus does not want to tell us something so much as He simply wants to give us Himself, to draw us more personally into relationship with Him. This is a transformational relationship that is also deeply and increasingly contemplative.

Prayer Transformed by Listening in Silence

In our sharing with the Lord in prayer, it is also important to leave space for listening. The first stage of listening is just being aware of Him as we are sharing our hearts. Our awareness includes an awareness of His Presence, His attention, His tender listening to our sharing, His posture of mercy and acceptance toward us. In human relationships, we feel loved when a person listens to us lovingly, even without saying anything. Our first step of listening is not so much trying to hear what He is saying but simply becoming more aware of God's loving attention towards us. After soaking this in, we can use the rest of our time in prayer for pouring our hearts out and listening. We should listen at least as much as we talk to God. While listening for Him, it is most important not to wait for anything in particular, such as words or signs, but simply to wait in loving receptivity. We are like baby birds awaiting a worm from the mama bird. "Open wide your mouth and I will fill it" (Ps 81:10). Sometimes we feel we are holding our mouths open for a long time and wondering if the mama bird will ever come. It can be difficult holding ourselves open and waiting for God. This is a very vulnerable position, and our attention is difficult to sustain. The word "attention" has the same root as "tender," "tendon," and "tension." The ancient root word, "ten" means "to stretch." We are stretching open our secret, darkest places to God who sees in secret and always fills with love.

The second step of listening involves entering into silence, which we discuss in more detail in the next chapter. As we open our hearts to the Lord, we can leave some silence for Him to respond. The response may come in different ways. As our relationship with God develops and becomes more personal, we become more aware of the ways that God responds to us personally, which may be different than the ways He responds to other people. Indeed, listening in silent love allows us to develop a new "love language," in which we not only listen for the special words of love we have developed together, but in which words are no longer necessary.[13] His response may come in the form of some insight which we may or may not be able to put into words. Sometimes it is simply a peace that rises up in our hearts, or we find that an image comes to us and possibly an interpretation of how that image applies to us. Other times we start to see a situation or a person differently, from God's perspective. We might sum up the ways in which God speaks to us by talking about "recognition." We come to a recognition deep within ourselves of how God is responding, perhaps how God sees things. This recognition is usually accompanied by peace. As we await some response, it is important that we simply focus our loving attention *on Him*.

In developing an ability to recognize God's voice and learning

---

[13] Haggerty, *Contemplative Provocations*, 62.

to listen to Him, journaling is helpful for many people. Especially for people who easily wander in their thoughts, journaling can help them to keep a more linear focus. It should have all the qualities discussed above—vulnerability, openness, sharing the deepest parts of our hearts, expressing our feelings, etc. The one praying should also be focusing on the Lord in prayer much more than on the journal. One must be careful not to get so caught up in writing that focusing on this task pushes God out of the process. A very helpful way to journal that deepens our personal relationship with the Lord is to address the journal to Him. This keeps us from writing the journal from the perspective of how others might think of us if they should read it, or if the journal should be read as part of our canonization process! After expressing our hearts in our journal, it is still important to leave further room for listening. It can even be helpful to try to write God's response in our journaling. We do not claim to become an oracle or a scribe for God in this, but allowing God's communication to us to be more concrete can be a great help.

As expressed earlier, we know that God will only communicate to us in ways that are in harmony with how He has revealed Himself to the Church through Scripture and Tradition, and this supplies a basic check on what we are writing. If we are recording things we feel have been spoken or revealed by God, we should not let them give us a sense of entitlement or make us focus more on ourselves. What God may actually be saying to us needs to be confirmed over time or in spiritual direction. Primarily, these inspirations should serve to deepen our listening to God and our communion with Him, rather than merely giving us lots of information. We should strive to make these journal entries part of a

Level III conversation.

Sometimes we wonder why God does not speak more loudly, more clearly. In fact, He does say some things very loudly. There are certain universal truths that are absolutely necessary for us to survive and grow in human society and God has written those on every human heart. As the Catechism states it, "The natural law, present in the heart of each man and established by reason, is universal in its precepts and its authority extends to all men."[14] The Catechism even follows that with a quote from Cicero to demonstrate the universality of this knowledge. Because our minds have been darkened by sin, God needed to reiterate this law, and He did so on Mount Sinai as He gave the Ten Commandments to Moses. When speaking that universal and fundamental truth, His voice came in thunder and lightning and was heard like a trumpet blast that made the people tremble (see Ex 19:16). The truths He spoke on Mount Sinai were necessary to provide the simple conditions for us to grow as a people and ultimately develop a personal relationship with Him, but they did not contain all the love that He wanted to share with us nor draw from us the love we are capable of giving to Him.

Love requires freedom. If God always spoke in such a thundering way that scared us into compliance, He would never leave the room we need for freedom, and without freedom there is no love. This is why God also speaks in whispers. When it comes to our personal calling, words of love meant for us alone, direction for specific situations or guiding us in the choice of two goods, His voice can be so quiet that we cannot hear it. That is to say, we will hear His voice only when we are ready to hear it, when

---

[14] CCC 1956.

we have already aligned our freedom with His will. We will discover that the call to marriage is most clear when it is also our desire. We will discover that we hear God drawing us to make a hard choice when we are finally ready to make that choice. This reminds us of the appearance of God to Elijah, not in the wind, the earthquake or the fire, but finally in "a still small voice" (1 Kgs 19:12). The personal word God spoke to Elijah could only be received in freedom, not imposed from without but quietly resonating in a heart that had been aligned to God's designs from within.

Ultimately, the language of God is silence, and it is only by allowing all the noise to settle in us that we are able to receive the Truth that God wants to communicate to us in prayer. Letting the noise settle and letting our hearts be filled with silence takes time, especially if one is living a noisy, busy life. It is important for us to speak to God from our hearts, but when we start going in circles, we need to stop and listen. None of this is a mechanical process, but rather it is guided by the Holy Spirit. He gently guides us in knowing when to speak and when to be quiet. "The Spirit helps us in our weakness; for we do not know how to pray as we ought, but the Spirit himself intercedes for us with sighs too deep for words" (Rom 8:26).

As our prayer develops, as with human relationships, the tendency over time is to move toward fewer words. We should not force this to happen artificially,[15] but we should also not be disturbed if we find ourselves needing fewer and fewer words. The

---

[15] Forcing oneself into premature silence, a kind of pseudo-contemplation, is the underlying problem of the Quietist heresy. It is also underlying the problems with the pseudognosticism of non-Christian forms of meditation as described in Ratzinger, *Orationis Formas,* no. 19.

key is that we are still very open and vulnerable in our prayer, exposing our hearts and sharing everything with Him. Likewise, our awareness of His Presence and His Love remains and grows stronger until we find ourselves mutually vulnerable with Him, open and loving in the silence of perfect love. No matter how much we grow in silence, however, it is always possible and desirable that I continue to speak to the Lord whenever that seems like the best way to draw closer to Him in love.

As this silence develops and our prayer transitions, it can lead to some difficult periods of purification. We can see this also in human relationships. As we have seen, at first we tend to project past relationships onto new ones. As relationships deepen, we see people more as they truly are and begin to interact in unique ways in this new relationship. Also, qualities that we overlooked at first may start to irritate us. Qualities in ourselves may start to emerge and enter into the relationship. Sometimes they cause problems. There is a need to transition into a more nuanced way of expressing ourselves that stretches us and makes us more sensitive and aware in ways we never were before. We have to learn to apologize for our shortcomings or forgive others for their failures. We learn how to leave space for others and to pick up on their more subtle cues. The key is that we cannot cling to the way we used to communicate. We have to let the relationship develop. The same is true in prayer. If we try to cling to our old way of communicating or imagining or meditating when the Holy Spirit is trying to lead us in a new direction, then we will prevent the relationship from developing.

Persevering in Prayer

The most important thing in order to grow in prayer and in our relationship with God is to begin to pray. The second most important thing is to continue, to persevere in prayer. The vow of stability taken by men and women living under the Rule of St. Benedict reflects a quality that every person should have. Perhaps more in our time than ever, there is a need for us to grow in stability. We move around so much sometimes because we are so afraid of being stuck or trapped! We also move around to chase illusions, because we are afraid that life is better somewhere else. The fear of missing out makes us restless. The same temptations face us when we settle into a dedicated time of prayer, but the only way to grow is through stability and perseverance. Stability and perseverance are just as necessary in prayer as in any other relationship that is going to develop.

One of the authors' mothers told the story of when she was a child and a stray cat birthed a litter of kittens under the porch, which, to say the least, were unwanted. Eventually her father boxed the kittens and went out and threw the box over a bridge to drown them. By the time he got home, the kittens were on the front porch waiting for him. They had clawed their way out of the box, swam to safety, and found their way home. They were only following their instincts for survival, but would that we had their determination! Would that we would seek the home for which we yearn with what is much more than an instinct; indeed, it is a burning desire for God. Instead, we shape that desire into other desires of all sorts. These desires destabilize us.

Abide in Him

The Gospel of John records Jesus's repeated invitations to us, most compellingly right before He instituted the Eucharist, to abide in Him. We know that God does not change. Everything else does. All around us is flux. In our times we have developed an incredible capacity to assimilate change, though at the same time we always feel rushed, always feel out of time, feel that time and life are slipping away. We are ambivalent about this, in the sense that while we clamor for change, we resist it when it comes. Only God does not change. The radical insecurity which we feel makes the interior life almost impossible. Our busyness is a way of pushing God away, keeping Him at arm's length. We'd prefer that God stay almighty and powerful in heaven rather than for Him to be in our midst. We would rather God work from the outside of us than from the inside of us.

To abide in Christ means to allow Him into our lives so deeply that we develop a union with the divine persons of the Trinity. It means to persevere in trusting Him and obeying Him. "If a man loves me, he will keep my word, and my Father will love him, and we will come to him and make our home with him" (John 14:23). This deep union slowly becomes a mystical reality; it is the fullness of the contemplative dimension of all prayer. Mystical does not mean less real, it means more real than ordinary reality. Likewise, a deeper contemplative prayer is not more abstract but more concrete and real, going right to the heart of everything. To live from this heart, we have to be willing to allow passing attractions not to make us fickle and easily distracted. How can we ever gain confidence in God and overcome our insecurity if we do not stay still long enough to hear Him, and become quiet enough to know what He is saying. When we do, grace is all around us. Detachment from passing things becomes second nature. These are the dispositions we assume when we pray, which ground us and center us.

St. Benedict spoke of gyrovagues who are so busy moving around and following their own will that they never settle in one monastery for long.[16] We are a bunch of gyrovagues! We all have a restless tendency to compare ourselves constantly with others, especially comparing what we have and what we don't have. This leads to complete instability and destroys any sense of focus. No wonder we are scattered! No wonder we are tired! The real problem may be that we do not trust God. We do not trust in His love, in His plans for our lives, in His Providence for all of our needs. Jesus made a promise when He declared, "I came that they may have life, and have it abundantly" (John 10:10). Prayer is abandoning ourselves to God with radical trust, and then remaining there in attentive vulnerability.

Abiding in vulnerable, trusting attentiveness leads to a disposition of obedience. This leads to bonding with the Trinity just as it leads to the bonding necessary for community. Community grows because we stay long enough to bond deeply with people. Above all, we become rooted not only among the people we are with, in the family, community, society, or church, but we become rooted in Christ. Many lessons can be learned when we grow in inner stability. The complaints that we cannot find the presence of God start to dissolve into finding Him everywhere.

---

[16] See Timothy Fry, O.S.B., trans., *The Rule of St. Benedict in English* (Collegeville, MN: Liturgical Press, 2018), 1:10–11.

Abiding in God does not take away human freedom! It teaches us how to surrender. In our fallen nature, we are born with an instinct and a desire to be our own masters. Nonetheless, we are capable of freely disposing our will to submit to the mastery of another. This happens in marriage, and in many other ways such as in family, in community, and in other relationships. It can happen most radically with God, and then we find ourselves in the present moment where God acts. Disheartened despair comes from always dwelling in the past or future. Finding life as gift in the here and now brings us to the heart of reality, to the Incarnation, the mystery more real than any reality, the Word made flesh.

This means facing ourselves, which inevitably means the need to embrace our poverty. Fear is often our worst enemy; what we usually fear most is ourselves. To face ourselves allows us to move beyond fear and find ourselves in Christ. We are created in the image and likeness of God. We were created by God out of nothing, and without God we become nothing. But God, like an attentive mother, is always listening. If we listen with the ears of our hearts, we will hear the word of the Lord and we will know Him in the abiding peace He gives us. Like a good mother who loves each of her children best, God loves each one of us as if each one of us were the only person in the world; He loves each one of us best! But we have to persevere in prayer before we can see that He is trying to show us this.

When we pray, we should seat ourselves at the lowest place, that is, at the lowest place in our hearts:

One time in prayer I faced the Scripture passage where Jesus advises his listeners not to vie for the highest place at the head of the table but to go and take the lowest place (Luke 14:7-11). . . . Then the Lord seemed to be inviting me to be more explicit about this, to actually do what he says here. I knew he probably wasn't asking me to actually go and take the seat farthest to the rear of the chapel in which I was praying alone . . . He wanted a response from my whole heart, with passion. So, in my heart I went to the lowest place I could find. How sweet and quiet it was, though rather lonely at first—waiting there, listening there. It seemed as if a long time passed, and then I remembered the further promise of Jesus that the one who invited me will come and say, "Friend, go up higher" (Luke 14:10). At that moment, in my prayer, there he was, very close, beckoning me to come not so much higher as closer.[17]

We can even take the lowest place in all of creation. "Then it occurred to me that I could ask the favor of being the last one seated at his banquet table in his kingdom at the end of time, being the one responsible to be sure first of all that every other person has been seated."[18] We can even consider ourselves less worthy than the fallen angels and lower than the worst sinners, even lower than Satan himself, lower than all God's creatures. Then we must stay there. We discover something true about ourselves there. We are capable of the worst things. We have the capacity to commit atrocious evil, but it is by the grace of God, and of course with our cooperation, that we have been preserved

---

[17] Thomas Acklin, *The Passion of the Lamb: The Self-Giving Love of Jesus* (Cincinnati, Ohio: St. Anthony Messenger Press, 2006), 25–26.

[18] Acklin, *The Passion of the Lamb*, 26.

from that, as St. Therese expressed in the concluding paragraph of her autobiography:

> But above all I imitate Mary Magdalene's behavior, her surprising—or rather her loving—audaciousness that charmed Jesus' Heart and captivates mine [Lk. 7:36-38]. Yes, I feel it. Even when I might have on my conscience all the sins that can be committed, I would go with a heart broken with repentance to throw myself into Jesus' arms, because I know how much He cherishes the prodigal who comes back to Him [Lk. 15:20-24]. It's not because God, in His kind mercy, has preserved my soul from mortal sin that I rise and go to Him in confidence and love. [19]

From the lowest place we can stop proving ourselves, acknowledge our terrible nothingness and then from there we cry out in our poverty! How could God not hear this cry? How could He not answer it? Surely He would have forgiven even our first parents had they asked, had they come out of hiding, had they disentangled themselves from the illusion that they could take the place of God, and if they had been willing to beg forgiveness like creatures, like children. Surely He would have forgiven them.

Challenges to perseverance

There are many different moments in any relationship. In any relationship or community, indeed in any communication with a person there are moments of distraction, transparency, intimacy, revulsion, doubt about the other person, deep love. There are

---

[19] St. Thérèse of Lisieux, *The Story of a Soul*, trans. Robert J. Edmonson (Brewster, MA: Paraclete Press, 2006), 296–97.

times when we feel a deep sense of being understood by another person, and times when we feel neglected or hurt. We may be in awe at the mystery of another person, or feel the relationship to be a waste of time. We can still feel alone despite being in the presence of another person. There are moments when we never want to leave persons with whom we are in relationship or communities to which we belong, and other times when we can't wait to get away from them. There are moments of deep peace. Just as these conflictual moments can be in human relationships, so they can be found in prayer because prayer is a human relationship. Those moments result from the fragility of our humanity because we always bring our human self into our relationships. Sometimes we are painfully aware of the burden of self. At the same time, we experience all of these moments in an even deeper way in prayer, because the other partner in that relationship is God. Fortunately, God who initiated our relationship with Him also provides for and sustains it.

Sometimes it seems that we are the ones doing all the work in our relationship with God. Because God speaks the language of silence, yet because this can leave us feeling exposed or empty, we feel that we need to keep the conversation going. We imagine that if we did not take the initiative and enter into prayer by striking up a conversation, prayer would just fade away and die out. The reality is that God is constantly attentive to us, always seeking us out, always drawing us and at the same time always waiting for us. This is illustrated beautifully in the three stories in Luke 15 that St. Ambrose associated with a threefold remedy for our wounds carried out by the Church and the Persons of the

Blessed Trinity.[20] In the parable of the Good Shepherd (Luke 15:3–7), Jesus describes the passion with which God urgently seeks out the lost sheep. In His urgency to find the lost one, He seems to have lost His mind even to the point of leaving behind the ninety-nine. In the parable of the lost coin we hear about the thorough search that God conducts through Mother Church, leaving no stone unturned in His search for a lost coin (Luke 15:8–10). Then in the parable of the Prodigal Son (Luke 15:11–32), we learn about a God who stays behind and waits, but not with indifference. He so anxiously looks for the return of His son that as soon as He catches sight of him at a distance, He humiliates Himself by running to meet him. Sometimes we experience the God who waits behind as a God who gave up or a God who does not care. We feel the distance and we translate it into indifference. We do not realize that if indeed the Father is waiting for us, the Son is seeking us out like the Good Shepherd and the Holy Spirit is systematically sweeping the house to be absolutely sure He will find us. God does not need us to initiate the relationship or keep it alive; He only needs us to give our free response to His intense, seeking love—a love which Pope Benedict XVI even boldly called *eros*.[21]

---

[20] "St. Luke has given three parables successively; the sheep which was lost and found, the piece of silver which was lost and found, the son who was dead and came to life again, in order that invited by a threefold remedy, we might heal our wounds. Christ as the Shepherd bears thee on His own body, the Church as the woman seeks for thee, God as the Father receives thee, the first, pity, the second, intercession, the third, reconciliation." Thomas Aquinas, *Catena Aurea: Commentary on the Four Gospels, Collected out of the Works of the Fathers: St. Luke*, ed. J. H. Newman (Oxford: John Henry Parker, 1843), 3:529–30.

[21] Benedict XVI, *Deus Caritas Est*, §9: "God loves, and his love may certainly be called eros, yet it is also totally agape." Pope Benedict XVI included in Footnote 7, "Cf. Ps.-Dionysius the Areopagite, who in his treatise The Divine Names, IV, 12-14: PG 3, 709-713 calls God both *eros* and *agape*."

In fact, not only is God the One who initiates, provides for and keeps alive our relationship with Him, but also the more that we let Him do that, the more quickly we will grow. If we give Him the time in openness, trust and, simplicity, we will be amazed at the growth that takes place. Simplicity in particular is an important quality to maintain. It is often the most unsophisticated and those who seem to be the "simpletons" who have the strongest relationship with God. The more we pray, the simpler things become. God is in charge of everything and the simple-hearted trust in that. The simple ones listen to God with open hearts, taking God's law at face value and learning the divine wisdom: "The law of the Lord is perfect, reviving the soul; the testimony of the Lord is sure, making wise the simple" (Ps 19:7). The simple ones let the Lord save them rather than insisting on saving themselves: "The Lord preserves the simple; when I was brought low, he saved me" (Ps 116:6). The simple make the logic of the Gospel their own and let that be a light for their path: "The unfolding of your words gives light; it imparts understanding to the simple" (Ps 199:130).

When we persevere and remain in prayer, when we persevere and return faithfully to prayer, we quickly grow in prayer. The more we pray, the more ready we are to enter into prayer. We maintain a prayerful spirit even outside of prayer. We develop a habit of recollection and we are able to keep our hearts open to God even as we are listening to others or engaged in other work. Our hearts develop a prayerful self-offering, laying our interior open before the Lord in a way that becomes virtually unbroken. Our communion with Him becomes more constant. Prayer in general requires less effort and develops into more surrender. The dominant note in prayer becomes passivity and receptivity—an "active passivity" or a "receptive expressiveness" as God allows us to combine those seeming opposites by His grace.

The noise in ourselves that destabilizes us is often being kept up by us since, as we have mentioned before, we often, without fully realizing it, are afraid of the silence and afraid of what He might ask of us if we really listen. We can even do this at the same time as we are lamenting all the noise outside us, and wishing we had more time to pray. What are we afraid He will ask of us? The Lord will really take nothing away from us because He is All. Maybe we are afraid that He will say nothing and ask nothing, that He will not speak at all. Will He forget us? What fears do we hold? We must let Christ enter into the depth of that fear. March into the midst of what we fear most and face it, with the Lord! Listen to God in the midst of our noise. Trust in God in the midst of our fears. Let nothing distress or interrupt us from remaining stable in the Lord. We must learn to face the restlessness or the apathy that comes up in prayer by persevering and abiding in Him.

Sometimes we fear that if we stay, we will be left behind, but God never leaves us or distances Himself from us. God is always nearer to us than we are to ourselves.[22] He will never withdraw from us or love us any less than infinitely. God is love and His love does not diminish, even for those who turn away from Him definitively like the fallen angels. He continues to love them even though in freedom He lets them cut themselves off from Him. He loves Satan no less than He has eternally loved him, and is no more distant from him than He has been since He created

---

[22] See St. Augustine, *Confessions*, bk. III, chap. 6, no. 11.

him.[23] The same is true of us. He will always love us. His love will never lessen. To allow him, then, to be the source of my strength, my love, my hope, of all my projects, is truly to live in a secure way. What is not initiated by Christ, what is not sustained by Him, what is not brought to completion by Him, was never really His will and never really meant to be. We must remember that Christ has conquered everything. There is nothing that will be lost which is good, and nothing that is good that will not be brought to fruition by God. Even in situations which appeared to end tragically, in loss and death, much fruit will come from them. This is a mystery to us, not only because we cannot see everything, but because we refuse to see what we can see, or do not stay long enough to see or come to recognize who God is and what is really happening. We just don't persevere. Maybe it is because we already have a sense of where all of this is leading.

One seminarian was very drawn into deeper, contemplative prayer and was considering entering a Trappist monastery. As that was happening, he was praying alone one night in the choir stalls. Suddenly his soul became totally dark and he became terrified. He was so horrified by that experience that he discontinued his plan to enter the Trappists. He was eventually ordained a diocesan priest, but he was so terrified by that experience that he never went that deep in prayer again. It took many years of priesthood before he could re-approach such deep prayer. He never doubted

---

[23] See St. Ephraim the Syrian: "Look too at Legion: When in anguish he begged, our Lord permitted and allowed him to enter into the herd; respite did he ask for, without deception, in his anguish, and our Lord in His kindness granted his request. His compassion for demons is a rebuke to that People, showing how much anguish His love suffers in desiring that men and women should live." St. Ephrem the Syrian, *Hymns on Paradise*, trans. Sebastian P. Brock (Crestwood, NY: St. Vladimir's Seminary Press, 1990), 163.

God, but he remained stunned by the darkness he encountered. Nature can have a bleak and stark quality as great, living creatures die and decay and leave no remains. There is a certain dark quality to such stark realities. In the blink of an eye, our whole life can change and everything can be radically different than we ever knew. A diagnosis of brain cancer, an accusation that ends priestly ministry, a collapsed economy, a sudden, accidental death can change everything, and even turning to God in those moments can seem so empty and useless. Prayer does not simply insulate us against these experiences, but if we persevere, we can find ourselves descending into the depths, even the hellish depths of human suffering, with Christ.

3

Silence and Prayer

T HE FATHER SPOKE ONE WORD, which was his
Son, and this Word he always speaks in eternal
silence, and in silence must it be heard by the soul.[1]

How do we learn? Through prayer. We talk to God,
listening then speaking, this is prayer. If we have not listened, we have nothing to talk about. So we must take the
trouble to listen. For this we need silence of the mind,
silence of the heart, silence of the eyes, silence of the
hands.[2]

What we need most in order to make progress is to be
silent before this great God with our appetites and our
tongue, for the language He best hears is silent love.[3]

Our relationship with God has similarities to human relation-

---

[1] St. John of the Cross, "Sayings of Light and Love" no. 100, in Kieran Kavanaugh, trans. and ed., *The Collected Works of St. John of the Cross, Revised Edition*
(Washington, DC: ICS Publications, 1991), 92.
[2] Mother Teresa, *Where There Is Love, There Is God: A Path to Closer Union with
God and Greater Love for Others* (New York: Image, 2010), 18.
[3] St. John of the Cross, "Sayings" no. 132 (Kavanaugh, *The Collected Works of St.
John of the Cross*, 95).

ships, but there are also significant differences. In our human relationships, we are accustomed to speaking with each other for a definite period of time in the form of an uninterrupted dialogue. Communication in our relationship with God can be a very different experience. In our relationship with God, there is much more silence. In fact, God *always* seems to be silent; yet God is always drawing us into that silence to become one with Him. Although such silent communion is more foreign to our adult relationships, we initially experienced silent communion in the beginning of our lives, and we can learn from our original experience.

Our relationship with God began in silence. From the moment of our creation, indeed from all eternity, He knew us and loved us beyond words. He has never stopped knowing us and loving us and willing us into being. All of that happens in silence.

Silence also marked the beginning of our most foundational relationships. Soon after our conception, God began to share His love for us with our mother, whose body started changing to accommodate us and nurture us, and who slowly became aware of our existence and then began to love us consciously. She carried us beneath her heart for nine months with growing awareness of our personhood and growing personal love for us.[4] Her love for us was communicated like God's, primarily in silence. Even after birth, as a baby who cannot speak, love was communicated in silence and simplicity. A mother knows her baby and loves her baby mostly without words. A father, too, learns the cries and needs of his baby. Holding, nursing, cleaning, cuddling—these

---

[4] St. John Paul II included this capacity to know and love her unborn child as part of the feminine genius that he lauded in his apostolic letter *Mulieris Dignitatem* (1988). See §18.

happen mostly without words. Even the words that father and mother begin to use to speak to their child are incomprehensible to the baby at first. Only over time does the baby come to understand those words and begin to speak and slowly to converse.

Before God we remain forever as little children. God is known as the Ancient of Days (see Daniel 7:9), and compared to Him, we are all very little and very young babies. His words are often incomprehensible to us, and we do not always recognize the ways He is loving us because they are so basic to our existence. We cry like babies when we do not get what we need, but we do not recognize that it is always God who provides everything for us. For a baby at rest in its mother's arms, there is the most profound communication of love taking place that gives life to the baby and fosters growth, but which the baby is not able to consciously acknowledge. Likewise, we spend our whole lives in the arms of God, being loved by Him, without realizing that we are in the arms of God. *The deepest prayer is a silent acknowledgement of that fact, expressed in a choice to receive His love and to rest in Him.*

Although we have a tendency to make prayer complicated as we try to be overly sophisticated in our approach to God, prayer is actually very simple. He has only one message: unconditional love. He has only one Word: His eternal Son. He speaks only one language: silence. We can get frustrated at God's silence, wanting Him to say something to us. But God's language is silence. As St. John of the Cross said, everything God has ever created or said, He has spoken with one Word, and it is eternally being spoken out of silence.[5] This is not silence as we know it—silence as the

---

[5] See St. John of the Cross, "Sayings" no. 100 (Kavanaugh, *The Collected Works of St. John of the Cross*, 92).

absence of noise—but this is the silence that makes any sound possible, any word meaningful and coherent.

As Pope Benedict XVI reflected beautifully in his message for the World Day of Communication 2012, silence is a necessary and fruitful part of ongoing human communication if it is to deepen in meaning and love:

> Silence is an integral element of communication; in its absence, words rich in content cannot exist. In silence, we are better able to listen to and understand ourselves; ideas come to birth and acquire depth; we understand with greater clarity what it is we want to say and what we expect from others; and we choose how to express ourselves. By remaining silent we allow the other person to speak, to express him or herself; and we avoid being tied simply to our own words and ideas without them being adequately tested. In this way, space is created for mutual listening, and deeper human relationships become possible. It is often in silence, for example, that we observe the most authentic communication taking place between people who are in love: gestures, facial expressions and body language are signs by which they reveal themselves to each other. Joy, anxiety, and suffering can all be communicated in silence – indeed it provides them with a particularly powerful mode of expression. Silence, then, gives rise to even more active communication, requiring sensitivity and a capacity to listen that often makes manifest the true measure and nature of the relationships involved.[6]

---

[6] Pope Benedict XVI, Message for the World Day of Communication 2012 (at http://w2.vatican.va/content/benedict-xvi/en/messages/communications/doc-

In that sense, God is always speaking, using the language of silence. When necessary, He uses words, and even then it is only to settle us down, move us along, and lead us back into His silent love. But it is His silence that also makes prayer universal. People who cannot speak, from infants in utero to elderly with dementia, from the severely disabled to the man drawing his dying breath, can all pray by being in relationship with God in silence. The one who is poor, hungry, lost, little, sick, or imprisoned can still be in silent union with Christ: "As you did it to one of the least of these my brethren, you did it to me" (Matt 25:40). And so each one of us ultimately experiences the deepest union with God not through words but in the silence of trust and surrender, like a baby in her mother's arms.

From Silence through Words Back to Silence

Our relationship with God began in silence. At a certain point in time, we were conceived and began our historical existence, but we were already conceived in the mind of God even before our creation. We became consciously aware of our relationship with God at a certain point in history when someone told us about God and taught us how to pray. We started to pray in words that people taught us. Over time our relationship with God becomes more conscious and freely chosen, but the relationship has always been there in the heart of God. In fact, we could not come to know God or even desire to know God without His grace already at work in us. We had already been tapping into our relationship with Him before we first learned about God and started praying to Him.

As humans, our being is always already in relationship with God, but as our free will and reason develop, we begin to have a choice about how much we will open ourselves to Him or how consciously our relationship with Him will develop. We can choose how much attention we will give Him or how we will guide our thoughts about Him. We do this at first by formulating those thoughts into words. Little children can also direct their attention to Him through how they play or draw or color, as Sofia Cavalletti capitalized on when she developed the Catechesis of the Good Shepherd.[7] Although at first we spend relatively little time choosing to think about Him and to speak with Him, He is constantly present to us in silence, sustaining us in being and dwelling in the depths of our souls.

As we become more communicative and choose to spend more time with God, we use words to focus our attention and to grasp His Presence and self-revelation. We reflect on the words of Sacred Scripture, translating those words into our modern expressions and personalizing them to receive them better. We formulate prayers and try to express our hearts to Him, but these prayers should always be like flowers rising up from a bed of silence. "Keep spiritually tranquil in a loving attentiveness to God, and when it is necessary to speak, let it be with the same calm and peace."[8]

---

[7] Sofia Cavalletti, *The Religious Potential of the Child: Experiencing Scripture and Liturgy with Young Children*, trans. Patricia M. Coulter and Julie M. Coulter, 2nd ed. (New York: Liturgy Training Publications, 1992).

[8] St. John of the Cross, "Sayings" no. 82 (Kavanaugh, *The Collected Works of St.*

Intermittently we come back to our relationship with Him in original silence. We find that we can share more with Him in a vulnerable openness than we can fit into words. Words are always an approximation, but the full gift of ourselves can only be given in a silence beyond words. We discover that God communicates with us the same way. Words express an approximation of Him, but the Eternal Word desires to give Himself to us completely in a silence that is beyond words. Like our original relationship with Him in infancy, we can prayerfully find ourselves together with Him in silence. Unlike our original relationship with Him, however, now it can be a silence that is freely chosen with all our faculties opened up to Him to receive Him in love.

As one Benedictine monk heard from Jesus in prayer:

> The purpose of any words that I speak to you is to unite you to Me in the silence of love. That is why friends and lovers speak one to the other: to express what they hold in their hearts. Once these things have been expressed, it is enough for them to remain united one to the other in the silence that is the more perfect expression of their love.[9]

Struggle with Silence

> So many souls are afraid of the silence into which I would lead them if only they would let Me. Fear causes them to hide behind a barrage of words and concepts, when My desire is to unite them directly to Myself by means of

---

John of the Cross, 91).

[9] A Benedictine Monk, *In Sinu Jesu*, 108.

faith, hope, and especially love. Love is the bond of My
union with you and with every soul whom I have chosen
to live in the gift of My divine friendship.[10]

We struggle with silence in our relationship with God.
There is an analogy here with human relationships. We speak
of an "awkward silence." Think of getting into an elevator with
strangers. Everyone stands silently, perhaps wondering what the
others are thinking or doing. We might become self-conscious,
wondering if our clothes match or our hair is combed. We focus
on the floor indicator and wish it moved faster to its destination,
and we wonder how many stops there will be before we reach
our floor. We seek an escape and reach for our phone or carefully
study the advertisements on the inside of the elevator.

Reflect on how different it is when we share the elevator with
someone we know. We are able to carry on an easy conversation, and we hardly notice the time going by. We are able to wait
peacefully in silence, not worrying about how we look or what
the other person thinks about us. When we are in silence with
another person and we do not know we are loved, our minds and
bodies become restless. This can happen in our times of prayer
as well.

When we are in silence in prayer and we do not recognize
we are loved by God, we can also become very restless. As with
strangers in an elevator, we can become self-conscious, especially
aware of our shortcomings and our weaknesses. When we think
about God, we can become uncomfortable in feeling insignificant
and unworthy. Alternately, we can bury that feeling of insignifi-

---

[10] A Benedictine Monk, *In Sinu Jesu*, 108.

cance beneath a self-assured pride that closes our hearts to God and refuses to acknowledge any need for Him, perhaps distracting ourselves with what is going on around us. Our smallness and aspects of ourselves that make us self-conscious become particularly painful in the silence. At those moments, the most fitting disposition is humility; the most incongruous is pride. The most appropriate attitude is submission or surrender. Even if our worst fears that we are a complete mess are true, we can give it all to God and trust in His unconditional love for us. We will always experience this as a breakthrough.

The problem is that human silence is ambiguous. Sometimes human silence involves withholding something, or as we say, "keeping silent." The awkward silence in the elevator full of strangers is like that. Everyone is silent because no one is willing to share more of themselves. We are silent and do not express our thoughts when we do not trust that they will be listened to with love. That silence has not even risen up to a Level I conversation. From the receiving end, we experience that silence as another person's refusal to share more or to be vulnerable. This happens when the other person does not trust us to listen and receive him or her with love. Then silence indicates a barrier in a relationship, a wall that we cannot penetrate. When we interpret God's silence this way, it hurts us and makes us fearful. Is He not really there? Why does He not speak to me? Did I do something wrong? Is there something wrong with me? Coupled with our deeply held awareness that there are indeed many things wrong with us, this brings out our insecurities and makes us want to leave prayer.

Another message we can derive from silence is disinterest. When someone refuses to say anything to me, perhaps that person does not care about me. Likewise, the silence we experience in nature is impersonal and seems disinterested in us. When we look at the beauty of the stars and the vastness of the sky, while it captivates us, it does not seem to care whether or not we exist. We can feel very small and insignificant in the face of this. It is so much greater and more timeless than we are, and we wonder if our personal existence has any significance at all. We wonder if the vastness of the silence of the universe has any personal reality at all, or if that silence simply dead silence. We wonder if the universe is boundless, and we fear how that makes us infinitesimally small.

In the ambiguity of human silence, silence can act like a wall that keeps us out: "You have the right to remain silent." On the other hand, silence can be the fruit of the deepest intimacy. Behind silence there can be defensiveness or condemnation, but there can also be unconditional love. When we know there is unconditional love, the silence takes on a radically different quality. Rather than me keeping silence, this silence keeps me. We can think of the earlier example of a mother's silent love for her baby, or we can think of the silent love that is shared by lovers who know and love each other so completely and who for periods of time have no more need of words. Those are the examples of the silence that God is drawing each of us into with Himself.

Silence Opens Up with Trust

In our prayers we often find we are confronted by God's silence, we feel, as it were, let down, it seems to us that God neither listens nor responds. Yet God's silence, as happened to Jesus, does not indicate his absence. Christians know well that the Lord is present and listens, even in the darkness of pain, rejection and loneliness.

Jesus reassures his disciples and each one of us that God is well acquainted with our needs at every moment of our life. He teaches the disciples: "In praying do not heap up empty phrases as the Gentiles do; for they think that they will be heard for their many words. Do not be like them, for your Father knows what you need before you ask him" (Mt 6:7-8): an attentive, silent and open heart is more important than many words. God knows us in our inmost depths, better than we know ourselves, and loves us; and knowing this must suffice.[11]

There is a breakthrough when we discover that God's silence is never ambiguous. God's silence is always silent love. Behind God's silence there is not disregard or disinterest but rather unconditional, total, self-giving love. God's silence is not the absence of words but the very possibility of words. In fact, silence communicates God's infinite self-gift, which cannot be reduced to finite words or fully communicated in any other finite way. There is neither defensiveness nor condemnation. He is not withholding anything from us. He is not refusing to speak to us or to answer our questions. Rather, His response is always Himself. He, Himself, is the answer to all our questions. His love is the fulfillment of all our longings. He moves us beyond yes/no answers to rest in His gaze upon us and accept His self-giving

---

[11] Pope Benedict XVI, Audience of March 7, 2012 (at http://w2.vatican.va/content/benedict-xvi/en/audiences/2012/documents/hf_ben-xvi_aud_20120307.html).

love for us. As we receive this answer, it makes us rethink our questions. We discover how trivial our initial concerns are and our minds slowly become more conformed to His. We discover in His silent love who we are and what we can become. We discover all this as we allow God to take us into His silence. Then we discover, as Archbishop Luis Martinez says, "the summit of love is silence."[12]

This is analogous to the experience of a human relationship such as spiritual direction, in which a directee brings a list of questions or topics, but as she begins pouring out her heart, the conversation quickly ascends from a Level I transactional conversation to a Level III transformational conversation. In being able to share herself and experiencing unconditional loving acceptance, she is moved to set aside her list and her questions and finds herself fulfilled in the loving encounter. The Lord is profoundly present in such an encounter and gives Himself generously through such conversations that often culminate in a peaceful silence.

As we receive God Himself in silence, we may find that conviction, insight, understanding, and even words and images start to overflow into our faculties—our feelings, imagination, and reason. We may find that we are able to put an idea into words or discern a concrete action to take in moving forward. The more deeply we go into silence, the more possible it is to hear words that rise up from the depths of our silence, which originate in the depths of His silence. These are merely the overflow of the most important gift of our prayer which is the gift of God Himself.

---

[12] Luis M. Martinez, *When God Is Silent: Finding Spiritual Peace amid the Storms of Life* (Manchester, NH: Sophia Institute Press, 2014), 67.

Rather than simply solving our problems, He helps us grasp the meaning of the problem and what is at stake in the situation that we face. He also takes us beyond that situation so that we can receive from His Providence. Sometimes we feel an initial dissatisfaction that God has not been more concrete or more specific. In fact, God communicates Himself and provides for us in a way that always takes into account the tiniest details of the reality of our lives, of who we are. At the same time, He always preserves the great gift of our free will. He shows us the true freedom of our will by inviting us to trust Him and let our human will flow into His divine Will. In His self-giving love for us, God is always opening us out, never closing us in. He leads us in deeper ways to a fuller perspective on ourselves, our lives, and particular situations that are going on.

In one experience of profound disappointment caused by a confusing rejection, one man named Timothy felt his loneliness, as there was no one he could call who would understand. This led to a reflection on the whole of his life and made him realize that there was no human being who had been with him throughout his whole life. His parents and childhood friends were dead and gone. Those who knew him during his college education were no longer involved in his post-graduate career, and practically no one knew that he was applying for a new position, let alone what it meant to be turned down. At the moment, as he felt the pain of no one really knowing his whole life or having been present for his whole life, he experienced a closeness with the Lord. As he lamented that no one was with him who had known him his whole life, he heard the echo of the Lord's words in his heart, "I was." That helped him accept the rejection, persevere through the pain, and surrender in deeper trust, knowing that the Lord was at work and would never leave him.

All of this depends on trust. There is no way to differentiate the silence of condemnation and the silence of love without trust. We can only open ourselves to receive God's self-gift by making the act of trust that He is Love, and His silence always contains the gift of His Love that, in its totality, is always more than we can grasp. This is not blind faith or wishful thinking. We have good reason for this faith in Christian revelation. We have a great cloud of witnesses throughout history, and we have the witnesses who shared the faith with us personally. We have the Church, the Scriptures, and the Sacraments as a concrete guide and support. All this gives us a reason to believe, but the choice to believe always remains personal and free. No one can make that choice for us. Each one must make it for himself, and he must make it again and again.

When we choose to believe and trust, and we enter and remain in the silence, we discover that the boundlessness of God is more infinitely personal than we could have imagined. We come "to know and to believe in the love God has for us" (1 John 4:16), and we discover that behind God's silence is only pure, infinite, unconditional love. Coming to trust in that can be a painful and purifying process, traditionally imaged as a desert or a dark night in our spiritual tradition. After we pass through it, as we continue to hold on to our faith that God is love (1 John 4:16) and that He never leaves us orphans (John 14:18), we come to discover that His love has always surrounded us, even in the silence.

St. Anthony of the Desert

The story of the father of monasticism, St. Anthony of the Desert, illustrates this powerfully. After a rigorous life of prayer and asceticism, Anthony entered into a deeper level of darkness and temptation. He was mightily tempted through bodily pain and a spirit of lust, through apparitions arousing his fears and the feeling that he was on his own, without God's help. He passed through these temptations with a prayer of faith in God's love and the words of St. Paul on his lips: "Who shall separate us from the love of Christ? Shall tribulation, or distress, or persecution, or famine, or nakedness, or peril, or sword?" (Rom 8:35). He also repeated the faith of the psalmist, "Though a host encamp against me, my heart shall not fear" (Ps 27:3). When he was nearly overcome, a ray of light shone through and took away his bodily pains, dispersed the demons, and gave him strength. Anthony immediately queried his Savior, "'Where were you? Why did you not appear at the beginning to end my pains?' 'I was here, Anthony,' a voice answered, 'but I waited to see your struggle. Because you have remained firm and have not yielded, I will always be your helper, and I will make your name known everywhere.'"[13]

St. Anthony was drawn into the Passion of Christ through the experience of suffering in silence. God was not present to him in the ways he had previously come to know. He had to learn a silent Presence, just as Christ had experienced in His humanity on the Cross. Christ was first drawn into silence and then placed His trust in His Father's silence. When Christ entered into His

---

[13] St. Athanasius, "Life of St. Anthony," in H. Dressler and R. J. Deferrari, eds., *Early Christian Biographies*, trans. M. E. Keenan (Washington, DC: The Catholic University of America Press, 1952) 15:145.

Passion, He fell silent—very few words were spoken from His arrest to His death. On the Cross He showed His solidarity with our pain at the silence of God as He cried out, "My God, my God, why have you forsaken me?" (Matt 27:46); but then He brings all who suffer with Him to a place of trusting surrender: "Into your hands I commend my spirit" (Luke 23:46). In this way, the hidden God hid Himself in our suffering and death, and He still maintains a hidden, silent presence to all of us in our suffering. In contrast to our complaints that God is far from human suffering and death, in Jesus, God enters into all of it, mostly in silence.

Christ has gone ahead of us and awaits us

Pope Benedict XVI explicated this mystery beautifully in his reflection on the Shroud of Turin as an icon of Holy Saturday:

> Jesus Christ "descended to the dead." What do these words mean? They mean that God, having made himself man, reached the point of entering man's most extreme and absolute solitude, where not a ray of love enters, where total abandonment reigns without any word of comfort: "hell." Jesus Christ, by remaining in death, passed beyond the door of this ultimate solitude to lead us too to cross it with him. We have all, at some point, felt the frightening sensation of abandonment, and that is what we fear most about death, just as when we were children we were afraid to be alone in the dark and could only be reassured by the presence of a person who loved us. Well, this is exactly what happened on Holy Saturday: the voice of God resounded in the realm of death. The

unimaginable occurred: namely, Love penetrated "hell." Even in the extreme darkness of the most absolute human loneliness we may hear a voice that calls us and find a hand that takes ours and leads us out. Human beings live because they are loved and can love; and if love even penetrated the realm of death, then life also even reached there. In the hour of supreme solitude we shall never be alone: *Passio Christi. Passio hominis.*[14]

Knowing that Christ has gone ahead of us and awaits us there gives us courage to face the darkness and enter into the silence. In fact, after we endure the trial of silence and experience the depths of our own weakness, we come to a deeper faith in God and the power of His strength to protect us and sustain us. What appeared to us to be silent absence turns out to be a silent presence, and we discover that God is always closer to us than what we could have dreamed possible. What appeared to be silence to us was in fact deafeningly loud and what appeared dark to us was in fact blindingly bright. As Pope Benedict XVI said, "The Holy Shroud acts as a 'photographic' document, with both a 'positive' and a 'negative.' And, in fact, this is really how it is: the darkest mystery of faith is at the same time the most luminous sign of a never-ending hope."[15] God is not giving us too little; He is giving us too much. This was the exclamation of St. Augustine after his conversion. What he had perceived as silence and distance was in fact God's presence. God was not far away but was so close to

---

[14] Pope Benedict XVI, Meditation on the Shroud during his Pastoral Visit to Turin, May 2, 2010 (at http://w2.vatican.va/content/benedict-xvi/en/speeches/2010/may/documents/hf_ben-xvi_spe_20100502_meditazione-torino.html).

[15] Benedict XVI, Meditation on the Shroud.

him that He was actually deeply inside:

> Late have I loved you, O Beauty ever ancient, ever
> new, late have I loved you! You were within me, but I
> was outside, and it was there that I searched for you. In
> my unloveliness I plunged into the lovely things which
> you created. You were with me, but I was not with you.
> Created things kept me from you; yet if they had not been
> in you they would not have been at all. You called, you
> shouted, and you broke through my deafness. You flashed,
> you shone, and you dispelled my blindness. You breathed
> your fragrance on me; I drew in breath and now I pant for
> you. I have tasted you, now I hunger and thirst for more.
> You touched me, and I burned for your peace.[16]

To discover this kind of presence requires us to allow our
trust in God to be deepened. When He said that He would not
abandon us (John 14:18), He meant it. When He said that He
would always be faithful (2 Tim 2:13), He meant it. When He
said that He is with us always (Matt 28:20), He meant it. When
He said He is in the sick, the stranger, the naked, the hungry,
the thirsty, and the prisoner, He meant it (Matt 25:35–40). We
believe it to an extent, but then our belief must be tested and
stretched in order to be strengthened.

One religious sister who prayed deeply, reflected often on
scripture, and had a beautiful faith, found her faith tested through
many trials of illness. Not only was the illness debilitating, but it
was also inscrutable, and many doctors were not able to cure her or
even properly diagnose the problem. Her concrete trust in God's

---

[16] St. Augustine, *Confessions*, bk. VII, chap. 10.

word was tested and strengthened through these trials. One day while she was in the hospital awaiting visitors, she reflected on the Lord's words in the Gospel, "I was sick and you visited me" (Matt 25:36). In that moment, she realized that in a mysterious way she had become Jesus because of her sickness. When people came to visit her, they received Him. This was a mystery that she could not wrap her mind around, but she could allow herself to be wrapped in this mystery in loving awe and contemplation of God's gracious goodness.

This requires us to have patience and remain in the silence. In its etymology, "patience" comes from the Latin *patior*, meaning "let it be done" as well as "to suffer" or "to be open." To deepen our trust, we must not only be willing to stay there in silence, letting it be done to us according to His will, but also to be patient in the sense of being open to suffering absence, aloneness, and doubt. We must choose to trust when familiar ways of presence disappear, and we are opened up to be able to receive the presence of God, which is silent, hidden, and mysterious. We discover that His presence is much greater than the forms of presence we are familiar with, but at first it seems to be an absence. It is a light so bright it is blinding, and the blindness made us think at first that it was darkness. It is a voice so loud it is deafening, and the deafness made us think it was silence.

The discovery of God cannot be entirely on our own terms. Silence teaches us to be willing to receive God on His terms. Surely God meets us halfway, like the Apostle Thomas who demanded a particular sign but then had to wait for God to decide the timing (see John 20:24–29). God's silence draws out the deepest patience and vulnerability from us. Our trust is stretched to its limits and we feel foolish wasting our time in this silent prayer. Perseverance wins the prize, however, and like St. Anthony, when we have reached our limit, a ray of light appears and all the shadows disperse, and we are restored by God's love to a state of innocence, peace, and joy like we had never known before. In that moment, we know that God had never left us, and in fact we never could have persevered without Him. He gave us exactly the grace we needed to endure the trial and to deepen in love.

Silence Requires Vulnerability and Weakness

If every one of us is in relationship with God, then why are there many people who deny God or who do not allow for a relationship with God? We can see this happening for all the obvious reasons. The silence and hiddenness of God make us doubt His existence. How are we to believe that someone is communicating Himself in silence? That seems like make-believe, like trying to imagine something that is not there. Regarding prayer, Jesus told us that God, who is secret and hidden, will hear us (Matt 6:6). But, while a Christian claims God is hidden, the agnostic or atheist demands evidence for God before he will believe there is anyone speaking or communicating Himself. Since God is silent, He seems non-existent. The atheist requires God to reveal Himself in particular ways. He is unwilling to let God reveal Himself on His own terms. God's silence makes it seem much more likely that He is not there at all.

We are convinced that every single human being who is

willing to be vulnerable enough to look silently into the depths of himself will come to know there is a God: "There is no place on earth where God is more present than in the human heart. This heart truly is God's abode, the temple of silence."[17] What interferes with our discovery is our refusal to be vulnerable, to lay ourselves bare, to look deeply enough into ourselves and beyond. A furtive glance or a skeptical outlook makes the atheist come up with nothing. He acts like a fisherman who barely dips his net in the sea, and when he catches nothing, complains there are no fish. Without patience and humility, he uses a net that can only catch what is finite, rational, or measurable. He will never come up with anything that way, and then he too hastily abandons his pursuit.

The disciples lowered their nets all night long and caught nothing (see Luke 5:5, John 21:5). Then one more cast and the nets could not hold the catch. The difference is that we must learn to keep fishing for what is greater than any net can hold rather than angrily claiming that our net is not being filled. When we encounter the empty net of silence, we must go deeper, cast to the other side, and not give up. We must listen for what is deeper and what is greater than the net of our understanding can grasp. If I only fish for what my net can bring up, then I will bring up some things that are not God, but when I cast my net to the other side in the sense of casting into what is beyond, then I will bring up more than I could ever handle on my own.

---

[17] Cardinal Robert Sarah and Nicolas Diat, *The Power of Silence: Against the Dictatorship of Noise* (San Francisco: Ignatius Press, 2017), 31.

Noise and Materialism Keep Us on the Surface

God is silent; the devil is noisy. Cardinal Robert Sarah offered a scathing critique of the modern world:

> Without noise, postmodern man falls into a dull, insistent uneasiness. He is accustomed to permanent background noise, which sickens yet reassures him. Without noise, man is feverish, lost. Noise gives him security, like a drug on which he has become dependent. With its festive appearance, noise is a whirlwind that avoids facing itself. Agitation becomes a tranquilizer, a sedative, a morphine pump, a sort of reverie, an incoherent dream-world. But this noise is a dangerous, deceptive medicine, a diabolic lie that helps man avoid confronting himself in his interior emptiness. The awakening will necessarily be brutal.[18]

The noise of the world remains on the surface, like a layer of shiny pollution. Perhaps one cast a net to seek God in the deep once, but having come up short, settled only for what could be gleaned from the surface. Noise keeps man at the surface of reality and the surface of himself. Noise makes man superficial. As long as man is determined to remain superficial, he will never make that miraculous catch and discover God in the depths of silence. He cannot simply yell at the sea until God emerges from it. He must keep casting his net, going deeper than the noise. God will not emerge amidst our noise; He is determined to draw

---

[18] Sarah and Diat, *The Power of Silence*, 39.

us into His silence. We are not made to live on the surface; our full potential is fulfilled only by going into the depths.

Postmodern man is fascinated with the surface of things, no longer taking time to seek the deeper meaning. The philosophies of materialism and positivism have taken hold of man through the enticements of instant power and entertainment offered by technology. Materialism says that there is no spiritual reality. Positivism says that only that which can be positively perceived by our senses actually exists. Focusing primarily on the positive, material realities, experimental science has been extremely successful in dazzling us with technological inventions that can perform incredible feats of strength and information discovery. Because science does not concern itself with the spiritual, however, we too quickly decide that we do not need the spiritual and perhaps it does not even exist. From the arrogant heights of our technological Tower of Babel, we demand that God reveal Himself on our terms, but we receive only silence in response. God does not submit Himself to our positivist, materialist reductions of reality.

When we reduce reality to what can be experienced with our five senses, we lose the best things. We lose the transcendental qualities of truth, beauty, and goodness, qualities that can only be grasped through our inner perceptions: our inner eye, our inner hearing, our inner feeling—through the heart. Compared to high cultures of other ages which had great literature, art, architecture, and philosophy, we have become very pragmatic. That makes finding God and the reality of God oblique because we are not interested in the hiddenness of transcendental reality or mystery. We presume that what is silent is simply non-existent, and we think, "Because God is not intruding into my life, He isn't saying anything, so I'll just go on with my life without any reference to Him." This happens even to people of faith. Faith becomes weak when prayer becomes weak. When we avoid silence, we stop praying, and we stop listening, and our sense of the reality of God and a relationship with Him becomes vague and oblique rather than becoming more real. Then we dismiss God as distant and unimportant for our lives, demanding that He reveal Himself on our terms before we will have a relationship with Him.

To return to the example of Timothy, he, in his profound disappointment, was casting about trying to understand his life. There were no human supports for him in his pain. He was deprived of responses that he could receive with his five external senses. He could have summoned up pious platitudes or clung to theological concepts, but they would have remained empty and uncomforting for him. God was taking him down into the silence. It was from the silence of his internal anguish that the words of God and the spiritual consolation of peace and stillness rose up, and he internally recognized the words, "I was." They were God's response. He heard those words in his own thoughts, and yet they rose up from a place of distinct "Otherness."

If God yielded to our demands, He would risk losing the best part of us. The invisible and the spiritual have primacy over the visible and material. Our capacity to love, to understand, to desire, to know truth, to develop science, to create art, is not rooted in our material reality but comes from the depths of our souls. And these are precisely the parts of us that emerge and grow in silence. An artist's greatest masterpieces rise up from silence. A scientist's greatest discoveries emerge from his spirit in silence. We come to realize our human potential not by calling God to the surface, but rather by casting our nets into the deep, not by bringing God to where we are, but rather by letting Him draw us into where He is.

Pope Benedict XVI summarized beautifully the way that silence draws us to see a deeper reality, to discover a meaning that underlies and transcends everything else:

> When messages and information are plentiful, silence becomes essential if we are to distinguish what is important from what is insignificant or secondary. Deeper reflection helps us to discover the links between events that at first sight seem unconnected, to make evaluations, to analyze messages; this makes it possible to share thoughtful and relevant opinions, giving rise to an authentic body of shared knowledge. For this to happen, it is necessary to develop an appropriate environment, a kind of 'eco-system' that maintains a just equilibrium between silence, words, images and sounds.[19]

Just a Little Faith Is Enough

How much silence are we able to tolerate? What happens if we take silence to its absolute conclusion? What happens when we begin to believe that the silence not only is the preparation for, but also is itself the abundance? Then the barren womb becomes fruitful. The empty sea becomes full of fish. What brings that transformation about? It is the invitation of Christ. Christ invites

---

[19] Benedict XVI, Message for the World Day of Communication 2012.

us, in the silence, and through the silence, to "cast into the deep," meaning to "listen." Listen in faith! There is no excuse to say we don't have enough faith—even the smallest amount of faith, the size of a mustard seed, is all that is needed (Luke 17:6). We will only draw up a great catch of fish if we continue to trust and step forward into the void. Our faith might seem too faint or too little. Peter and the apostles were skeptical at best when Jesus said to cast their nets again, but they cast them out all the same! Do I have enough faith simply to cast out my net? Doubt, darkness, dryness, emptiness, and silence can become so great. Sometimes the Church seems cold, dark, and empty. No one is there but me. Listening seems useless, silence feels barren, the sea appears empty. But simply cast out the net—listen, make an act of faith. However little our trust is, let us cast out the net anyway.

Even when the Lord knocks us to the ground like St. Paul, it is only to get our attention. He pushes us to do the most unlikely things—stand up and walk, open our eyes and see, cast out into the deep. If a person trusts and tries—to stand, to cast out the net, to open his eyes—that is the mustard seed of faith. Faith steps out in vulnerability, a vulnerability that allows a miraculous catch of fish. Silence becomes fullness. The empty sea brings forth more fish than the net can hold. As with the loaves and fishes, there was more left when they picked up the leftovers than they started with! That's how faith works. When we take the smallest step in faith, the Lord multiplies that faith and tells us to take another step, "Give them something to eat yourselves!" (Mark 6:37). That's how silence works. It also brings out our poverty and summons our protests, "Two hundred denarii would not buy enough bread for each of them to get a little" (John 6:7).

When we feel our poverty and our need, we might finally take the risk to believe. They had nothing to eat. We need the silence of failure and hunger. We need the vulnerability of asking people to sit on the ground and expect to be fed, without having enough in our hands to give them (John 6:10). We need to be empty in order to be filled, silent in order to receive. We need the tiniest bit of silent faith to allow the Lord to multiply and expand and to reveal a Love for us that is beyond our imagining.

God already has this relationship with us in the depths of ourselves, but we are tempted to deny it and not attend to it. Our denial can arise from several places. We can be limited by what makes sense to us and reduce the power of God to common sense, or to the laws of nature and the limits of human reason. We can be limited by fear. The risk of spending our time in silence and hoping that God will show up can be frightening. This makes us feel very vulnerable! What if He does not show up? When we come before the Lord in silence and remain there it can expose our loneliness and doubts, and we might give in to impatience and give up in a lack of faith. Silence seems counterintuitive to us. We want to scream, "Why don't you say something?" It is necessary for us to be silent and listen before we can hear God say something, but we are afraid that we will listen and hear nothing, and so we avoid silence. This is the fear of the Apostles before casting their net into the empty sea one more time. They had tried all night and caught nothing. There is no way to get around this risk. We have to dare to listen to Jesus, cast into the deep, and make a miraculous catch.

A Greater Fullness of Prayer through Silence

Sometimes we are held back by the fear that it *is* all real and that God *will* speak! Sometimes we resist silence because we are really resisting an encounter with God. Perhaps He will turn my life upside down. Perhaps I will lose my feeling of comfort or even my very self. Perhaps He will consume me and take away my freedom, and everything familiar will disappear. It is good to examine our hearts and not only ask whether I will hear anything but ask precisely, "What am I afraid that I *will* hear?"

When we encounter God, it is a *mysterium tremendum et fascinans,* to use the phrase of Rudolf Otto.[20] We are terrified and fascinated. It is horrifying and thrilling at the same time. We experience alarm and fear, but we are excited at the same time. The Gospels say that when the disciples made the miraculous catch of fish, the nets were about to break. We can feel stretched to our limit by our encounter with God. It makes us feel both humbled and exalted simultaneously. We feel chosen and precious but also unworthy and sinful. The words of St. Peter are easy for us to echo, "Depart from me Lord, for I am a sinful man" (Luke 5:8). We will always be overwhelmed by the greatness of God and also feel how small we are. In this way, the encounter in silence also leads us back into silence. We are stupefied and do not know what else to say. Even when we babble something in praise or adoration, it always feels inadequate. Peter's incoherent

---

[20] Rudolf Otto, *The Idea of the Holy: An Inquiry Into the Non-Rational Factor in the Idea of the Divine and Its Relation to the Rational,* trans. John W. Harvey (Pantianos Classics: CreateSpace Independent Publishing Platform, 2017).

request at the Transfiguration to build three tents makes us laugh because we can recognize ourselves in his tongue-tied eruption (see Luke 9:33).

When we encounter God, we lose our feeling of self-importance. As we persevere through these moments in silence and we realize that God does not leave us or withdraw His love, that He does not accede to Peter's request to depart from him, then we start to understand God's mercy. God's mercy is so great that it throws us off-balance in our self-sufficiency. Having a deep awareness of our unworthiness can allow us to welcome and receive the experience of God as what we have been longing for. We discover answers to questions we did not know we had. We receive directions for paths we did not even know existed and the solution to riddles we have not yet encountered. It is the fulfillment of our heart's desire.

The truth is that absolutely nothing on this earth can really satisfy us. This is the dirty secret our world does not like to face. Our hearts have been made for Him, who is not a creature but is rather the Creator. He is the ground of our existence. He is the reason for our existence. This is why we can never locate the Creator among the other creatures. My existence is not necessary but completely gratuitous. For reasons I will never understand, He chose to create me. It was an intentional choice, not an accident. He chose to create me. Sometimes we protest about the presence of evil in the world, but we fail to ponder in awe that there is goodness in the world, or, indeed that there is anything at all! But even greater awe overcomes us when we recognize the total gift of our own creation and even more so the reason for it. God chose to create me for Himself,[21] and so He alone is the answer to all my longing.

In the moments that we encounter Him in all His superabundant fullness and we know deeply that only He can satisfy us, the only adequate response is spontaneous gratitude, praise, and adoration. Words may come up and come out, but ultimately no word can express what we want to say in moments like this. Prayer like this can also be ecstatic. We can be lifted out of ourselves or end up blacking out in a semi-unconscious, wordless surrender. We often have no way of grasping what we are experiencing. We have the feeling of being grasped, being lifted up, consumed, exalted, but in no merely human way. We have glimpses of what is happening, but we do not experience God in a way that can easily be explained. In these experiences, we abandon any effort at explanation, and in silence we seek to glorify Him and love Him. In these moments we experience a love that goes beyond any other love that we have known.

We encounter reality in prayer

This is a reality we know in prayer that is more real than the ordinary reality we live in. It is more concrete, not in a creaturely way, but in the sense of being the basis or ground of all things even in their concrete forms. We see God in all things. There may be some images in our mind's eye or some words from God's self-revelation, but there is normally nothing we can carry away from these experiences other than a vague memory or two. We are left with a feeling, but not like ordinary emotions. We feel overloaded with diverse, even conflicting feelings. If we try to

---

[21] CCC 356.

express these conflicting feelings, we feel poor, incapable of capturing the experience. Every word seems to reduce it or limit it. The essence of it remains silent and inexpressible.

When there are words that come to us in these moments of ecstatic prayer, they do not have the same quality as ordinary words do. They are tokens or symbols that are much more than words. The same is true with images.[22] These words and images are not bad. Language is a divine gift, but language meets its limits in these experiences. This does not mean that God is too abstract for language, but rather that He is too *real* for words and images. Images and words are tokens that refer to ordinary reality and are but echoes of what is going on deep within us. When we encounter God, we encounter sheer reality. St. Paul of the Cross guided one of his spiritual directees along this path of prayer:

> Listen, my daughter, your present stage of prayer, in which God has placed you, has no need of many words. Love speaks little; the tongue of Holy Love is the heart on fire, which flames, consumes itself, melts entirely in God, and cannot express in concepts the ardor which compels it to make a continuous sacrifice of love of its loving soul. And this sacrifice is a holocaust, that is, it is entirely consumed, it reduces itself to ashes in that divine fire of infinite love and, in a word, one glance of love in pure faith understands great things, etc.[23]

---

[22] See Cardinal Ratzinger, *The Message of Fatima*, 2006 (at http://www.vatican.va/roman_curia/congregations/cfaith/documents/rc_con_cfaith_doc_20000626_message-fatima_en.html).

[23] St. Paul of the Cross, *The Letters of Saint Paul of the Cross, vol. 1, 1720-1747*, ed. Laurence Finn and Donald Webber (Chicago, IL: Passionist Provincial Office, 2000), no. 342.

In the Resurrection encounter with Jesus, when the Apostles cast into the deep at Jesus's command, they caught 153 fish (see John 21:1–14). This has been interpreted by the Fathers as being every known variety of fish.[24] In other words, they caught *everything*, and then on the shore they encountered the Infinite. God is One, and His oneness encompasses everything and beyond. He is the One that makes any other one possible. He is the foundation of all reality. The amazing claim of Christian revelation is that this foundation is also infinitely personal and wants to be intimate with us. If we allow Him, He brings out, in relationship with Him, the most radically unique sense of who I am as an individual person. God in His own being comes through in these moments, and we encounter Him in a way that is personal, intimate, and loving at the same time as it is transcendent. His transcendence comes through in being beyond and in everything. We are not a step removed from everything, but a step closer to everything when we encounter God. He is radically Other, but His Otherness is not a distance from reality—it is absolutely real. God is the center and wellspring of reality. There is a definite dissimilarity between ourselves and Him, but not one that alienates us from Him. Instead it opens up into a profound intimacy. We know He is God and we are not God, but amazingly we see that we are like Him even as we see that we are different from Him.

This is all sheer gift, and in the face of it we fall into silence.

---

[24] "A hundred and fifty-three: The number of fish hauled ashore is symbolic. St. Jerome claims that Greek zoologists had identified 153 different kinds of fish (*Comm. in Ez.* 14, 47). If this is the background, the episode anticipates how the apostles, made fishers of men by Christ (Mt 4:19), will gather believers from every nation into the Church (Mt 28:18–20)." *The Ignatius Catholic Study Bible: The New Testament*, eds. Scott Hahn and Curtis Mitch (San Francisco: Ignatius Press, 2010), 200.

Cardinal Sarah wrote, "The love that says nothing and asks for nothing leads to the greatest love, the silent love of God. The silence of love is the perfect silence in the presence of God that sums up all goodness, all beauty, all perfection."[25] This is the path the mystics and contemplatives invite us to walk. They have always sought out silence and solitude in order to be alone with the Alone. They never cease their pursuit for the One who alone is able to fill us with the presence, communion, and relationship that we have been created for and that we long for. Each one of us is invited to take a risk and become a mystic by opening ourselves to this wonderful mystery that we have come to know in Christ.

"Silence is more important than any other human work." That is where the true revolution comes from.[26]

---

[25] Sarah and Diat, *The Power of Silence*, 62.
[26] Sarah and Diat, *The Power of Silence*, 68; emphasis added.

4

Praying in Loving Faith

I N T H I S P A S S I N G O V E R, if it is to be perfect, all intellectual activities must be left behind and the height
of our affection must be totally transferred and transformed into God. This, however, is mystical and most
secret, which *no one knows except him who receives it*, no
one receives except him who desires it, and no one desires
except him who is inflamed in his very marrow by the fire
of the Holy Spirit whom Christ sent into the world. And
therefore the Apostle says that this mystical wisdom is
revealed by the Holy Spirit.[1]

What if I Feel I Am Praying Poorly?

Archbishop Luis Martinez wrote brilliantly about feelings in
prayer in his book, *Worshipping A Hidden God*.[2] He noted how
reliant we are upon whether we feel consoled or desolate, devout

---

[1] St. Bonaventure, *Bonaventure: The Soul's Journey into God, The Tree of Life, The
Life of St. Francis*, trans. Ewert Cousins (Mahwah, NJ: Paulist Press, 1978), 113.

[2] Luis M. Martinez, *Worshipping a Hidden God: Unlocking the Secrets of the Interior
Life* (2003; repr., Manchester, NH: Sophia Institute Press, 2014), 123–130.

or indifferent, and whether God feels close or distant. What we need is faith: "Faith assures us that God is there, and if we would comport ourselves in harmony with what faith tells us, how different our prayer would be!"[3] Likewise, the Catechism of the Catholic Church looks to the teaching of St. Therese in defining prayer: "For me, prayer is a surge of the heart; it is a simple look turned toward heaven, it is a cry of recognition and of love, embracing both trial and joy."[4] This "surge of the heart" that gathers up all our feelings ("trial and joy") and directs them to the Lord is a fundamental movement of prayer that we must learn and practice again and again as our union with God grows stronger and deeper.

Imagine going to pray. We naturally begin to get our bearings by checking to see how we are as we try to compose ourselves. We reach out to the Lord with an act of our will to pray, and with faith we connect with Him. Remembering this is a personal relationship, we intentionally imagine or visualize Him, however vaguely, whether connecting with all three divine persons or one of them, with the Blessed Mother or one of the saints. We begin perhaps to talk to the Lord and may find that we have more to say than we had realized. But our disposition of loving faith makes us listen as we speak, makes us focus on Him more than on ourselves. Eventually we want to listen more than we want to speak. We become calmer and more focused. Then the thought may come: "Is He really there; does He really hear me?"

We have spoken of these types of doubts before, which are obviously matters of faith and the need for deeper faith. In this

---

[3] Martinez, *Worshipping a Hidden God*, 128.

[4] St. Thérèse of Lisieux, *Manuscrits autobiographiques*: C 25r, quoted in CCC 2558.

chapter we want to consider faith. Our faith at any given moment may be stronger or weaker, and accordingly we have a confident feeling or a sense of not being at ease. This generates feelings of consolation or desolation, of devotion or indifference, of progress in the spiritual life or stagnation. One day we feel good about how we are doing, and the next day think we have lost everything. If on a given day, we seem focused or feel contrite or prayerful, we feel happy that we are on the road to sanctity. On the other hand, if we are distracted or tired, we feel far from God and fear that we are wasting our time.

These feelings will ascend and descend, soar and plummet. We cannot avoid them, nor should we want to. It is helpful to note how we are feeling and even to glance at the possibilities of why we are feeling this way in case there is something we need to attend to, such as getting more sleep, rising from our kneeling posture and sitting down, or laying something out before the Lord that is bothering us.

But feelings are not totally reliable in assessing where God is or where we are in relation to Him. We should not try to suppress or control our feelings. What we must do is savor or endure how we feel, at the same time taking the focus off ourselves and putting it onto Him. What is needed is faith. In prayer as well as in our daily activities, over and over again, we need to remove the focus from ourselves and how we feel and turn to Him in loving faith, renewing this act of loving faith each time we stray from it.

Feelings in prayer

What do we do about the feelings? Nothing. Just have them, and do not take them as a serious indication of what is really going on, of how well prayer is going or of what God is doing. In the *Summa Theologica*, St. Thomas Aquinas noted that we do not have much direct control over our feelings. We can influence them with our reason, but the influence is only partial.[5] We should try to love Him with our whole heart, soul, mind, and strength, focusing not on ourselves or our love but on Him. When we are feeling sad, we should not focus on the sadness but hold it out to Him. We should not overanalyze our feelings, for by holding them out to Him, we will understand what we need to know about our sadness without indulging or getting swallowed up in it. The same is true if we are happy or feel a union with the Lord. We should be glad but not focus on how elevated this union is, or focus on ourselves as being gifted with union. Rather we should focus on Him and love Him in faith.

Nonetheless, in our acceptance that we must pray as human beings, we must also acknowledge that feelings are part of being human. How do we handle our feelings and what role do they play in prayer? By noticing them without becoming absorbed in them, we can go even deeper into our relationship with God in prayer, and we can begin to make sense of our experience and also begin to shape it by conscious choices. Ultimately, our emotions can be trained and transformed to become a powerful support to our virtues and part of a more perfect act of love, worship, hope, or faith. We must be patient with ourselves, and slowly,

---

[5] "Hence the Philosopher says (Polit. i, 2) that the reason governs the irascible and concupiscible not by a 'despotic supremacy,' which is that of a master over his slave; but by a 'politic and royal supremacy,' whereby the free are governed, who are not wholly subject to command." *The Summa Theologiae of St. Thomas Aquinas*, Second and Revised Ed., trans. Fathers of the English Dominican Province, (1920; Kevin Knight, 2017), I-II, q. 17, a. 7, http://www.newadvent.org/summa/2017.htm#article7.

through the exercise of the intellect and the will, we can guide our emotions in the right direction. "Emotions do not exist for the purpose of being extinguished or repressed or even simply to be curbed. The emotions are not dangerous wild horses, as Plato held. Rather, they are docile, like a child with its parent, who must be taken by the hand and guided in the right direction."[6] Of course, we cannot wait for our emotions to be well trained before starting to pray. To the contrary, our prayer will become an important training ground for the emotions.

As Pope Benedict XVI taught in his first encyclical *God is Love*, our sentiments, intellect, and will are all transformed together as we encounter God in prayer, "Contact with the visible manifestations of God's love can awaken within us a feeling of joy born of the experience of being loved. But this encounter also engages our will and our intellect. Acknowledgment of the living God is one path towards love, and the 'yes' of our will to his will unites our intellect, will and sentiments in the all-embracing act of love."[7]

A basis for understanding this is recognizing that our emotions are rooted in the bodily part of us, but they also affect and are affected by the soul. We are designed in such a way that the body is meant to express the soul, as Pope St. John Paul II explored in depth in his catecheses on the Theology of the Body.[8] This will be fully the case in our glorified bodies. We experience it only partially now because sin has caused the body and the soul to be disintegrated. There is a process of partial integration

---

[6] Conrad W. Baars, *I Will Give Them a New Heart: Reflections on the Priesthood and the Renewal of the Church* (Staten Island, NY: Alba House, 2007), 83.

[7] Benedict XVI, *Deus Caritas Est*, §17.

[8] See Pope John Paul II's Audiences nos. 103–107, for example.

that takes place in this life under the influence of grace and the life of virtue. However, as we move closer to death, there is also the opposite process of further disintegration that takes place due to the decay of our mortal flesh. For example, think of the delight that can be seen on the face of a child who receives his first puppy—that face gives us a glimpse into the child's soul. On the other hand, think of the fake smile of the charlatan or the expressionless face of the stroke victim. These bodies obscure the reality of the soul rather than revealing it.

We give examples of facial expressions, but the internal experience of the emotions function similarly. We may experience delight, sadness, or nothing in prayer. Our feelings may distort or reinforce the true image of God and subsequently affect how we feel. Moreover, our feelings can be influenced by a good or bad spirit. Any range of emotions, positive or negative, may come up as our experiences and imaginations emerge in prayer. Negative emotions could arise, such as anger, frustration, inadequacy, self-contempt, lust, envy, etc.; or positive emotions could emerge, such as joy, delight, satisfaction, affection, desire, longing, gratitude, etc.

But the point of prayer is not to understand or focus too much on our feelings. The worst trap is always the same: self-absorption. I can get preoccupied with what is going on in my prayer or keep assessing how I am doing. I can become fascinated with something I am imagining or visualizing and wonder if it is a special sign for me from Him. I can marvel at the feelings of warmth or fervor, or at how holy I must be. These feelings are perfectly natural and perfectly useless. If I commend these feelings to Him, the wheat will be separated from the chaff. As

I simply bring all this to Him, along with any other distractions or random feelings and thoughts, and focus in loving faith on Him, what I need to know or understand or whatever God may be saying to me will stand out in the periphery of my attention. I can discern this better from the periphery than by focusing directly on it.

The point of prayer: a loving relationship with God

It is not uncommon for a person making a directed retreat to come to the spiritual director after a day of four hours of prayer with a simple report that prayer was difficult, dry, and empty. And yet, as he begins to describe the experience in more detail, the presence of the Lord emerges. One young man met with his retreat director at the end of the day after many hours of prayer and had no idea what to say. He was aware that he had been uncomfortable in prayer throughout the day. He had been alternately impressed with how much time he had spent in the chapel and disgusted at his inability to focus. He squirmed in the hard pews and fought to stay awake at different times. There seemed to be nothing that could provide refuge from the bleakness of the chapel, only lit with the dim light that came in from the dreary day through the stained-glass windows. But as the retreat director invited him simply to talk about his experience, and as he humbly admitted the inane thoughts that had coursed through his mind, he also became aware of how present the Lord was through all of it. Furthermore, he became aware of how profoundly the Lord was loving him through all of it. He never felt so inadequate and incapable, and as he shared the experience, he also never felt so unconditionally loved. It was a turning point in his life of prayer.

What stands out in prayer may begin to present itself in a way that lets me know it comes from more than me, from beyond me. I still should leave it on the periphery of my attention and continue holding it out to the Lord, focusing in loving faith on Him. The point of prayer is not to produce feelings or experiences that I like or that are encouraging to me. The point of prayer is not even primarily what God has to say to me or what I have to say to Him. The point of prayer is a loving relationship with God. Within that relationship I can say or express anything I want, but I should do so in faith that remains passionately open to Him and whatever He may be doing, without letting it lead back to absorption in myself. It is a diversion if I try to figure out what He is doing or saying. God communicates very clearly, but it takes us time, even a long time, to understand. God respects the time it takes us, and so should we. But if we are always relating to God like an oracle who will give us a word or a sign by which we can tell the future or read God's mind, we will be squandering intimacy for the sake of self-satisfying curiosity or self-assured security.

Think of how we impair our ability to understand another person more deeply if we are always trying to second-guess what the person means. If we get out ahead of God, we are always confused and feeling poorly connected with Him because we are hampering our ability to be truly attentive. It is as if we do not trust Him enough to wait for Him. This waiting is faith. If we simply wait in loving faith, all the things we need to know, the answers we want, "all these things will be [ours] as well" (Matt 6:33).

Moreover, our feelings can easily mislead us. Sometimes our feelings tell us God is far away, but in fact God is never distant. He is always closer to me than I am to myself.[9] As God, He can only love infinitely, meaning that He never loves us less. His love for every creature is infinite. His love even for Satan remains infinite and has never or will never lessen. As we have also noted, He infinitely loves every creature in an absolutely unique and personal way, as only a divine person can. Prayer in loving faith lets me connect relationally with the Lord in such a way that I begin to know His unique love for me. To chase after my feelings or impressions is to distract myself from the truth of how uniquely He loves me and what is really going on in the relationship He has with me. My feelings about Him, based on such things as what mood I am in or how I currently feel about myself are not only unreliable but can even be deceptive.

God is always waiting for me. He has waited for me from all eternity. This is true whether I feel like it or not. What we are saying here is all the more important to remember in modern times when there has been such a major epistemological shift. People today are more likely than ever to think the truth of something is based on their feeling about it. "It's true for me!" On what basis? "Because I strongly feel it is true!" In our times, most of us unknowingly approach reality this way, accepting subjective intensity as surely true, discounting the question of what is really or objectively true. But God really loves me infinitely, whether I feel like He does or not. He is closer than I am to myself, even if today I am not feeling that He is. How do I know that? By loving faith. That is, love, sustained by how God has revealed Himself

---

9   See St. Augustine, *Confessions*, bk. III, chap. 6, no. 11.

to us as passed on by Sacred Scripture and the Church, and nourished by the experience of Him opened up to me by that faith
which perdures no matter how I might be feeling, and which may
inform and correct what I am feeling.

The role of feelings in spiritual discernment according to St. Ignatius of Loyola

St. Ignatius of Loyola was a master of spiritual discernment and
noted the role of feelings such as joy, tears, and peace as signs
of spiritual consolation.[10] Likewise, he noted the way feelings
of interior agitation, disturbance, sadness, tepidity, and darkness
can be signs of spiritual desolation.[11] St. Ignatius did not reduce
the experience of spiritual consolation and desolation to feelings,
however. He also noted that these states could be characterized
by an increase in theological faith, hope, and love (or result in
a diminishment of those). He likewise observed the effect on
our reason, noting the lies that can accompany spiritual desolation and the truth that can come during spiritual consolation.
Above all he was describing human spiritual states that affect
both the material and spiritual parts of the person, indeed, the
whole psychology including intellect, sentiment, and will. These
states do not consist merely of feelings, nor are they devoid of
feelings. Feelings are a meaningful part of our discernment of the
authenticity of a religious experience, but by no means the sole
determinant of that experience. Furthermore, St. Ignatius found
it necessary to have a second set of rules for spiritual consola-

---

[10] St. Ignatius of Loyola, *Spiritual Exercises*, trans. Louis J. Puhl (Westminster, MD: Newman Press, 1960), no. 316.

[11] Ignatius of Loyola, *Spiritual Exercises*, no. 317.

tion,[12] because the positive feelings of religious experience can so easily lead us astray.

A careful study of the approach of St. Ignatius, held up to our personal experience, can provide an excellent guide in the spiritual life. There is a subtlety in his descriptions that must be carefully observed, however. The contrast between spiritual consolation and non-spiritual consolation as well as the contrast between spiritual desolation and non-spiritual desolation are critical distinctions for applying his rules of discernment. Ultimately, St. Ignatius expected the rules to be fully understood and used by those advanced in the spiritual life who would lead others in the Spiritual Exercises. He only encouraged the spiritual director to share the rules with the exercitant at appropriate times based on what he is experiencing during his retreat.[13] That way the exercitant would be able to understand them specifically against the applicable experiences in his prayer. When properly understood, the teaching of St. Ignatius provides a wonderful synthesis of the work of the demons and angels on our human feelings and thoughts, and he carefully guides the intellect and will of the one praying to navigate those experiences in such a way as to remain faithful to God's will.

What if My Faith Is Weak?
Confident Hope

My faith may not feel strong enough to believe in God's infinite love for me, but it is the truth and He loves me anyway. I may not

---

[12] Ignatius of Loyola, *Spiritual Exercises*, nos. 328–336.
[13] Ignatius of Loyola, *Spiritual Exercises*, nos. 8–10.

feel like I even know what love is, but through thick and thin, all I need to do is use my free will and choose to make an act of loving faith in Him. I choose to believe that He has always and will always love me infinitely. There is a saying in Alcoholics Anonymous: "Fake it till you make it." I may feel that my love and faith are fake, but I can choose lovingly to have faith anyway. I can keep blindly loving in blind faith whether I feel like it or not, perhaps praying as the father in the Gospel did, "I believe; help my unbelief!" (Mark 9:24).

Faith and love, as well as hope, are *infused* theological virtues, which means they are given supernaturally as gifts rather than being conjured up by our own efforts. Without the supernatural assistance of God, we would not even be stirred to faith and would not even know how to begin to approach God. It is so important always to remember this. When we reach out and speak to God or love Him, He is already there ahead of us, drawing us to Himself. God is partially accessible to our natural reason even without supernatural faith, and so we can know Him to some degree and seek Him using our natural faculties, such as when our experience of the world allows us to rationally infer the reality and goodness of God. But our natural efforts are always met and sustained by God's love for us and His sharing with us His own life in supernatural grace and the supernatural infused virtues of faith, hope, and love. We first received these virtues at Baptism, and they are strengthened and increased with every Sacrament we receive. Remember also that grace builds on and does not cancel out nature. God's supernatural gifts of faith, hope, and love do not make our efforts unnecessary but work together with them and enable the natural to reach what it could never reach without the supernatural love of God. No matter how I feel, I need only to open my heart to receive the gift of loving faith, though it may take some time and healing for me to grow in loving faith. This is where hope and confidence come in.

Confidence is sustained by the three theological virtues: faith, hope, and love. "The word, 'confidence,' summarizes the three theological virtues: faith, hope, and charity—sovereign virtues which bring all the others in their train. But if these are the highest virtues, then the greatest heroism is demanded of us in order to realize them in the face of the mystery of a 'hidden God.'"[14] We will talk further of the mystery of the hidden God in the next chapter, but for now let us see how faith becomes stronger and bears the fruit of love. This happens through hope and the confidence it generates.

Confidence happens when faith expands into loving hope. Slowly, as we live in a hopeful way, in this faith, love increases to a measure that leads to the conviction that grounds confidence. How confident can our faith become? There is no limit. But as we practice faith, faith is given. As we reach out in hope, hope grows. Faith and hope give rise to love, which then abounds. Soon confidence abounds, which generates stronger faith and hope, and deeper love. God then pours out more of His grace, faith upon faith, hope upon hope, and love upon love. Confidence grows beyond measure.

One very successful woman began discerning a call to a contemplative vocation and struggled for many years to find the confidence to make such a radical shift. She was a confident

---

[14] Jean C. J. d'Elbée, *I Believe in Love: A Personal Retreat Based on the Teaching of St. Thérèse of Lisieux*, 2nd ed. (Manchester, NH: Sophia Institute Press, 2001), 25.

woman and had done many noteworthy things in her field, but she struggled with a hesitancy to let go of everything and enter into a cloistered, contemplative life. Perseverance in spiritual direction and in prayer gradually strengthened her from within. She invested her little bit of faith and hope and love, and God increased these graces gradually, almost imperceptibly. Eventually she came to the point on a retreat that everything fell into place. She heard a word spoken at Mass by the priest that resonated in her heart, and she was able to make a decision to move forward in faith. She decided to enter the convent, and from that point on, she never looked back.

What would happen if we abandoned ourselves in *complete* confidence, to the point that anything we ask the Lord in faith, He will do. Here we will remember how Jesus was constantly seeking out faith among His disciples and those who sought healing from Him. It is astonishing how pervasive the occurrence of healing is in the New Testament.[15] All of it was grounded in faith, the faith that can move mountains, a faith that allows us not only to receive miracles but even to receive the forgiveness of sins. It is as if He is saying, "You have stolen my Heart; you have stolen my will from me by your faith filled with love; I can refuse you nothing."[16] Confident faith knows this. It knows that the Lord wants to refuse us nothing.

But our confidence falters, like Peter stepping out onto the water with Jesus but beginning to sink when he realized what he was doing (Matt 14:30). Jesus almost sounds sad when He rebukes Peter and others for their lack of faith (see Matt 14:31). At the

---

[15] See, for example, Mary Healy, *Healing: Bringing the Gift of God's Mercy to the World* (Huntington, IN: Our Sunday Visitor, 2015).

[16] d'Elbée, *I Believe in Love*, 38.

appearance of Jesus, when He sent His disciples out and when the Spirit was poured out, we see a confidence and faith that seem to suggest the heights to which Jesus is summoning us. This is confirmed not only by the many healings and exorcisms, but also by preaching. When we look at history, sometimes it seems that this faith was missing in different periods, and correspondingly, evidence of miracles or miraculous healing was missing. Perhaps various communities of faith at various points in history have had a more abstract or weak faith, or maybe the faith and confidence took other forms at other times, such as in mysticism or martyrdom.

Have you ever wondered if you would have the faith to give your life if you were facing martyrdom? Have you ever wondered if you pray with a person who has an infirmity whether you have the faith to pray for healing and to believe it will take place? The total confidence it takes to be a martyr or to believe totally that the Lord wants to answer our prayer is the same total confidence that animates our loving faith in prayer. Indeed, it is not going too far to say that loving faith is the very substance of prayer. Prayer must be practiced, and by becoming free from riding the roller coaster of fluctuating feelings, we can be free to grow in faith and hope, bearing fruit in love and confidence. Practicing this can lead to a habitual faith that dismisses doubt and yields an increasingly firmer confidence as well as a deeper love. This confidence becomes total in a way that could never be achieved except through grace.

Where Do Faith and Hope Lead? Self-Emptying Love

It would seem that to grow in confidence, one needs to accumulate it, save it up, preserve it until finally one has enough. In reality, rather than growing through filling up, the confidence coming from faith grows through emptying. Rather than coming from a strong self-certainty, this confidence comes from self-emptying. It might seem that to be confident, I must be fiercely independent, but the truth is that I must know my poverty and be totally dependent on God. This is where the love borne by the practice of prayer bears fruit, for this love is self-emptying love. This love grows until it is the very substance of my relationship with God, as I love the Lord my God with my whole heart, soul, mind, and strength. If I truly pray, I will fall deeply in love with the Lord until He truly is the center of my life rather than myself being in the center. As I no longer focus primarily on myself, now God becomes truly present.

Furthermore, this love flows into every area of our lives, into every relationship. Loving the Lord so totally makes love of neighbor and a proper self-love easy; indeed, they are given besides, and in appropriate measure. I find myself loving, understanding, and accommodating in my relationships with others. My life becomes joy filled, even if I am suffering deeply in other ways. Patience and solicitude become natural, and in the midst of an even greater investment in others, self-forgetfulness grows, exceeded only by growth in love of God. As Pope Benedict XVI put it so beautifully:

> In God and with God, I love even the person whom I do not like or even know. This can only take place on the basis of an intimate encounter with God, an encounter which has become a communion of will, even affecting my feelings. Then I learn to look on this other person not

simply with my eyes and my feelings, but from the perspective of Jesus Christ. His friend is my friend. Going beyond exterior appearances, I perceive in others an interior desire for a sign of love, of concern. . . . Seeing with the eyes of Christ, I can give to others much more than their outward necessities; I can give them the look of love which they crave.[17]

Then the best moments of the day are the moments given to an exclusive, one-on-one relationship with the Lord. This prayer is illuminated by love, like all my relationships, and it is a self-emptying love. Such prayer proceeds in the following way: whatever distractions there are, no matter how or what I am feeling, I can bring it all to the Lord and focus on Him in loving faith. This is the "communion of will" Pope Benedict XVI spoke of, which even transforms our feelings. This is adoration, and it is the best disposition with which to enter into a prayer of thanksgiving. Likewise, the other moments of prayer, petition, and atonement are best prayerfully assumed in loving faith.

This prayer allows the Lord to work powerfully in us, whether we feel Him working or not. Indeed, our faithful perseverance in loving faith is how we are best and most totally transformed. The consistent acts of self-emptying, loving faith eventually cease being individual acts and become a habitual disposition. Then we discover that we are being carried and that it is all grace! We stop focusing on ourselves, repeatedly taking our spiritual pulse, and we forget ourselves as we become resolute in faith which is received as a gift. There are then no bad times of prayer or wasted

---

[17] Benedict XVI, *Deus Caritas Est*, §18.

time in prayer. If I am besieged by sad feelings and tormented by distractions, if I have no consolation or seem to be unfocused, it makes no difference as long as I have returned again and again to loving faith.

Here we have what we can call the ascetical-mystical practice of the "sacrament of the present moment," wherein we simply take each moment in faith as an occasion of grace and expect the power of divine love in it. Asceticism is a discipline by virtue of which we become detached and transformed. In this case, the detachment is from self. Like asceticism that involves fasting or some other discipline, here the discipline is one that allows me to live in the present moment in a prayerful way. It is not easy to live in the present moment. The less absorbed in self I am, the more easily I can be free to just receive prayerfully and gratefully what is given by life, by others, and by my own efforts. Freedom also comes because we come to carry our past without being burdened by it or feeling cheated, and to hope for the future without being anxious about it. Whatever comes up from the past or the future, whatever memories or anticipation, we commend it to Him and focus on Him. Whatever comes in each present moment we receive as God's will and greet it with hope and faith. "Endeavor to remain always in the presence of God, either real, imaginative, or unitive insofar as is permitted by your works."[18]

Indeed, when we enter into more protracted periods of quiet prayer, it sometimes seems we have lost track of time, and even lost a sense of where we are. At times it may seem like we have blacked out or felt nothing. In fact, if one spends substantial

---

[18] St. John of the Cross, "*Degrees of Perfection*" no. 2 (Kavanaugh, *The Collected Works of St. John of the Cross*, 729).

amounts of time in prayer, soon he will often feel that time stops and all is present. The asceticism of this prayer is an asceticism of faith through which we live in the confidence that the Lord is infinitely loving us each moment of our lives and into eternity. And so, we live in loving confidence.

What about Feelings of Guilt and Negativity in Prayer? Divine Mercy!

Sometimes in prayer we are beset by thoughts or imaginings. They often seem to be simply nonsense, such that we begin to doubt if we are praying at all. At other times we are plagued with negative thoughts and feelings which seem to indicate there is no hope of reaching recollection, and that no matter how hard we try we only see the dark side of things. At other times we may be aware of our sins, of our weaknesses, of our temptations, all of which St. Paul calls "the flesh" (see Rom 7:18). It may seem that I am overwhelmed with such guilt that I do not even feel worthy to pray or to approach God.

Here again we are dealing with feelings. Ultimately, they cannot be trusted, especially if I am a person who tends to be negative about myself, or even negative about everything. If there is reason for guilt, such as over my sins, then I need still to pray the same way. I should hold out my sins, along with any guilty feelings I have about them, and then confess them unless I have already done so. Then I should focus not on my sin or guilt but upon God. My loving faith can include sorrow for my sin, and I may want to speak to God and ask for forgiveness, but my focus should not be on myself nor on my sin. I leave these things at the periphery of my awareness.

Thus, I should never wallow in guilt in a self-absorbed way. It is unchristian to think of my sin apart from God's mercy. I should be sorry for my sins and experience any guilt only in light of the infinite love and mercy of God and in faith that all is forgiven. Here again, if I do not feel forgiven or do not feel contrite enough, I can express my sorrow to the Lord in the faith that I am indeed forgiven. As is always the truth with faith, as I simply look to the Lord in love, whatever my feelings, my attitude begins to change; I see my sins in a new light and understand them in the light of faith in the Lord's mercy. I may also begin to see any unrepentant parts of myself, and I can bring those parts before the Lord's mercy as well.

Sometimes guilt is really our keen disappointment over our resistant tendencies toward sin or our weaknesses. I may find myself fantasizing about lustful things and then suddenly realize what I am doing. As long as I do not deliberately choose to pursue these thoughts, they are not sinful, though I may feel contaminated by them or guilty for having them. However, there is no sin without deliberate, conscious consent. Weaknesses or temptations should be taken seriously, but I should not feel guilty over them unless I encourage them or give in to them.[19] Those who are trying to grow in prayer and in the spiritual life and who are conscientious about rooting out sin need to be reminded of this. The best thing to do with weakness and even temptations is not to try to suppress or ignore them but to actually bring them before the Lord in prayer, focusing not on them but on Him, asking Him for relief from the

---

[19] See St. Thomas Aquinas, *de Malo*, Article 9, in *On Evil*, trans. Richard Regan and ed. Brian Davies (New York: Oxford University Press, 2003).

temptations and total reliance on Him in our weakness.

Sometimes the darkness is spiritual dryness or desolation, a seeming absence of faith. We can feel we have lost our way in a spiritual fog without any consolation, in which we seem not to know how to proceed or how to endure. I may find it hard to believe in myself, or to believe in God. I may even feel I cannot make an act of faith. This condition may lie deeper than feelings, and reach into the very innermost depths of heart and soul. Unlike mere negativity or guilt, this is a more pervasive condition and is not so easily bypassed by faith. But here is where faith, while seeming to flounder, is really being purified. Many of our human supports are being stripped away in this process. Our shallow beliefs about how life should be, how people should behave, how God should be acting, or other conventional beliefs of everyday life are all being purified to lead us to depend on God alone.

The earlier consolations which partially motivated prayer disappear or become less frequent. The one who prays now sees his own flesh in its most raw form. Boredom is replaced by a repugnance toward prayer, and the only infinite that seems real is infinite emptiness. We come face-to-face with our own interior nothingness and sin. Those who spend much time in prayer, such as cloistered contemplatives, hermits, or ordinary people who persevere in prayer for many years, have the same experience: faith deepens.

Loving faith may seem to be impossible in such desolation, but in fact it is greatly purified there. "Never give up prayer, and should you find dryness and difficulty, persevere in it for this very reason. God often desires to see what love your soul has, and love is not tried by ease and satisfaction."[20] This is especially true if the suffering of the dryness is made into an offering of love, and if this offering is made to the Lord even if He cannot be felt or found. Again, in this way, loving faith is purified. "To arrive at transformation, we must see with other eyes and love with another heart; and to see with other eyes, we have to pass through that darkness. After passing through that most dark passageway, we open our eyes and now we no longer see as before. We have a new way of seeing, of loving, and of understanding."[21] Now we see with eyes of deeper faith, a faith that can see in the dark and love in the dark, that can see through suffering and love in suffering.

It may seem that I cannot pray in desolation or because of negative feelings. All I need to do is to pray anyway. It is often the case that in the times when it seems impossible to pray or find God at all, that when we reach out anyway, suddenly we realize that He is there and we experience consolation. In such desolate times, we can only sit quietly, but then we discover that we are praying to Him after all. It is at times such as this that the Holy Spirit prays in us (Rom 8:26).

For the love among the persons in the Trinity is the source of the relationships we have with God and with each other. It is the Holy Spirit who engenders the relationship between ourselves and the Son, and through Him with the Father. This union is real whether we can feel it or not, and faith is able to touch its reality, however delicately.

---

[20] St. John of the Cross, "*Degrees of Perfection*" no. 9 (Kavanaugh, *The Collected Works of St. John of the Cross*, 730).

[21] Martinez, *Worshipping a Hidden God*, 203.

Does Prayer Make Me Suffer More?
The Wounds

"Pure love is realized in pure faith, and pure faith is realized in darkness in the same way that strength is perfected in weakness."[22] Nonetheless, sometimes the darkness is so great that it causes great pain, and the most painful thing of all may be prayer.

There is suffering that comes from self-absorption. This suffering is not to be borne but should be eliminated if possible, and that happens by dying to self and becoming absorbed in the Lord. It happens every time we turn away from self and turn toward the other. Some suffering comes from deprivation, and this often can and should be eliminated. Suffering that comes from outside myself and which cannot be eliminated can be assimilated during prayer by being accepted and possibly offered up rather than becoming a cause for self-pity or self-absorption. But the suffering that comes from love, while being purified, should not be eliminated and usually serves to deepen love even further.

Suffering is transformed when it is taken up into love. Indeed, there is an exquisite quality to the suffering that comes from love. This may be a suffering from unrequited love or lack of love, but there is a suffering in *all* love, even when it is fulfilled. For love can never be satisfied completely, and often the deepest, most fulfilled love has at its heart a profound pain. This cannot be eliminated, at least this side of death. Moreover, it is an essential part of deep love, and suffering from love deepens love.

Nowhere is this experienced more profoundly than in love

---

[22] d'Elbée, *I Believe in Love*, 78.

of God. We said that the loving faith in which prayer consists is really a gift. We also pointed out that the awareness of how extraordinary the love of God is causes us to be taken up into that love. Love always singles out the beloved from all the others. "Simon . . . do you love me more than these?" (see John 21:15–17). The loved one becomes absolutely unique, and my love, our love, is absolutely unique. Exclusivity is one of the perfections of love. This creates a certain solitude between two lovers, a relationship exclusive to them and shared by no one else, making them both say: "You are my only one!" This unity is consuming and absorbing, isolating us from everyone else. We experience this overwhelmingly when we fall in love; but even if the love is mutual, and however fully expressed, there is still sorrow and something lacking because we long for more. This is not only true of erotic love, but also of friendship and charity. In the beauty of love there is always a lack and a longing, and a certain solitude that persists even while united with the beloved.

In the love of God there is a silence and a solitude: "The silence of God is a form of speech. His Word is solitude. The solitude of God is not an absence, it is his very being, his silent transcendence."[23] One would think this suffering is due to the fact that only God can satisfy us, for "you have made us and drawn us to yourself, and our heart is unquiet until it rests in you."[24] Yet the love of God bears within it the deepest suffering of all. It starts with a longing, and even when there is some fulfillment, the longing simply seems to grow. A pain starts, moving from emotional pain to a pain deep in the innermost self. This can sometimes take the

---

[23] Sarah and Diat, *The Power of Silence*, 88.
[24] St. Augustine, *Confessions*, bk. I, chap. 1, no. 1.

form of what seems to be an actual physical pain, often where the heart is, sometimes seeming to be constant, becoming more intense when love is flowing freely. This is true when we love another person but especially when we love the Lord.

Love always involves suffering, because love can never completely express or fulfill itself, even when it is sexually consummated. Sometimes the deepest pain is then. Prayer involves this suffering in an unabated way even when love is joyful and gratified, when there is contentment as well as when there is separation, or unfulfilled or unfulfillable love. This suffering surely purifies love, but it is about much more than purgation. It is about the realization and perfection of love. Love is infinite and eternal, but in our humanity we are finite and temporal. As long as we are on this side of death, we are rooted in time and we continue to face the inevitable reality of death, which appears to be the end of love.

This opens to us the mystery of the Cross. "Greater love has no man than this, that a man lay down his life for his friends" (John 15:13). This is the love that conquers death, sin, time, and every limit. It is a love that is stronger than death and that reaches into eternity by passing through the suffering of total self-offering, even to the point of death, which is eternal. And the death on the Cross was finalized in the descent into the most absolute solitude of abandonment, the descent among the dead. Love is only satisfied with what is infinite. In our love of God we taste this, and in suffering we long not only for more love, but for infinite love, a love that includes every tear ever shed and every loss ever felt. This is already embraced in loving faith: every groan we make along with all creation as we await the fulfillment of love. We can see all this in the powerful reflection of St. Paul in his letter to the Romans:

> I consider that the sufferings of this present time are not worth comparing with the glory that is to be revealed to us. For the creation waits with eager longing for the revealing of the sons of God; for the creation was subjected to futility, not of its own will but by the will of him who subjected it in hope; because the creation itself will be set free from its bondage to decay and obtain the glorious liberty of the children of God. We know that the whole creation has been groaning with labor pains together until now; and not only the creation, but we ourselves, who have the first fruits of the Spirit, groan inwardly as we wait for adoption as sons, the redemption of our bodies. For in this hope we were saved. Now hope that is seen is not hope. For who hopes for what he sees? But if we hope for what we do not see, we wait for it with patience. (Rom 8:18–25)

Even mystical, transforming union here on earth still longs in suffering for total consummation, and loves the Cross as the only way to enter such love. This side of death, love longs to die with Him so as to rise with Him (see Rom 6:5).

To summarize, we must take up the cross of our finitude and in faith set our direction for a consummation that lies beyond the limits of this life. We can only make progress if we allow divine love to fill us and hope to move us in a way that even increases our suffering as we long for eternal union with the Beloved. In the face of our personal weakness and sinfulness, we can let this love move us out of ourselves as we abandon everything to Him for whom we were made. As St. Paul said, we stretch forward in hope and at the same time we wait in patience, which always involves a form of suffering. We humbly accept that we are not worthy of Him, and yet we know that we need Him and cannot live without Him. As the Catechism expresses it:

> The most common yet most hidden temptation is our lack of faith. It expresses itself less by declared incredulity than by our actual preferences. When we begin to pray, a thousand labors or cares thought to be urgent vie for priority; once again, it is the moment of truth for the heart: what is its real love? Sometimes we turn to the Lord as a last resort, but do we really believe he is? Sometimes we enlist the Lord as an ally, but our heart remains presumptuous. In each case, our lack of faith reveals that we do not yet share in the disposition of a humble heart: "Apart from me, you can do nothing."[25]

"It is no longer I who live but Christ who lives in me" (Gal 2:20). Jesus transforms us into Himself. I now want to do everything for Christ and in Christ, love in His love, breathe in His breath, pray in His prayer, suffer in His suffering, offer myself in His offering to His Father. This must be lived out in my daily life here on earth, and involves the suffering of abandonment by which I surrender to doing His will. Abandonment to God's will, in a faith that strips away the veil of secondary causes as well as attachments to anything but God:

---

[25] CCC 2732.

Abandonment, rightly understood, includes everything. It requires great humility, since it is a submission of ourselves to creatures and events, seeing Jesus Himself in them. It requires an immense faith, confidence at every moment, to tear open the veil of secondary causes, to break through the screen of creatures which too often prevents us from seeing Jesus behind them, who governs everything, since nothing—nothing—happens without His having willed or permitted it.[26]

---

[26] d'Elbée, *I Believe in Love*, 84.

5

Praying to a Hidden God

T RULY, you are a God who hides yourself, O God of Israel, the Savior. (Isa 45:15)

One of the great and saving truths that prayer brings home to us is this: God is always present. God is present to us even before we take our first, baby breaths in the spiritual life. Our five senses, of course, simply cannot grasp this truth. To them it seems like an illusion. But if we take time, in prayer, to step away from the immediate noise of the senses, if we dare to go down to the root of our desire, then gradually, in that place of silence and darkness, something like an awakening occurs, and we realize that the God whom we felt or thought was absent, has in fact always been present, and is so close to us now we can dare to speak – amazing thought! – of God dwelling within us.[1]

---

[1] Paul Murray, O.P., *In the Grip of Light: The Dark and Bright Journey of Christian Contemplation* (London: Bloomsbury, 2012), 22–23.

The Hiddenness of God

One of the greatest scandals to faith is that God is a hidden God. Why is He hidden? Why does He hide? We talk to Him though we can't really see Him or hear Him. An agnostic on television once spoke of his faith journey, explaining he was born Jewish, switched to Christianity in a more established denomination which had beautiful liturgy, and then moved to a more fundamentalist and charismatic non-denominational form of Christianity. Finally he gave up. Then, to make his point more vividly, he said, "If there is a God, show yourself to me!" Then he looked at his audience and observed, "Nothing!" Then he said, "God, show me somehow that you are here if you are here!" Again only silence! And he concluded, "Then if you can't do that for me, I give up on you!"

Woody Allen once observed in one of his movie monologues, "You know, if it turns out that there *is* a God, I don't think that He's evil. I think that the worst you can say about Him is that, basically, He's an underachiever."[2] Who *is* in charge here? Why doesn't God show Himself? Why is He so hidden? After all we have been saying about prayer, how do we know He's really there? We claim we can know what He wants and that He is there. We have talked all about how even these consolations can be taken away, how dark it gets and how dry. We say that this is because God is deepening our love by deepening our faith. But why are we required to have faith rather than to have sight? This scandal becomes all the more severe when things happen which are hard

---

[2]   Woody Allen, *Love and Death*, (Beverly Hills: MGM Studios, 1975).

to imagine a merciful God would allow: the torture and abuse of innocent children, the slaughter of people of faith, the violent and destructive acts which traumatize and damage a woman for the rest of her life, the heartfelt and faith-filled prayers which seem to go unanswered.

As faith tries to make sense of this, we need to realize first: God's ways are not our ways (see Isa 55:8–9). What does this mean? In the first place, as we have already seen, we do not find God in the usual way in which we know naturally, using merely our five external senses. Clearly God is not available to our sense perception, to be experienced in the way we experience sensible reality. Most of us will agree that there is more to reality than what can be experienced with our external senses. The internal senses, for example, tell us things about what is real which go beyond and are deeper than what is empirically verifiable. As Joseph Ratzinger observed, "In point of fact, we cannot see God as we see an apple tree or a neon sign, that is, in a purely external way that requires no interior commitment. We can see him only by becoming like him. . . . We can see God only if we turn around, stop looking for him as we might look for street signs and dollar bills, and begin looking away from the visible to the invisible."[3] But why is God not simply accessible to our senses like the other creatures in the world? Why, if He wants us to recognize Him, is He hidden?

One reason we cannot see God is that He is not one creature or being that can be found among others. Rather, He is the very ground and possibility of any other beings. For this reason, some

---

[3] Joseph Ratzinger, *Dogma and Preaching* (San Francisco: Ignatius Press, 2011), 325.

philosophers and theologians speak of individual beings but name Him "Being" or "being-in-itself."[4] He is beyond all creation and at the same time within every particular being there is or has ever been. He cannot be located in space and time as you and I and every other creature can, because He is the Creator and beyond any particular space and time, indeed beyond any definition whatsoever. Because God is God, He is infinite, without limit. That means that unlike every creature which is limited and defined by being the kind of creature it is, God the Creator is without limit, beyond limit, beyond definition. Even created things are unfathomable, and Immanuel Kant and others demonstrated that we never know the "thing in itself."[5] St. Thomas Aquinas would actually agree, and points out that there is much that is unknown about every object of knowledge, and that, in his terminology, we do not know the substantial forms of things as they are in themselves.[6] How much more, then, do we find ourselves at a disadvantage when we try to know God or even to locate or find Him? The problem with God becomes all the greater since we are unable to even see or hear Him! Why didn't God do something about this if He wants us to know, love, and serve Him?

He is hidden because He does not exist in a particular way as a particular being in a particular space at a particular time like we do. He is everywhere at once. How do we penetrate this veil of hiddenness? Actually we cannot see Him with our eyes except through the eyes of our heart, and we cannot hear Him except

---

[4] In Latin: *ipsum esse subsistens*.

[5] Immanuel Kant, *Critique of Pure Reason: Unified Edition*, ed. James W. Ellington, trans. Werner S. Pluhar (Indianapolis, IN: Hackett, 1996).

[6] St. Thomas Aquinas, *Quaestiones Disputatae de Veritate*, 4, 1 ad 8, in Josef Pieper, *Silence of St. Thomas*, 3rd ed. (South Bend, IN: St. Augustine's Press, 1999), 65.

through the ears of our heart. In other words, we can only see Him in blindness or darkness and can only hear Him in silence. But what if we're hearing nothing at all?

This leads to the question, why isn't there only nothing? Why is there anything at all? Why is there something rather than nothing? Where did I, where did all of this come from? No being, not even human beings, are self-originating, self-sufficient, and self-sustaining, though we might like to think we are! If life can be produced in a test tube from some non-living elements, where did those elements come from? Who designed all this? Is it really possible to believe it was random chance rather than intelligent design?

While God is not locatable as one being among others, He is mysteriously the source and destiny of every creature. Eliminate the question of source and destiny before and beyond life, and it all becomes absurd. Moreover, God is somehow mysteriously in all creation and in every creature. The internal senses, the intuition for example, seem to perceive or know a presence surrounding and grounding everything that is, flowing in everything that is. This presence permeates the innermost depths of myself, of my soul. The concerted effort to tune in to this presence and live in accord with it is a primary focus of every religion. This universal intuition gives even more credence to faith than the logical necessity of Being that is the source of all beings.

The wonderfully surprising discovery of God's self-revelation to Abraham and Moses is that this ground of all being, the unlocatable reason there is something rather than nothing, is *personal*! If He is less than personal, human beings surpass Him, though we clearly are not the reason there is something rather than nothing. God is not a "what" but a "Who"! Our human "I," or self, stands always before an eternal I, an eternal person. My "I am" makes sense only before the great "I AM" who revealed Himself from the burning bush to Moses. God lets us be, lets us stand before Him, because God "is the Almighty, but at the same time, he wants to permit man to be truly free . . . The infinity of God is not an infinity in space, a bottomless, scoreless ocean; it is love that has no limits. Creation is an act of love . . . a kind of divine 'self-restraint.'"[7]

In God's revelation in Jesus Christ, we know that as part of His divine "self-restraint," God has become incarnate in the Person of the Son, but in space and time, in history, as one of us. In the Person of Jesus Christ, God has come out of hiddenness to limit Himself to a particular face and a particular voice. Paradoxically, He can emerge from hiddenness while still also remaining hidden in the mystery of the Incarnation. The mystery of the intimate union of divinity and humanity in the person of the Son is the mystery of how our relationship with God can become a union that transforms our soul into Christ. The mystery of the Incarnation is consummated in the Paschal mystery. The Paschal mystery furthermore bears the fruit of the Eucharist—the bread and wine that became the Body and Blood of Christ, which, when received, transforms us too into Christ.

Consider the writings of St. Paul on this hiddenness of God, even after the Incarnation and His gift of Himself in the Eucharist: "We walk by faith and not by sight" (2 Cor 5:7), hoping for that which we do not see (Rom 8:25). But St. Paul also writes mysteriously that at his coming again, our seeing will be "face

---

[7] Sarah and Diat, *The Power of Silence*, 91.

to face" when "I shall know even as I am known" (1 Cor 13:12). The Eternal Son of God became Incarnate in order to let us see ourselves in Him. The Son is the image of the invisible God, the Father, who sees Himself in the Son (Col 1:15). Out of His bountiful love He created human beings capable of knowing and loving Him. So that we could see Him and see ourselves in Him, He became flesh. We see ourselves in the innocent babe of Nazareth; we see and hear about ourselves in the words and teaching of Christ and continue to do so in Scripture and Sacrament. And nowhere do we see ourselves mirrored in Him and He in us more than in the paschal mystery of the passion, death, and resurrection of Jesus Christ. "If then you have been raised with Christ, seek the things that are above, where Christ is, seated at the right hand of God. Set your minds on things that are above, not on things that are on earth. For you have died, and your life is hidden with Christ in God. When Christ who is our life appears, then you also will appear with him in glory" (Col 3:1–4).

God's Hiddenness in Darkness and Silence: Supernatural Faith

What are the depths of our hidden God into which we are entering when we pray? The greatest saints have not penetrated to the depths of themselves, nor the greatest psychoanalysts, nor the greatest mystics or gurus. When we consider that we are made in the image of God and we have immortal souls, we know we have an infinite capacity. This helps us imagine how exponentially greater must be the proportion of our heart or human spirit which we do not know or ever tap into. Indeed, we are a bottomless pit! We know this when we try to fill or fulfill ourselves. There is a place deep in us where God is most present. We come to know that place in knowing Him. We never exhaustively know that place; only God does, for it is God who sustains everything, knows everything, loves everything, from the inside out. Then we discover that God has loved us first! It is not we who make room for God, it is God who makes room for us. If God is infinitely beyond us, only He can unite us with Himself, and He does so by making us totally one with Him who is closer to us than we are to ourselves.

Two of the things we dislike most about prayer are when we pray and don't hear anything, or when we pray and it is all dry and dark. We feel that prayer then is not good, is not working. In fact, these are two of the things that indicate we are truly praying to God and connecting with Him who is hidden, and not just entertaining our own thoughts and feelings. We actually should seek the darkness and seek the silence, not try to avoid them! Because God is infinite, because He is not locatable to be found or seen in space and time, He can only be seen in the darkness of my senses, both exterior (the five senses) and even interior (the imagination and memory). God is hidden because He is greater than these and cannot be contained, localized, or objectified in a finite way, and He is only available to faith which sees in darkness, sees in secret. Likewise, faith only sees or hears God hidden in silence and in darkness.

Catholic doctrine has shown us that God's existence is reasonable, but reason and concepts only give us hints of Him, not a direct knowledge of Him any more than the five senses give us a direct perception of Him. Our imagination likewise cannot grasp Him. We can use images of the imagination and concepts of reason only to achieve analogous knowledge of Him, not direct comprehension. Dionysius said, "Since [God] is the Cause of all beings, we should posit and ascribe to [Him] all the affirmations we make in regard to beings, and, more appropriately, we should negate all these affirmations, since [He] surpasses all being."[8] Only faith is capable of directly knowing God, and that is in a darkness of the understanding and imagination. Therefore, reading about Him, even in the scriptures, and imagining Him can only lead us into prayer and deeper into faith. When faith is darkest, then we are closest to understanding. God speaks in the faith that is fostered by the most absolute silence, for in fact the darkness is overwhelming light, infinite light, and the silence is not the mere absence of noise but the silence of potential sound. It is not a silence that stifles words, but a silence that makes sounds or words possible, the silence that allows us to hear at all, to hear God at all.

As we have seen, God's pure gift of supernatural faith builds upon our own natural efforts. Because faith as a supernatural gift is infused, or directly "poured in," the obscurity in faith contains its greatest certitude. Such supernatural faith is obscure because it is given in the darkness of the interior and exterior senses. It is certain because its certitude and authority rest in its giver, God. This is therefore not a natural certitude but a supernatural certitude, just as the obscurity is not a natural obscurity but a supernatural obscurity. The certitude does not remove the obscurity because God cannot be known or seen by anything but

8 Pseudo-Dionysius, *Pseudo-Dionysius: The Complete Works*, ed. J. Farina, trans. C. Luibheid and P. Rorem (Mahwah, NJ: Paulist Press, 1987), 136.

supernatural faith, and then He is seen in darkness and heard in silence. Thus the silence and obscurity are not a deficit or deprivation in prayer but are the only way in which we can make the direct contact with God which supernatural faith alone provides.

These are not word games or sleight of hand maneuvers. This is not taking refuge in mysticism and unknowing. It is an attempt to see why God is hidden. It demonstrates the contemplative mystical element of all prayer. It shows why the saints and mystics claim that, in order to reach such supernatural contemplation, one must enter into a night of internal and external senses in which it seems we are losing faith, for indeed natural faith does fade as supernatural faith takes over. If nothing that can be seen reveals God or is God, God can only be seen by entering into darkness or "unseeing." If God cannot be heard in the ordinary way, He must be heard in silence.

St. John of the Cross distinguishes between active and passive phases of the purification that come through the night of the senses, the will, and the soul. Initially we have some experience where our effort (I'm active) and God's movement (I'm passive) are running in tandem. Slowly our emotional life begins to drag behind what is going on in prayer, and later our will, and even our very soul! It feels not only like I do not want to pray, but as if I cannot! This in fact is the time of great purification. "Not every suffering is night. But any suffering can become night."[9]

No matter how dark the night, God is always pure shining light, and no matter how dry and empty the soul, God's love is always flowing in. Passivity deepens to the point of seeming almost to be total as we let ourselves be carried by God and be

---

[9]   Matthew, *The Impact of God*, 72.

sustained in Him in a way in which we discover He has always been carrying us. Then we know that all we need to do when we pray is "show up." The simple attentiveness of passive prayer is a naked trust which allows for more total gift on the part of Divine Love. At such moments of darkness, we must simply believe, trust, and love (i.e., faith, hope, and love, which are the infused theological virtues), knowing that we are receiving the gift even if we cannot perceive it or feel it. All we need to do is turn to God, believe in Him no matter what, trust in Him no matter what, and love Him with all our hearts! "Turn to God present within you, and love him. You may not feel his presence; but want him, value him, give yourself to him, say yes to him, adore him. Love him, and you are experiencing God."[10]

It is hard to be passive because we are afraid of losing God, but God never withdraws or is absent. He never loves us less. He never leaves us in darkness simply to purify us, but He is always closer to us than we are to ourselves. This is what we must believe, this is what we must trust, and this is how we must love! This love is much greater than any experience we will ever have of it, including supernatural consolations and gifts. This passivity is increasingly letting go by denying ourselves and entering into a deeper abandonment to God's Will. It leads to a deepening of humility which engenders a dying to self and an entering into a greater simplicity, silence and love. It leads ever more deeply into God's hiddenness. God is hidden also in order to draw us into His hiddenness with Him, to draw us to let go of all that keeps us from knowing in His hiddenness that He is nearer to us than we are to ourselves. It is not Who He is to be one of us, though He

---

[10] Matthew, *The Impact of God*, 111.

became one of us in the Incarnation. But He wants us to freely decide to come to Him, to be drawn through His hiddenness in mystery to come to Him, to yearn for Him, seek Him, and be transformed in becoming more like Him in coming to Him. "We can see him only by becoming like him, by reaching the level of reality on which God exists; in other words, by being liberated from what is anti-divine: the quest for pleasure, enjoyment, possessions, gain, or, in a word, from ourselves. In the final analysis it is usually the self that stands between us and God."[11]

We have said that supernatural faith allows a direct contact with God. As St. John of the Cross writes in his *Ascent of Mount Carmel*, faith is "the only proximate and proportionate means to union with God" because "the likeness between faith and God is so close that no other difference exists than that between believing in God and seeing Him. Just as God is infinite, faith proposes Him to us as infinite; as there are Three Persons in One God, it presents Him to us in this way; and as God is darkness to our intellect, so does faith dazzle and blind us. Only by means of faith, in Divine Light exceeding all understanding, does God manifest Himself to the soul. The more intense a man's faith, the closer is his union with God."[12]

This naked faith can become the experience of the dark night of purification of which St. John of the Cross speaks and for which he is most famous. The thing about the dark night is that when one is in it, one does not usually think of it as a spiritual phase one is passing through, for the deepest dark night may

---

[11] Ratzinger, *Dogma and Preaching*, 325.

[12] St. John of the Cross, *Ascent of Mount Carmel*, Book II, ix, (Kavanaugh, *The Collected Works of John of the Cross*, 129); See also Matthew, *The Impact of God*, 530.

seem that it is not spiritual at all and that it will never end, that night is all there is. This dark night may bring about a mystical death culminating from a process of detachment, a detachment which began in the self-denial and ascetical practices through which the spiritual purification begins. Dark nights of the senses and faculties lead to a dark night of the soul and to a mystical death to self so that it is no longer I who live but Christ who lives in me (Gal 2:20). The night of pure and naked faith brings us to the point of almost being able to grasp God by being able to grasp nothing, grasping Him only by surrendering myself to love that is infinite and infinitely dark.

And yet the infinite darkness is infinite light. St. Thomas Aquinas says that there is an obscurity to our knowing even finite objects of knowledge, but that this obscurity is because finite knowledge cannot grasp the luminosity even of natural, much less of supernatural reality: the reality of things is their light, but they are also darkness because they have been created out of nothing.[13] It is because the truth of every limited, finite reality has such a depth of being and light that it exceeds our finite faculties of knowledge such that we never know any creature, not even ourselves, in the full reality with which God knows it or me. How much greater the luminosity of divine light? We know Him only in the darkness of faith, only in His hiddenness. Yet because faith is a supernatural gift, it in fact gives us a contact with God and union with Him that is greatest when it feels like contact has been completely lost. The abandonment of all things, most especially of self, in love leaves an emptiness that is at first disarming,

---

[13] *Quaestiones Disputatae de Veritate*, 18, 2 ad 5, in Josef Pieper, *The Silence of Saint Thomas*, 60, 67.

then perhaps terrifying, then simply empty, and then the fullness of love in union.

Seeing Him and Seeing Ourselves in Him

Of all creatures, human beings are created in the image and likeness of God. This likeness in image becomes more fully union as we discover we are like Him and become more and more like Him. Our likeness to God indeed continues to increase as we go more deeply into union with Him in the darkness of loving faith. This union is an abiding in Him which already was initiated in Baptism and which makes us long ever more intensely to see His face. When we do, the union and the likeness will be complete. The mystery of creation in His image and likeness has been fulfilled in the mystery of the Incarnation in which the eternal Son of God became human precisely to reveal to us much about God that could not otherwise be known, and much about our likeness to Him that we could otherwise never have known. How awesome that God, in the person of the Divine Son, became one of us so that we could see in Him how like us He is and how much He loves us, that He would become one of us and make it possible for us to see His face! Yet even His contemporaries who saw Him and heard Him were still summoned by Jesus to faith, and to abide in Him in faith, hope, and love. Even they sometimes faltered in faith and failed to recognize Him. As we have noted, only when we see Him face-to-face in the fullness of vision will we see Him as He is, and then we will be like Him. How Jesus appeared transfigured and risen still required faith which will no longer be required when we see Him in the fullness of vision.

The mystery of the Incarnation in turn is consummated in the Paschal mystery of the passion, death, and resurrection of Jesus. Until He comes again, at the moment of full vision, we live in what will lead us to that vision as here we already see ourselves in His Paschal mystery as we see Him like us in our sin and death. Jesus gave us through the Paschal mystery the ongoing sacramental presence of Himself in the Eucharist where He is hidden mysteriously beneath the accidents or appearances of bread and wine. This presence and "seeing" ourselves in Him in the Eucharist requires faith: as St. Augustine says, before the words of consecration what you see on the altar is bread and wine; after the consecration what you see on the altar is the body and blood of Christ.[14] But even that does not quench our longing. Even after we are fed by the Eucharist, we are left longing to see His face and abide even more deeply in Him.

We see our likeness in Him enough to know that we are Christ's brothers and sisters, that we are children of the Father! We also recognize what the Son has revealed about God, that He is Abba. As Jesus has told us, no one sees the Father except the Son and those to whom the Son gives the power to see Him, since we are unable to see the Father in space and time as the Son was during His earthly life and as He is in the Eucharist. The Father eternally begets the Son in eternal Love, and the third, the Spirit proceeds from the Father and the Son and is Himself the Divine Love flowing between them. It is the Spirit, again unlocatable in space and time, through whom the eternally begotten Son of the Father became flesh and through whom the bread and

---

[14] See St. Augustine's Sermon to Neophytes (#227), in Lawrence Feingold, *The Eucharist: Mystery of Presence, Sacrifice, and Communion* (Steubenville: Emmaus Academic, 2018), 158.

wine become the Body and Blood of Christ.

God's self-revelation as three persons in one seems to pass from the invisible, unnamable God to the visibility of the Son who names God "Abba," and back into invisibility in the Spirit who explains and reminds us of what the Son has revealed, without being able Himself to be located or perceived in space and time. "The Holy Spirit reminds us that God is mystery. The Son is 'truth' (Greek *aletheia*: not hidden). He is God who is no longer hidden, he is the God who is revealed. The Spirit, however, is God who is still concealed. He is the unfathomable depth of God, which is unreachable and incomprehensible. St. Paul associates the Spirit with the depths of God: 'The Spirit searches everything, even the depths of God' (1 Cor 2:10)."[15]

Rather, the Spirit is seen in the light of all that is illuminated in Him, particularly the Fatherhood of God who cannot be called Abba except in the Spirit (see Rom 8:15) and the Lordship of the Son who cannot be called Lord except in the Spirit (1 Cor 12:3). No one sees the Father because the Father is beyond objectification, is indeed the eternal infinite source of all Being, is hidden. It is the Spirit who reveals the Father's eternal Word and explains Him, not Himself being visible as Spirit, but as the one who lets us see God. As we become "divinized by the Spirit . . . We shall see God to the extent that it is at all possible to see Him. His mystery will be the light in which we shall see His light that is twilight in the mystery,"[16] twilight in the mystery of creation, the mystery of Incarnation, and in the Paschal mystery.

---

[15] Wilfrid Stinissen, O.C.D., *The Holy Spirit, Fire of Divine Love* (San Francisco: Ignatius Press, 2017), 15.

[16] Hans Urs von Balthasar, *Creator Spirit*, trans. Brian McNeil, C.R.V., vol. 3, *Explorations in Theology* (San Francisco: Ignatius Press, 1993), 112.

Our Hiddenness Gives Greatest Access to God Who Is Hidden

Thus, it is only in our hiddenness and in the littleness of humble loving faith that we "see" Him in His hiddenness. As Jesus said, "When you pray, go into your room and shut the door and pray to your Father who is in secret [hidden]; and your Father who sees in secret [hiddenness] will reward you" (Matt 6:6). It even seems that God prefers hiddenness! These are the mysteries revealed to mere children and to the littlest ones. In our relationship with Him, we need to become like little children, indeed, like the humblest one taking the lowest place, desiring to be the lowest of all creatures, even lower than Satan himself![17] Hiddenness and littleness go together with humility into one perfect disposition of hiddenness in which to better see and hear Him in His hiddenness. This is the kind of love shown and given to us in the poverty and suffering of Christ who lays down His life for us and never comes down from the Cross by engaging Divine power. We see ourselves in Him through the hiddenness of the selfless love of laying down our lives for our brothers and sisters, through which we remain hidden in Him (1 John 3:16–18). It is by loving Him from the hiddenness of our own heart that we know God (1

---

[17] Consider the experience of St. Paul of the Cross: "I recall that I kept praying to my Jesus to grant me the highest degree of humility. I desired to be the last of men, the scum of the earth, and I kept praying to the Blessed Virgin with many tears to obtain this grace for me. I remember that I asked my Jesus to teach me what degree of humility is most pleasing to Him and I heard it said in my heart: 'When you cast yourself in spirit under the feet of every creature, even beneath the feet of demons, this is what pleases me most.'" Jude Mede, C.P., *A Source/ Workbook for Paulacrucian Studies* (New Rochelle, NY: Don Bosco Publications, Saint Paul of the Cross Province, 1977), 31.

John 4:7–8) and that we see Him.

When He is fully revealed, then we shall be like Him as sons and daughters of God, for we will see Him no longer hidden but as He is (1 John 3:1–2). We were created in His image and likeness, but this likeness was tarnished and obscured through sin. It is love that restores us to that created likeness of God through the forgiveness of our sins (1 John 3:1). It is love that causes an ongoing transformation which likens us more to Him through a deification which makes us sons and daughters. No longer hidden, we will see Him as He is and see we are like Him, sons and daughters of God like the Son of God. Before God's face, man receives his own true countenance. No longer as in a mirror dimly but face-to-face, understanding Him fully as I am fully understood (1 Cor 13:12). We will see Him face-to-face and see that we are like Him, fully understanding and being understood through love.

Then, in the fulfillment of the intimacy we have known in sharing hiddenness with Him, we will behold the mysteries with unveiled faces as they transform us into his likeness from one degree of glory to another (2 Cor 3:18). In addition to Moses's glorious encounters with God that caused his face to be radiant (Exod 34:29–35), there are several other magnificent foreshadowings in the Old Testament of the way we are meant to be transformed by beholding the face of God. For example, when one like a Son of Man was manifested to Daniel (10:4–12:13), clothed in linen like the appearance of lightning and a voice sounding like the noise of a multitude (10:4–6), or when one seemingly in human form appeared to Ezekiel as the likeness of the Glory of the Lord (1:26–28), then He indeed looked like us, like a man, though there were Divine qualities to Him. The Beloved Disciple, John, likewise saw the Lord in vision, first as a lamb who had been slain (Rev 5:6). Glorious as these glimpses are, they are merely foretastes of the revelation of how God is like us as seen in the incarnate Son who became one of us. And they are only foretastes of the glory that awaits us: "What no eye has seen, nor ear heard, nor the heart of man conceived, what God has prepared for those who love him" (1 Cor 2:9).

Even now in prayer, we mysteriously see the Face of Jesus. We meet His eyes; even in hiddenness now, He already takes us into Himself and makes us like Himself. A practical, mystical, contemplative way to seek God in prayer involves awareness of how my seeking Him is only possible in losing myself, denying myself, dying to myself. We have already spoken of how we do this in generous, selfless serving of others, and how in prayer to make frequent acts of self-offering. Bl. Paul Giustiniani wrote of how to pray or be in a nothingness which is hidden. He writes, "Finally, the soul is 'reduced to nothing' and 'it does not know it.' When it's very intense, the love of God so transforms it in God that it no longer loves itself in itself, nor itself in God, nor God in itself, but only God in God. No longer does it know self in self nor self in God. It no longer knows God in self but only God in God."[18]

We can draw close to a hidden God by going into those hidden places within ourselves and inviting Him to be there with us. He loves to be in hidden places, and He will never pass up that invitation. Our best way to abide in Him is to abide in hid-

---

[18] Dom Jean Leclercq and Paul Giustiniani, *Camaldolese Extraordinary: The Life, Doctrine, and Rule of Blessed Paul Giustiniani* (Bloomingdale, OH: Ercam Editions, 2002), 375.

denness ourselves, and denying and emptying ourselves; dying to ourselves happens as we hide, as we disappear. The soul IS reduced to nothing, and in a way that is not self-conscious or self-focused but self-forgetful. When self-centeredness fades into self-forgetfulness, the love of God greatly increases to the point that I want to be nothing. My nothingness allows my Beloved to be everything. There is not even enough of myself left for me to any longer imagine God entering into me and being in me, nor even for me to enter into intimacy by being in Him. Reduced to nothingness, I want to be where God is in God. No longer do I imagine God loving me as I am in myself; in the hiddenness of my nothingness, I no longer want to focus on myself and be the object of my own greatest love. I no longer want to love myself in myself. In the intense love of God, in my own nothingness, I do not even want to see God loving me in me or loving me in Him. Rather, I discover this hidden place where love is the most intimate, where I am nothing yet still pray to be with Him where I am nothing and where He is everything, where He is in Himself!

To know myself where I am in myself is not necessarily a narcissistic place. It can be that place in myself, my innermost self, where I am alone with myself, where no one knows me but me. This is the place we seek to enter in another person, where he or she is most intimately and personally who he or she is. The drive of sexuality properly expressed wants to penetrate into this hidden sanctuary of the beloved. Hence it can be a most erotic place, a place reached in a spousal mutuality and intimacy, as well as in friendship or loving intimacy with any person. If someone tries to force his way into this place against the will of the other, this act is violent and violating. This can be the place of deepest unity but also loneliness, one where I am alone with myself, or can be the place of intimacy and self-love. It can be the place of narcissism or the sanctuary of deepest self-giving love. Most importantly, it is the place where my hiddenness and God who is hidden can meet in secret. It is the place of prayer.

Prayer can be a loving of God hidden in myself, or can be loving God where I am hidden in Him. This is the place of prayer. To enter into God where God is hidden in God is to enter into the most intimate place in God. To enter there, I must become so hidden that I am nothing so that He can take me into His hiddenness. This is a deeper, totally graced prayer.

St. Elizabeth of the Trinity had a special devotion to the Trinity indwelling in hiddenness, and she described such prayer in her Last Retreat:

> "They fall down and adore, they cast down their crowns.
> . . ." First of all the soul should "fall down," should plunge into the abyss of its nothingness, sinking so deeply into it that in the beautiful expression of a mystic, it finds "true, unchanging, and perfect peace which no one can disturb, for it has plunged so low that no one will look for it there."[19]

She described the poverty of the human person as an "abyss of its nothingness." And quoting from the Flemish priest and mystic, Johannes Ruysbroeck, she counseled plunging so low that no one would look for it there. This deep, low place, where God is hidden in the soul's abyss of nothingness takes us to the Heart

---

[19] St. Elizabeth of the Trinity, *Last Retreat*, no. 21, in *The Complete Works of Elizabeth of the Trinity, Vol. 1*, trans. Sister Alethea Kane, O.C.D. (Washington, DC: ICS Publications, 1984), 150.

of the Trinity where God is in God. That leads us to a silent adoration that anticipates the silent love of heaven:

> Then it can "adore." Adoration, ah! That is a word from Heaven! It seems to me it can be defined as the ecstasy of love. It is love overcome by the beauty, the strength, the immense grandeur of the Object loved, and it "falls down in a kind of faint" in an utterly profound silence, that silence of which David spoke when he exclaimed: "Silence is Your praise!" Yes, this is the most beautiful praise since it is sung eternally in the bosom of the tranquil Trinity; and it is also the "last effort of the soul that overflows and can say no more." (Lacordaire).[20]

St. Paul of the Cross

To illustrate the points earlier in this chapter, we turn to one of the masters of prayer, St. Paul of the Cross. St. Paul of the Cross was the founder of the Congregation of the Passion. He centered his own spirituality and the spirituality of his religious order around the Passion of Christ. St. Paul wrote volumes of letters of spiritual direction to his religious sons and daughters, but also to many among the lay faithful who were seeking to grow in prayer. In all of his writing and preaching, he urged meditation on the Passion of Christ. More than simply meditating on the Passion of Christ from the outside, however, he also urged participation in the Passion of Christ. In some cases that participation would

---

[20] St. Elizabeth of the Trinity, *Last Retreat*, no. 21 (Kane, *Complete Works of Elizabeth of the Trinity*, 150).

be through intentionally seeking out such loving union. In other cases, St. Paul of the Cross helped his directees see that through their physical and mental sufferings, they were already participating in the Passion of Christ. They only needed to plunge themselves into that more intentionally. He saw participation in the Passion of Christ as the path to union by first leading to a mystical death and then bringing about a divine nativity.

In his writings, one finds three levels of participation in the Passion of Christ. The one who participates in the Passion of Christ as a son experiences the highest level of participation, which St. Paul of the Cross calls *naked suffering* (*nudo patire* in Italian). "In this most intense form of participation in the *passio Christi*, the person shares in the desolation of Jesus on the cross and surrenders himself full of confidence into the hands of the Father."[21] This "naked suffering" is a suffering without consolation that even experiences the pain of Jesus's cry on the Cross, "My God, my God, why have you forsaken me" (Matt 27:46). Part of the suffering is the hiddenness of God and the felt uncertainty of its value or meaning. This is the path of ultimate transformation, by which the Christian may enter into the depths of the Heart of Christ:

> Undoubtedly, this naked suffering is experienced existentially as more difficult and painful than suffering accompanied by consolation. Precisely because of this, *nudo patire* permits the person to have a more intimate and deeper share in the Lord's passion. Certainly, God does not give suffering amid desolation to every person.

---

[21] Martin Bialas, *The Mysticism of the Passion in St. Paul of the Cross* (San Francisco: Ignatius Press, 1990), 281.

Those to whom he does give it, however, the all-good and all-merciful God prepares and strengthens to endure it.[22]

We find more detailed descriptions of naked suffering in two of St. Paul's letters. Both were written to those who were experiencing this suffering. The first was to Dominic Panizza, about whom little is known, unfortunately, but it contains an excellent description of naked suffering and mystical death. He begins with the description of "naked suffering":

> Here is poor Paul in Rome for two hours, and I am coming to visit you in spirit on the holy Cross of Jesus, on which you are tasting the fruits of the holy tree of life. If these fruits have no attraction for sensibility, nevertheless, for you they are, for that very reason, the more blessed and beneficial, since in that way you are more like our Divine Savior, who called out from the cross: "My God, my God, why have you abandoned me?" In that way he expressed his naked suffering without any comfort.[23]

St. Paul of the Cross describes suffering without sensible attraction, without any comfort, and acknowledges it as more blessed for that reason since we are sharing in the desolation of Jesus on the Cross. He continues his letter urging Dominic to give himself willingly to that suffering, accepting everything and even rejoicing in doing the will of God:

> Oh, blessed is that soul that remains crucified with Jesus

---

[22] Bialas, *The Mysticism of the Passion in St. Paul of the Cross*, 280.

[23] St. Paul of the Cross, *The Letters of St. Paul of the Cross, Volume 2, 1748–1758*, ed. Laurence Finn and Donald Webber (Chicago, IL: Passionist Provincial Office, 2000), no. 694.

Christ without knowing him and without seeing him because he is deprived of all sensible consolation! Oh, fortunate that soul who in such a loss of comfort within and without feeds itself on the Divine Will, bows its head and says with Jesus: "Father, into your hands, I commend my spirit." . . . Rejoice in doing the Will of God in your sickness, with which the blessed God has visited you, and, above all, do not give way to scruples; rather, exterminate them and consume them in the fire of divine love.[24]

This is the path to transformation that brings the one suffering into a deeper union with Christ and with Christ brings him, as he prays, into the hidden bosom of the Father. Similar to the descriptions of Paul Giustiniani given earlier in this chapter, in this way the one praying is hidden away with God in the depths of God. Such hiddenness is only possible if one is "entirely clothed with Jesus Christ Crucified" because such hiddenness and intimacy requires such total self-emptying like that of Christ who became obedient to death, even death on a Cross. This is the place where Christ was hidden in the bosom of the Father:

> That soul dies mystically to all that is not God in order to live in God that divine life in the bosom of the Heavenly Father, entirely clothed with Jesus Christ Crucified, that is, entirely united to his pains, which the loving soul makes its own through its union in love with the Highest Good. So, dear Dominic, celebrate in your rich suffering.[25]

Because St. Paul of the Cross considered this to be a special

---

[24] St. Paul of the Cross, *Letters Volume 2*, no. 694.
[25] St. Paul of the Cross, *Letters Volume 2*, no. 694.

grace, not intended for everyone, he discerned it carefully in those he wrote to, and he could encourage them genuinely in the gift that God was giving them:

> God loves you; oh, how much he loves you! Be of brave heart and have great resignation. The one who is most resigned is the most holy, for true resignation contains in itself perfect love.[26]

Lastly, he offers Dominic Panizza a sweet image which seems at first so contradictory to the image of Christ Crucified, but in the writings of St. Paul of the Cross he often placed the Incarnation and Crucifixion together, seeing the total self-emptying of Christ in both. In this way, he envisioned a sweetness even in the worst sufferings, namely the image of beloved infancy:

> Take your rest then, like a child on the bosom of Jesus Christ, and partake of the food he ate: "My food is to do the Will of the Father who sent me."[27]

St. Paul of the Cross offered another description of naked suffering in a letter to Agnes Grazi as she suffered greatly with an illness that led to her death less than a year later. In this poem, we see the movement from a suffering union that starts with the consolation of love but enters into the darkness of desolation. Such suffering brings "ripe perfection" through purification (letting go of "non-divine dilection"):

> Only, only on the Cross
> Comes the soul to ripe perfection

---

[26] St. Paul of the Cross, *Letters Volume 2*, no. 694.

[27] St. Paul of the Cross, *Letters Volume 2*, no. 694.

Fervent, constant counting loss

Every non-divine dilection.[28]

He also uses the image of hiddenness, seeing that the one who suffers can enter into the hidden place where God Himself dwells with all the Treasure of His Divinity:

Oh, if I the news might bring

How the One-in-Trinity

Hides in bitter suffering

Treasure of Divinity.[29]

He highlights the importance of love in order to enter into this secret place and acknowledges that although this poem shines the light of explanation on the experience, the experience itself is darkness and the feeling of the one who is in this place is darkness:

Since it is a secret thing

Only to the loving known

I, in darkness, wandering

Hail afar the fair unknown.[30]

Although the experience is darkness, abandonment, and even the feeling of shame, the act of faith can "know" the blessing, the embrace, and the consuming flame:

Yet I know that heart is blessed,

Abandoned on the Cross of shame,

In a high embrace unguessed,

---

[28] St. Paul of the Cross, *Letters Volume 1*, no. 364.

[29] St. Paul of the Cross, *Letters Volume 1*, no. 364.

[30] St. Paul of the Cross, *Letters Volume 1*, no. 364.

Burned in Love's consuming flame.[31]

But then the experience becomes even more desolate, losing even the warmth of the flame, of the love, of the knowledge and entering into purest agony. This is the point of deepest transformation, where the Christian becomes one with Christ:

> Yea! And double blessed is he,
> By this flame no longer warmed,
> Who in purest agony
> Into Christ is thus transformed[32]

In the next stanza, St. Paul of the Cross describes the paradox of Crucified love, namely that the one who wounds is also the Great Lover. When one can learn to accept the Cross as a gift of love from the Great Lover who demonstrated His love on that Cross in naked suffering, then the transformation is complete. All worldly things are left behind, even the treasure of consolation and the Christian enters into deepest union with the Great Lover:

> Happy he who suffers pain
> Yet this treasure would forego
> Counting self and all things vain
> Save His love Who wounds him so![33]

St. Paul of the Cross concludes with two important points. One is that there is a shared experience among those who are called into this naked suffering, and so he can offer a lesson from

---

[31] St. Paul of the Cross, *Letters Volume 1*, no. 364.
[32] St. Paul of the Cross, *Letters Volume 1*, no. 364.
[33] St. Paul of the Cross, *Letters Volume 1*, no. 364.

the Cross. At the same time, there is something radically personal and unique about it, and so the further instruction must come from Christ Himself as a perfect Friend.

> Take this lesson that I send
> From the Cross that Jesus bore.
> But in prayer your perfect Friend
> Will instruct you more and more. Amen![34]

As we learn from St. Paul of the Cross, there are layers of hiddenness and layers of suffering that we experience in Christian prayer. In the mind of St. Paul, not everyone is called into naked suffering, but for those who are, it is highly valuable to have some idea of what is happening and a guide who can remind the one praying that this is a sign of success, not of failure. We are not in control of the path the Lord has prepared for us, but as we accept His path with deeper resignation, we find ourselves entering into a deeper, loving union with God. Throughout every discussion of suffering, desolation, and abandonment, the Christian spiritual masters always emphasize the centrality and principle of divine love as the guiding force. When we experience the searing pain of fire in prayer, it is always a flame of divine love that burns only because it desires to transform us into itself.

---

[34] St. Paul of the Cross, *Letters Volume 1*, no. 364.

6

Poverty

I REMAIN VERY LITTLE in the depths of my poverty. I see my nothingness, my misery, my weakness; I perceive that I am incapable of progress, of perseverance; I see the multitude of my shortcomings, my defects; I appear in my indulgence. I fall down in my misery, confessing my distress, and I display it before the mercy of my Master.[1]

A fundamental building block in our prayer life consists in the interior movement of allowing God into the different internal parts of us. Our interior life is fragmented. For example, we act differently around strangers than around friends. A different part of us emerges in a formal setting than in an informal setting. We behave differently when we are in crisis or in pain than when everything is calm and peaceful. Transformation takes place when we allow God to shine His Light and pour His Love into all the different parts of our interior life. The deeper and darker the interior places, the more profound the transformation will be.

---

[1] St. Elizabeth of the Trinity, *Heaven in Faith* no. 12 (Kane, *The Complete Works of Elizabeth of the Trinity*, 97).

The beginner in prayer generally brings his or her best self-presentation to God. Many people learned this as small children. Their parents taught them to be quiet, sit up, fold their hands, and look holy. At first, our behavior in prayer tends to imitate our behavior in the most formal settings. There is a purpose to this, and sometimes it helps us feel better to know that we can at least behave well in Church. On the other hand, our formal self-presentation is often superficial. We behave in Church in a pious way, and yet we know there are broken and sinful parts of us that lie underneath this pious appearance. This hypocrisy is hard to handle, and if we do not learn how to expose our deeper and darker parts to God, we may simply quit praying as a result. Furthermore, as we pray for more extended periods, we have a hard time keeping up the pious exterior. It tends to disintegrate into restlessness, fidgeting, and falling asleep. At best, we learn how to substitute in some other respectable behavior, such as reading, in order to pass the time in prayer, but we do not allow God's love to transform the deeper parts of us.

Even if we move beyond a formal, superficial prayer and let God into some parts of our lives, we may struggle to let Him into the deeper parts. In fact, simply finding the deeper parts of our interior lives can be challenging for us. What do the deepest parts look like? How do we find them? How do we bring God into them and bring them into God? In this chapter, we look at the areas of every human heart that come to the forefront as we persevere in prayer. The most terrifying is the dark abyss of our sinfulness. Due to original sin, we are capable of horrible things, and we must learn to face that and let God love us there. We must also learn to face our poverty, starting with the basic limitations of our contingent existence and then looking at all the unique limitations each of us has. Finally, we can learn from St. Therese how to believe that God can love us in our poverty by seeing it as the limitations of a little child who always remains infinitely loved by her father.

The process of opening up ourselves completely to God, laying everything bare and remaining vulnerably naked before Him is the only way to discover how totally and unconditionally He loves us. As long as we keep something hidden from Him, we will always wonder, consciously or subconsciously, whether He really loves us or whether He simply loves the persona we have presented to Him. The deepest intimacy between lovers happens when they let each other into their deepest secrets. At that point the intimacy even becomes an unbreakable union. That is what God wants for us and that is the deepest longing of our hearts as well. It is the highest consummation of prayer, but it must first go all the way to the depths of our souls.

The Descent into Hell: Letting God into Our Internal Abyss

In his rules for discernment, St. Ignatius offered the insight that in a time of spiritual desolation, the Enemy attacks our greatest weaknesses.[2] No one likes spiritual desolation, but the upside is that we can come to a deeper knowledge of our weaknesses if we pay attention to the kinds of temptations and lies that assault us in those times of spiritual desolation. It also gives us a sense of the

---

[2] St. Ignatius, *Spiritual Exercises*, no. 327.

parts of us that need the Lord's healing, strength, and support. The temptations that come up and the lies that we are prone to believe when we are struggling are the best places to bring before the Lord to receive the healing medication of His Love.

The place we go to in times of spiritual desolation is a kind of "default" place in our interior. Depending on how deep the desolation is, the experience can be especially dark. We go into that place when we are in sin, when we are hurt, when we are doubting. As St. Ignatius explained in his rules for the first week of the spiritual exercises, God lets us go into that place to humble us, deepen our patience, and keep us dependent on His grace as well.[3] We really experience the depths of our human poverty and human misery in those times. Mystical teachers like St. Paul of the Cross or St. Faustina called it our nothingness or the abyss of our misery.[4] In one letter, St. Paul of the Cross exhorted a directee, "For now I would like you to exercise yourself much in perfect knowledge of your nothingness, and then I would have you lose this nothing in that Immense All that is our good God. Oh! happy loss! in which the soul, losing itself completely in God, is so perfectly found!"[5] It can be terrifying to face those dark depths of ourselves. It is impossible to face those depths without faith that the abyss of God's love and

---

[3] St. Ignatius, *Spiritual Exercises*, nos. 320–22.

[4] St. Faustina wrote in her Diary no. 237: "I saw the abyss of my misery." And in no. 256: "Thank You, Jesus, for the great favor of making known to me the whole abyss of my misery. I know that I am an abyss of nothingness and that, if Your holy grace did not hold me up, I would return to nothingness in a moment. And so, with every beat of my heart, I thank You, my God, for Your great mercy towards me." No. 334 mentions abyss of misery and abyss of mercy, and there are many, many more references. See Maria Faustina Kowalska, *Diary: Divine Mercy in My Soul*, 3rd ed. (Stockbridge, MA: Marian Press, 2005).

[5] St. Paul of the Cross, *Letters Volume 1*, no. 342.

mercy is greater than the abyss of our misery.

To make this more concrete, consider the experience of a small child, who at the age of three or four years old was yelled at and felt crushed. Even at that age, it was not a new feeling. He went to the vacant lot next door to his house and sat down in the weeds. The weeds were high enough and he was small enough that he felt that the weeds concealed him. He felt completely rejected and unloved. There was an interior pouting and wanting his parents to prove they loved him. It was an attitude of, "Come and get me if you really love me." It was as close to running away and helplessness as a three-year-old can come to. The life of his home seemed so distant, the radio in the kitchen faintly playing far away. He sat there for what seemed like days, though in fact it was only a few minutes, and suddenly his father, who had been alerted by the neighbors, was there standing over him.

In that early experience, he discovered a place in himself that was sheer, unbridled self-centeredness, but totally disguised because there was so much pain in it. It was a refuge. An early, formative experience like that forms a kind of "default" position, which we tend to fall back into when we experience a similar kind of hurt. This default position becomes a refuge in us when we are stunned, hurt, discouraged, disappointed or feel a lack of love or a lack of response. It is a place we fall back into when we do not receive the love we want or when we experience unrequited love.

We are transformed when we start to let God into that place within us. This is very hard because He does not seem to be there. It is a desert place, a place of loneliness, isolation, and solitude. That interior place is like the exterior wildernesses where God seems to be absent. Even out in the woods or in the fields, places which have their own beauty, we can experience those places in such a way that the raw reality in them seems so invincible that they seem to be an impersonal emptiness where maybe there is no God. They just are. They seem to be a reality without God. We are tempted to believe that this reality consists of nothing more than just dry ground and plants, and it seems that we are so isolated that if we cry out, there is no one to hear us. It seems that death is as cold and final as reality presents itself as being. There seem to be so many unanswered prayers, and the cold, hard reality of life seems to be unforgiving and uncaring. Death seems to have the final word. In the end, it seems there is only nothingness.

In that default place (even if we have not always gone all the way into it), it can seem infinitely deep and hopeless. In the face of this, self-pity can arise and lead to self-loathing and hopeless-ness. It is a place where, a number of times, the only thing I can do is to cry out to the Lord in absolute helplessness. I go there when I don't know where to turn or what else to do in my life. Bitterness and even hatred can settle in where love has been, since all love has pain at its core, and so there is a possibility of bitterness or even of hatred. Hatred is never far from love and can easily be the flip side of love. Often it comes from long stretches of darkness, loneliness, helplessness, and inversion. It can be sub-conscious and projected onto others. Sometimes it turns into an angry self-righteousness. In all cases it inflates self, especially when it is self-hate. Likewise, in all cases it destroys self, espe-cially when hate is sustained by a hidden enjoyment of hate, and the default position can become habitual.

In that place I am split down the middle, and there is a huge hole in the center of myself. Around that hole I see every sin, every bit of duplicity, every bit of greed in me. I see all the capital sins that I am capable of or have actually committed. In fact, there is no depravity impossible for man. Because I know that place in myself, I can never, for example, look without compassion at the faces (even horrifying faces) or eyes in pictures of those who are "Wanted" because I recognize myself in those mug shots. I can look into the eyes of those people who are extortionists, molesters, murderers—all guilty of horrible things—and, if I forget the grace of God, I could see myself as one of them and feel that I am irredeemable. It is a place where Satan has a lot of power. If he could coax me into it, it is the place from which despair and suicide could come.

Every one of us has such a place in us. Some people live there all the time. Some people have some awareness of that place but only fall back into it infrequently. Most of us live around the jaws of that hell but do not fall into it very often. Others of us get snapped right into it as soon as there is heartbreak and disappointment or personal sin, shame, or failure. All of us taste it when there is personal or emotional pain.

Usually prayer brings us out of this better than anything else. In faith I discover that Jesus has entered into that place in His descent into hell and I can learn, in prayer, to bring God into that place with me, although my shame works against that. Likewise, I can bring that place to God, though I would rather leave it hidden and buried as long as I am not in it. It is a place in me that is profoundly vulnerable. It is the place in me where I feel I am most likely to be rejected, dubbed irredeemable, and discarded. It is also the place where I can be hurt the worst, perhaps especially with pain that is self-inflicted.

Allowing God to fill the deepest holes in me, those caused by pain, shame, sin, and failure, is the ongoing work and fruit of prayer. When we are not in those desolate places, we want to avoid them, but it is only by allowing the mercy of God to fill those places in us that we can find healing and wholeness. Likewise, when we have fallen into those places, we want to find a quick way to escape. Some people use the Sacrament of Confession as a quick escape, without really allowing the shame and failure to be touched by divine mercy. Some people beat themselves up as a way of climbing out of that place. Our good works and self-flagellation can become a way to try to earn salvation or to prove to ourselves that we are better than the pit into which we have fallen. But that is only a form of denial and avoidance.

The truth is that there is an abyss in each of us that is ugly and dark until we let God's light shine on it, and we let Him fill it with His love. To use the expression of St. Paul of the Cross, there is an abyss of nothingness and misery in us, but we can plunge it into the greater abyss of God's merciful love and it will be transformed. We can have the same experience as a small child who is terrified by his moonlit bedroom with its shadowy specters that seem to move on their own. As soon as we turn on the light, we discover that the shadows disappear and the gentle hues, carefully arranged furniture and the other signs of our parents' love for us are still there. This is similar to what happens when we allow God's love to shine in the depths and darkness of our hearts. St. Benedict described the steady transformation of the spiritual life beautifully when he spoke about the truly humble monk who learns to depend totally on God's grace:

Now, therefore, after ascending all these steps of humility, the monk will quickly arrive at that, "perfect love," of God which "casts out fear," (1 John 4:18). Through this love, all that he once performed with dread, he will now begin to observe without effort, as though naturally, from habit, no longer out of fear of hell, but out of love for Christ, good habit and delight in virtue.[6]

These are states that are essential to contemplative prayer and the spiritual life. As we persist in prayer, inevitably we are led to face these parts of us. We can only hold up a facade before God for so long. It is often manifested first of all as dryness or darkness. We feel that God is distant and prayer is fruitless. We may start to feel our unworthiness and the reasons start to come up why it makes sense that God would not want to spend time with us to help us or respond to our prayers. At that point we are tempted to quit praying or to grit our teeth and persevere in white-knuckled insistence or to lose ourselves in activities that seem to be more productive. Spiritual direction can be extremely helpful in these times. The turning point may come in opening up these dark places first to a spiritual director through whom we experience God's love and acceptance. It takes courageous vulnerability to share the darkest parts of our souls, but when we do, we can learn it is possible to be loved all the same. That gives us courage to believe that we can open up those areas in prayer as well. We are more convinced than ever that we are indeed unworthy, poor, broken, and sinful, and yet we come to accept that we are also profoundly loved, even in the ugliest depths, by our Heavenly Father.

---

6 *Rule of St. Benedict*, 7:67–69.

As we explore these places in ourselves, we also gain a deeper insight into the meaning of the Cross. What we experience as ugly and sinful is only a drop in the infinite ocean of this place that was experienced by Christ in His descent into hell. Christ descended into the place of depravity of the worst sinners who have done the most perverse and despicable deeds. He descended into the hell of absolute godlessness and entered deep into every human soul that has ever been and will ever be. This helps us begin to grasp the depths of human experience and also the depths of prayer that are possible as we allow Christ to guide us into a deep communion with Himself. We may find ourselves accompanying Him in some very dark places as He leads us through the darkness in ourselves and draws us into the darkness that exists in other human hearts as well. This seems to have been the experience of St. Therese in her last year, and the fifty-year experience of St. Teresa of Calcutta, who accompanied Christ into the dark holes where the Poor dwell—physically and spiritually.

Even when people are not conscious of it, they generally know this place in themselves. This is a place of true solitude with God in which we can be alone with Him in our unadorned poverty. There is a kind of war that rages within us, a microcosm of the war between heaven and hell spoken of in the Book of Revelation (Rev 12). The Catechism asserts that prayer is a battle.[7] The human heart is the battlefield. The war has been won by Christ, but we must repeatedly decide whether we will truly be on His side. Believing in the victory of Christ and seizing that victory for ourselves is the fruit of a long, hard life of prayer and not just a cheap word on a holy card. Our life of prayer oscillates

---

[7] See CCC 2752–2753.

between a place of consolation and a place of desolation. After feeling close to the Lord in prayer, almost taken up into heaven, we may then find ourselves falling and feeling terribly alone and wondering if there is anyone or even anything in the Tabernacle. Similarly, our thoughts may be diverted to mundane things that draw us away from prayer, and we look for excuses to leave early and do something more "useful":

> In the battle of prayer we must confront erroneous conceptions of prayer, various currents of thought, and our own experience of failure. We must respond with humility, trust, and perseverance to these temptations which cast doubt on the usefulness or even the possibility of prayer.[8]

If we persevere, we find that healing comes from bringing these places together in ourselves. This happens under the direction of God and by the grace of God. We are able to let the heaven in ourselves flow into the hell that is also in us, and we experience how darkness has no power over the light. Hope begins to well up from the hopeless places in us and we begin to find peace in the midst of our deepest struggles as we enter into a union with God in the starkness of pure faith.

We see this dynamic illustrated in Sacred Scripture in the healing and commissioning of St. Peter (John 21:1–19). Jesus opened up the place of poverty, pain, and betrayal in St. Peter when He appeared to him on the Sea of Tiberius. He built a charcoal fire on the beach so that after swimming to the shore, St. Peter saw the charcoal fire at the same time as He saw the

---

[8] CCC 2753.

Risen Lord. The evangelist highlighted the significance of this fire by using the word *anthrakia*, which is used in only one other passage in the whole New Testament—the passage describing St. Peter's betrayal (John 18:18). To effect Peter's healing, the Lord needed to draw out the place of betrayal from his heart and touch it with mercy. He exposed more of the wound by asking Peter three times if he loved Him—the same number of times as Peter betrayed Him. Finally, the mode of His asking exposed Peter's self-doubt as He asked Peter whether he loved Him with a divine, self-sacrificing love (*agapao*). Now faced with his worst failure, his greatest sin, Peter could only admit a love of friendship (*fileo*). Jesus's intention is not merely to shame Peter, however, but to heal Him, and so He continued:

> The third time Jesus only says to Simon: "*Fileis-me?*", "Do you love me?". Simon understands that his poor love is enough for Jesus, it is the only one of which he is capable, nonetheless he is grieved that the Lord spoke to him in this way. He thus replies: "Lord, you know everything; you know that I love you (*filo-se*)". This is to say that Jesus has put himself on the level of Peter, rather than Peter on Jesus' level! It is exactly this divine conformity that gives hope to the Disciple, who experienced the pain of infidelity. From here is born the trust that makes him able to follow [Christ] to the end: "This he said to show by what death he was to glorify God. And after this he said to him, 'Follow me'" (Jn 21: 19).[9]

---

[9] Pope Benedict XVI, General Audience of May 24, 2006, (at http://w2.vatican.va/content/benedict-xvi/en/audiences/2006/documents/hf_ben-xvi_aud_20060524.html).

In the same way, Jesus meets us in our poverty, drawing forth our weakness and even our greatest sin, and He touches it with His unconditional love and mercy in order to heal us and give birth to new trust as He draws us into a deeper union with Him.

Original Sin

Original sin created that "default" position in us. Adam felt the wretchedness of his disobedience and so he hid himself. He was afraid to face his naked poverty, including his sin, and he plunged himself into isolation. When God, in His mercy, sought Adam out, Adam tried to justify himself by blaming God and Eve, while Eve blamed the serpent. In doing that, they asserted their right to have that place of darkness and isolation in themselves in which they could hide from God and be miserable. For God's part, He gave them a reason for hope in the future redemption. He also gave them permission to hide, though in His mercy He offered them soft animal skin coverings instead of rough leaves. In the end, though, He wants us to let Him into our hiding places and leave our animal skins behind as we follow Christ, who was ultimately crucified in naked vulnerability. God wants us to trust Him completely, not to protect ourselves from Him. He gave us hope, Himself as an example, and even an outstretched hand to help us out of the darkness so that we could trust Him and follow Him into new life.

The journey of trust is difficult and can be painful. When we let the light into our default places, we see the ugliness there and we fear the reaction. In our fear to let Love stand before us in our vulnerable nakedness, one approach we often take is denial.

We push down and hide away that part of ourselves. We stuff it beneath our over-functioning, hide it behind procrastination, bury it with anger, or conceal it with blame; we medicate it with chemicals or numb it with binging. Another approach is worse: self-justification. In self-justification, we pretend that it's okay to have that place in us. Rather than recognizing that there is a sickness there, we pretend that the sickness is part of being normal. We try to reassure ourselves by looking at statistics and seeing that everyone else is just as bad off as we are, and apparently some people are even worse. Then we start to call good evil and evil good.

This is what the current secularization of our world is trying to accomplish en masse. Ours is a secular age and our society has been built on the rejection of God. In individuals, in the classroom, in higher education, in politics, in laboratories, and in marketplaces, there is not only a resistance to religion but a complete obliteration of references to God. Our modern world fosters the illusion that we can create a society without God. We justify that for good purposes, for the sake of peace and harmony, personal freedom, and an end to violence. But history has shown repeatedly that the societies that try to build a humanism without God become the most inhumane of all societies. They have the highest rates of crime and the greatest human atrocities. In them loneliness, addiction, despair, and suicide abound. Enlightenment France, Nazi Germany, and Communist Russia come to mind immediately in this regard. These are the societies that ridiculed religion, treating it as a circus sideshow for the weak and the ignorant. They made it out to be a form of bread and circuses to appease the masses or a curious museum display to titillate the sentimental.

Despite their arrogant dismissal of religion, those societies had no way to face the consequences of original sin. They could not confront the darkness in the human heart, and they had no power to redeem the wretched poverty we find in ourselves. In effect, they faced the interior desert of man's original sin by giving vent to it, unleashing its horrible potential under some falsified self-justification that "might makes right" or that some are chosen to be superior to others. Ultimately, however, those who live by the sword die by the sword (Matt 26:52), and the plague of original sin has the final word as each one must still face his own final judgment.

Salvation only comes by letting love in and letting ourselves be seen. We must learn to embrace our poverty, knowing the wretchedness we are capable of, recognize that we do not deserve to be loved and then decide whether we will accept anyway the freely offered love of God as the greatest Gift.

Embracing Poverty

Contemplative prayer is the poor and humble surrender to the loving will of the Father in ever deeper union with his beloved Son. . . . It is a gift, a grace; it can be accepted only in humility and poverty.[10]

The afore-mentioned materialist movements of atheistic, secular humanism seek to create a perfect humanity, but one without any reference to God. They refuse to accept the fundamental limitations of being human. Insofar as we allow the

---

[10] CCC 2712–13.

poison of this thinking to infect us, it inevitably undermines our prayer. We can only pray as human beings. If we do not accept the fundamental limits of our humanity, we will not be able to pray. The remedy for this is learning to embrace our human poverty. We can see our poverty in several forms.

The most obvious form of our poverty is found in the reality of death. Death is the ultimate proof of the limitation of our humanity. Secular humanism avoids looking at death in two ways. First it turns to medicine to fight back death with new technologies, pharmaceuticals, and therapies. This has its limits, but if those limits are not recognized and medicine is applied to the greatest extent possible, it can actually ruin the final years of life.[11] The other way secular humanism avoids death is through euthanasia. With euthanasia, we pretend we are more powerful than death because we can inflict death on our own terms. We believe we can become the masters of death. This is obviously an illusion. What is worse is that the final days of life, especially when a person experiences the deepest dependency and even great suffering, can be days of the greatest intimacy, holiness, and beauty when they are lived with love and prayer. Many of the saints have witnessed to this,[12] and many of us have experienced it with our own loved ones.

On the other hand, when we face the great poverty of our mortality, we can come to know God in a new way as the Lord and Giver of Life. We discover that our life is an undeserved gift and that it was freely given by a God who loves us. This pro-

---

[11] Atul Gawande, *Being Mortal: Medicine and What Matters in the End* (New York: Metropolitan Books, 2014).

[12] For example: St. Therese of Lisieux, St. Gabriel of Our Lady of Sorrows, St. Elizabeth of the Trinity, St. Anselm, St. Martin of Tours, and many more.

foundly affects the way that we pray. When we come before God in prayer, we can always be thankful for the gift of life. He loved us and created us before we had any opportunity to earn His love or prove ourselves in any way. When we remember our death, we can also recognize how fundamentally powerless we are. This recognition changes our interior disposition before God.

We should not come before Him with haughty demands. We should always come before Him as beggars who cannot even secure for ourselves the most fundamental thing—our own existence. We have no backup plan and no way out. We have no tricks up our sleeve. We are helpless before Him, and we need Him desperately, even for our next breath. Poverty that is truly human is inescapable for "hunger becomes a human hunger only when it can never be fully allayed; desire becomes a human desire only when it can remain unfulfilled. And nearness to the abyss becomes a human experience only when one can no longer call upon helping hands for protection."[13] This is what Jesus embraced when He emptied Himself of divinity and truly embraced our humanity. When the devil took him to a high tower and tempted Him to use His divinity to take control and remove His human helplessness, He did not allow Himself the escape route of His divine power (see Luke 4:9). He definitively entered into our humanity all the way to His last breath on the Cross. "The Cross is the Sacrament of Poverty of Spirit."[14]

If we do not accept this fundamental poverty of our existence but feverishly grasp after the illusion of controlling our lives, we choose to live a life of anxiety rather than a life of relationship

---

[13] Johannes Baptist Metz, *Poverty of Spirit* (Westminster, MD: Newman Press, 1968), 16–17.
[14] Metz, *Poverty of Spirit*, 14.

with God. But God never stops pursuing us in love. God even gives us anxiety as a gift[15]—a felt experience that alerts us to ways we are reaching for control that we know is beyond our power. If we read anxiety in this way, it can become a pathway to prayer that leads us into a deeper, trusting relationship with God. For this we must learn to show the anxiety to God with the heart of a beggar who has no power but only need. This approach is the opposite of the temptation to overcome anxiety by regaining control through a manipulative form of prayer that more closely resembles magic. We cannot control God by saying certain prayers. We must surrender all efforts that seek to self-medicate our anxiety through compulsive forms of prayer.

In addition to the poverty of our mortality, there are many other forms of human poverty that we can bring into our prayer. Johannes Metz noted several forms in his insightful work, *Poverty of Spirit*. There is a *"poverty of the commonplace.* There is nothing heroic about it; it is the poverty of the common lot, devoid of ecstasy."[16] Jesus, Mary, and Joseph were poor in this way, and a meditation on the simple life of Nazareth invites us to reflect on how completely ordinary they were. It gives us the courage to live an ordinary life and also to bring our ordinary life into prayer. Prayer is an extraordinary thing in one way, but unlike the prayer forms of ancient religions, our God who became flesh also wants to interact with the commonplace things of our humanity. Jesus was not in a rush to get to His extraordinary public life. He spent

---

[15] "He . . . inspired you with a devout anxiety," wrote St. Augustine to Proba. Philip Schaff, ed., *The Confessions and Letters of St. Augustin with a Sketch of His Life and Work*, vol. 1, *A Select Library of the Nicene and Post-Nicene Fathers of the Christian Church* (Peabody, MA: Hendrickson, 1994), 460.

[16] Metz, *Poverty of Spirit*, 37.

the majority of His life immersed in completely ordinary humanity. Even His three years of public life were largely ordinary, with the Bible recording only some exceptional moments.

"Related to this poverty is the *poverty of misery and neediness.*"[17] Jesus did not spurn the misery of our human condition, and He does not spurn us when we bring Him the misery of our human condition. God knows how needy we are and, like any good Father, He loves it when His children trust Him with their needs. It is so vulnerable to recognize and admit our neediness. There are so many things we cannot provide for ourselves. The virtue associated with this poverty is hope. Our hope is at its greatest when we have absolutely no other means to provide for ourselves than to beg God for help. We must learn to look up to Him with big, glistening eyes, showing Him our deepest hunger. From her time in the slums of Calcutta, St. Teresa experienced the glistening eyes of a starving child on many occasions. The poverty of such neediness always moves the Heart of God. We bring this into our prayer with simple gestures, allowing ourselves to feel our neediness and simply holding that neediness up to God. Our temptation is to hold onto some form of control. Rather than the totally poor Level III conversation[18] of sharing our hearts, we try to assert some power and maintain some dignity with a Level II conversation by seeking to convince God or manipulate God. We tell Him the reasons we deserve His help. On the other hand, sometimes we simply give up and close up our needs, and try to continue on our own without God's help.

"In contrast to the above forms [of misery and neediness],

---

[17] Metz, *Poverty of Spirit*, 38.
[18] See Chapter 1.

there is the *poverty of uniqueness and superiority.*"[19] This poverty is the lot of the great ones in history, but it is also the lot of each of us. We all carry a secret in our hearts that is tied to our uniqueness. It may be the unique relationship one has with a spouse or a child. It may be a unique intellectual gift or a combination of talents that no one else has. It is also in the unique experiences we have had, or in things that no one else has seen. Possibly it is a dimension of myself I don't understand, which confuses and puzzles me. We carry memories in our hearts that cannot be fully shared or understood by another. There is a poverty in this of not being completely understood by anyone. No one knows what it is like to live inside me, to experience the world as I experience it. Only God can fully understand. Only God can be fully inside me to see life through my eyes. He is capable of this but He also waits for our invitation. He waits for us to welcome Him into our secrets, into our deepest interior places where this poverty of uniqueness lives.

> Every *genuine human encounter* must be inspired by poverty of spirit. We must forget ourselves in order to let the other person approach us. We must be able to open up to him, to let his distinctive personality unfold—even though it often frightens or repels us. We often keep the other person down, and only see what we want to see; thus we never really encounter the mysterious secret of his being, only ourselves. Failing to risk the poverty of encounter, we indulge a new form of self-assertion and pay a price for it: loneliness.[20]

---

[19] Metz, *Poverty of Spirit*, 39.
[20] Metz, *Poverty of Spirit*, 45.

What is true for every genuine human encounter is also true of prayer. God receives us as we are. He allows us to be ourselves. He made us uniquely, and He loves and desires that uniqueness. Likewise, we must learn to let God be God. If we allow ourselves to encounter God as He is, we will be comforted by His consistency and also continually surprised by His creativity. If we allow ourselves to experience the poverty of admitting that we do not fully know Him and even after many decades humbly say like the Apostles, "Teach us to pray," we will continue to delight in our discoveries of an infinite love that comes to us from the Heart of God (Luke 11:1).

Fundamentally Poor: Little Ones

St. Therese of the Child Jesus and the Holy Face developed her spirituality around human poverty. She reframed the concepts of poverty around the Gospel notions of childlikeness and littleness. Jesus repeatedly lauds the childlike and makes childlikeness a necessary criterion for entering the Kingdom of Heaven (Matt 18:1–3) and the greatest in the Kingdom are the ones who are most childlike (Matt 18:4). He identifies with a little child when he says that those who receive such a child in His Name receive Him (Matt 18:5). He allies Himself with little children, delivering His most serious threats to those who would lead a little one into sin (Matt 18:6). He also connects the Father directly and constantly with every little child through the angels of those little ones who always gaze on the face of the Father (Matt 18:10). From this passage and many other related ones in the Gospels, the love that God has for children is unquestionable.

Reframing poverty as littleness is very helpful for our prayer lives, because we generally find littleness to be more lovable. We often turn away in disgust or horror when we face poor and deranged people, but most of us coo spontaneously over infants. We also often describe love in terms of littleness. Expressions of affection between lovers often involve adding the diminutive to a name or a descriptor. For example, the shortened names Annie, Maggie, Tony, Joey all have an affectionate quality to them, and they become even littler and more affectionate as "my little Joey" or "my littlest Maggie" or just "my little darling." While poverty brings up starker thoughts and images (people don't often find toothless beggars to be cute or lovable), littleness almost always summons to mind thoughts of cute and lovable creatures. When we learn to see our limitations as littleness, we find it easier to imagine that they could be loved.

A common struggle in extended prayer is staying awake. Most people feel they should try harder and chastise themselves for falling asleep in prayer. On the contrary, St. Therese made the connection to little children who are even more adorable when they are sleeping:

> I ought to be extremely sorry at sleeping (for seven years) during my prayers and *my times of thanksgiving*. Well, I'm not sorry ... I think that *little children* please their parents as much when they're asleep as when they're awake. I think that in order to perform operations, doctors put their patients to sleep. Finally, I think that the Lord "knows how much we are formed, he remembers that we are dust" [Ps. 103:14].[21]

---

21 St. Thérèse of Lisieux, *The Story of a Soul*, trans. Robert J. Edmonson, 185.

She imagined that her failed efforts to stay awake while adoring her Heavenly Father were even more endearing to Him. In saying this, she was building on our own reactions to watching a little child fall asleep in the arms of her father. She had the above Scriptural evidence to support this faith conviction. Although it should not be our intention to go to prayer in order to fall asleep, St. Therese helps us to see how little and loved we are when we are startled awake by our own snorting in the middle of a holy hour.

A misconception about littleness is that we should grow out of it. There is no indication in Jesus's words that He expects the little children to grow out of it. In fact, we get the idea that heaven is for children. We certainly grow up in some ways, but there remain parts of us that are limited, unformed, and weak. God loves these childlike parts of us, and He loves when we bring them before Him. That includes childlike desires, childlike adventures, and childlike romances. It also includes childlike distractions, childlike forgetfulness, and childlike anxieties. Rather than condemning these parts of us or despising them until they grow up (perhaps echoing the ways that others have treated us) these parts of us become the best starting points for prayer. God delights in us especially in the littleness that is evident in all our limitations.

Understanding ourselves *fundamentally* as little is the cornerstone of St. Therese's little way of spiritual childhood. It is the ultimate acceptance that we cannot do it on our own. Ever! It takes Jesus's statement literally, "apart from me you can do nothing" (John 15:5b). St. Therese's most mature reflections on this, expressed on her death bed, explained the permanency and universality of what it means to be little. It encompasses our whole being and it lasts from the beginning of our conception through eternity. Even our virtues are only on loan to us, and in the end they belong solely to God. The little child knows that everything is a gift, all is grace:

> To be little is not attributing to oneself the virtues that one practices, believing oneself capable of anything, but recognizing that God places this treasure in the hands of His little child to be used when necessary; but it remains always God's treasure.[22]

St. Therese knew deeply how little she was and saw this way of littleness as her only hope. She knew she could not climb the steep stairway by which the great saints ascended to heaven. Being so little she needed an elevator! In her autobiography she described how she found her answer in Proverbs 9:4, which she recorded as, "Whoever is a LITTLE ONE, let him come to me."[23] The Hebrew gives us insight about the Scripture passage she chose for illustrating her little way:

> In the verse from Proverbs that Therese quotes, the original biblical Hebrew phrase for "little one" is *haser lev*. These two words have a range of meanings throughout Scripture. *Haser* usually means to decrease, diminish, strip off, disappear, or be lacking. *Lev* refers to the heart, mind, will, or inner man. As such, the "little one" conveys not so

---

[22] St. Therese of Lisieux, *St. Therese of Lisieux: Her Last Conversations*, trans. John Clarke (Washington, DC: ICS Publications, 1977), 138–139.

[23] St. Therese of Lisieux, *The Story of a Soul*, trans. T. Taylor (London: Burns & Oates, 1912), 136.

much someone who is small, childish, cute, or stupid but someone who is fundamentally *missing* something. The "little one" has an impoverished heart, an inner self that is decreased, diminished, almost nothing in its obscurity. The little one is, in a sense, unable to even function on his or her own.[24]

St. Therese was not afraid to embrace her littleness in the most radical way. She did not try to hide behind her accomplishments, her knowledge, or even her virtues. She was not afraid to admit that she was fundamentally missing something, was almost nothing in her obscurity, unable even to function on her own. For those who are constantly competing, comparing, hiding insecurities, or trying to prove themselves, this teaching is very challenging, but then also a balm to the soul. We can admit how fundamentally weak and flawed we are. When we see how little we know how to pray, how poorly we practice the Christian life, how interminably distracted we are, how ignorant we are, or how many mistakes we make, we can remember that we are little, lovable, and indeed infinitely loved by God. After we fail many times, and we are tempted to give up and afraid that God will not accept us into the heights of holiness and contemplation, we can remember this simple call, "Whoever is a little one, let him come to me."

This is the idea Therese expressed so simply in describing herself as an "obscure grain of sand trampled underfoot by passersby." She cheerfully contemplated the radical

---

[24] Gina Loehr, *The Four Teresas* (Cincinnati, OH: Franciscan Media, 2010), 13.

depth of her personal poverty because she wasn't afraid of the truth about human frailty, incapacity, and weakness. She knew how far our shrunken hearts are from being able to love Jesus as we should.[25]

St. Therese was not afraid to extend this to our moral weaknesses and even our sins. While we are immediately moved like Adam to hide ourselves or like Peter to protest, "Depart from me, for I am a sinful man, O Lord" (Luke 5:8), St. Therese encourages us just to stay little and keep going. In that same conversation from her death bed she explained about littleness, "Finally, it is not to become discouraged over one's faults, for children fall often, but they are too little to hurt themselves very much." [26]

Although this spirituality of St. Therese can seem too cute, it has seized the hearts of Popes and professors along with simple, uneducated people, both young and old. Her declaration as a Doctor of the Church was requested and joyfully received by members of the Church of every rank in every country. It can be understood in light of the teachings of her spiritual "father" and "mother," St. Teresa of Avila and St. John of the Cross, as a kind of "short cut" on their itinerary into divine union.[27] St. Therese's little way skips neatly past the first three mansions in St. Teresa's terms. The most difficult transition in the path of the seven mansions of the Interior Castle is the transition from the third to the fourth mansion. That transition consists primarily of recognizing

---

[25] Loehr, *The Four Teresas*, 13.

[26] St. Therese of Lisieux, *St. Therese of Lisieux: Her Last Conversations*, 139.

[27] Two excellent works that detail the spiritual itinerary of St. Therese in light of the teachings of St. John of the Cross and St. Teresa of Avila are *Therese, the Little Child of God's Mercy* by Angel de les Gavarres and *John and Therese: Flames of Love* by Guy Gaucher.

that we cannot achieve that passage on our own. The passage into the fourth mansion opens up as our own hard efforts and prayer begin to fail and all we have achieved in the first three mansions turns out to be miniscule. That leads us to an abandonment which is necessary for God's grace of infused contemplation to replace our own efforts.

When we follow the Little Way of St. Therese, this abandonment is our starting point. When we choose to embrace our littleness rather than insisting on the Gospel of "try harder," we quickly move from failed efforts to surrender as little children. In this way we open ourselves to the elevator of God's grace that picks us up in the first, second, or third mansion and moves us quickly at least to the fourth, if not beyond.

Practically speaking, St. Therese's Little Way alters the way we enter into prayer and the way that we navigate the distractions and difficulties that come up in prayer. When we choose the Little Way, we enter into prayer with childlike hearts, coming before our heavenly Father with tender love and the helplessness of infants. In fact, like the word implies, as "infants" (meaning literally "non-speakers"), we do not even need to speak but we can remain speechless in the Face of a Daddy who loves us. Rather than entering into prayer with a proud, sophisticated regimen to impress God, we come with the confidence of a little child, a *haser lev,* who is fundamentally incapable and yet still infinitely loved. When we face difficulties, dryness, and darkness in our prayer so that we feel disturbance, distraction, and temptation, we do not condemn ourselves but remember that we are little children after all. What did we expect? And when we are embarrassed by failures and sins, we come shame-faced with our heads drooping but ready to be forgiven, picked up, and squeezed close to the Face of a Father who unconditionally loves us.

Pope Emeritus Benedict XVI, in a post-retirement interview with Peter Seewald, encouraged this approach of littleness and humility when handling darkness and difficulties in our lives of faith. It is a humble decision to stay inside a problem, remain in prayer, recognize our smallness, and then open our hearts to our good God, trusting that He will give us what we need when we are ready for it. When asked, "How do you deal with such problems of faith?" he responded:

> Primarily by the fact that I do not let go of the foundational certainty of faith, because I stand in it, so to speak, but also because I know if I do not understand something that doesn't mean that it is wrong, but that I am too small for it. With many things it has been like this: I gradually grew to see it this way. More and more it is a gift; you suddenly see something which was not perceptible before. You realize that you must be humble, you must wait when you can't enter into a passage of the Scriptures, until the Lord opens it up for you.[28]

The wise Pope Emeritus counseled us to remain in the darkness of faith when we are confronted with mysteries that we cannot penetrate. He advised from experience that the mysteries tend to open up as we wait in patience. Our faith is brought to the level of the saints however, when we are able to rejoice in hope even when the mysteries do not open up. St. Therese

---

[28] Benedict XVI with Peter Seewald, *Last Testament in His Own Words*, trans. Jacob Phillips (New York: Bloomsbury, 2016), 10.

described such patience as "perfect joy." In the last year of her life, she described perfect joy by using the poetic image of a little bird looking up to the Sun, the "Star of Love," but seeing only dark clouds. When the little bird can accept the uncertainty, the darkness, even without felt consolation, it becomes an experience of perfect joy:

> At times the little bird's heart is assailed by the storm, and it seems it should believe in the existence of no other thing except the clouds surrounding it; this is the moment of *perfect joy* for the *poor little weak creature*. And what joy it experiences when remaining there just the same! and gazing at the Invisible Light which remains hidden from its faith![29]

We are not content to be poor. When we feel the poverty of our mortality, we want eternal life. When we feel the limits on our relationships, we want them to be infinitely deep. When we feel the poverty of our strength, we want a strength without limits. When we encounter the poverty of our minds, we want divine knowledge. And we believe God wants to give us all these gifts! "How much more will the heavenly Father give the Holy Spirit to those who ask him" (Luke 11:13)! Like the persistent beggar in Jesus's parable, our poverty is what prepares us best to receive these gifts.

---

[29] St. Therese of Lisieux, *Story of a Soul*, 197–198, quoted in Bernard Bro, *St. Therese of Lisieux: Her Family, Her God, Her Message* (San Francisco: Ignatius Press, 2003), 235.

7

Liturgical Prayer: Mass, Other Sacraments, Liturgy of the Hours

THERE IS A NEED for liturgical formation or, rather, for spiritual formation in general; searching for the ways and forms for this should be a major task of liturgical commissions and bishops' conferences. A majority of today's Christians are de facto in the catechumenate state, and it is high time for us to take this fact seriously in pastoral practice.[1]

In the preceding chapters we have sought to describe the life of prayer in terms of a relationship between human and divine persons. That human-divine relationship has many similarities and also some fundamental differences to human relationships. We have sought to describe both the similarities and the differences in terms of how we experience them as we persevere in a life of prayer. In doing so, we have not focused on any particu-

---

[1] Joseph Ratzinger, *Theology of the Liturgy: The Sacramental Foundation of Christian Existence*, vol. 11, *Joseph Ratzinger Collected Works* (San Francisco: Ignatius Press, 2014), 585.

lar form of prayer, but we have looked at our relationship with God in general. In the next three chapters, we focus on particular forms of Christian prayer.

We begin with the highest form of prayer, namely liturgical prayer. Although it is a public and communal form of prayer, the personal, relational dynamics described in the preceding chapters still govern the way each individual enters into and prays the liturgy. The liturgy does not exhaust the prayer life of the Christian but is naturally and necessarily complemented by personal forms of devotional prayer. We discuss some of the more common forms of devotional prayer in Chapter 8, explaining how the dynamics in the first chapters come into play in our personal prayer. Lastly, in Chapter 9 we look at more extraordinary forms of prayer. These are called "extraordinary" in that they are not necessarily part of the prayer life of every saint. At the same time, we can see how they still follow the paths of prayer described in the first part of the book and how they are contemplative in the way they lead the faithful recipient of these gifts into a deeper loving union with God.

Heaven on Earth

Like the Church, the Liturgy is both a divine and a human reality and thus a mystery. Through our prayer in the Liturgy, we do not need to abandon our humanity in order to be taken up into the divine reality. Neither do we need to abandon the divine reality in order to make the liturgy more "realistic," more accessible, or more meaningful. Rather, as we have expressed throughout this book, the divine and the human meet in the mystery of the Incarnation of Christ who was *both* true God and true man, and the mystery of the Incarnation is consummated in the Paschal mystery. Our prayer of the Liturgy rightly enters into this mystery in that we become more aware of the divine reality made present through the power of God and the official prayer of the Church. At the same time, in such an elevated form of prayer, we do not need to be ashamed of our humanity in all its limitations or pretend to pray in a way that is anything other than fully human.

The divine reality of the liturgy was beautifully expressed by the Second Vatican Council in the first Constitution that she promulgated using the following lofty words:

> In the earthly liturgy we take part in a foretaste of that heavenly liturgy which is celebrated in the holy city of Jerusalem toward which we journey as pilgrims, where Christ is sitting at the right hand of God, a minister of the holies and of the true tabernacle; we sing a hymn to the Lord's glory with all the warriors of the heavenly army; venerating the memory of the saints, we hope for some part and fellowship with them; we eagerly await the Saviour, Our Lord Jesus Christ, until He, our life, shall appear and we too will appear with Him in glory.[2]

In the Liturgy we are lifted up into heaven, we are united with the saints in praise of God, and we share their inheritance already through the virtue of hope. That is the reality we acknowledge in faith but that we do not necessarily experience fully in our humanity. In this same Conciliar teaching, the Church acknowledged her limited yet essential human realities and how they

---

[2] Vatican II, *Sacrosanctum Concilium*, §8.

must be oriented to the divine and supernatural realities which are also made present in the Liturgy:

> It is of the essence of the Church that she be both human and divine, visible and yet invisibly equipped, eager to act and yet intent on contemplation, present in this world and yet not at home in it; and she is all these things in such wise that in her the human is directed and subordinated to the divine, the visible likewise to the invisible, action to contemplation, and this present world to that city yet to come, which we seek.[3]

This orientation of the visible to the invisible, action to contemplation, human to divine, and presence in this world yet with a destination in heaven, is a work that we carry out through our minds, wills, and bodies, including our sentiments. The word "Liturgy" implies our work (*Laos* + *ergon* = the work of the people). Indeed, our efforts matter when we follow the human/divine liturgical rituals provided for us by Christ through the Church. Our efforts lie in the realm of physical, mental, and emotional presences. We strive to carry out the ritual faithfully at a human level while we also muster our human faculties to the proper attitudes and openness to the work of grace. With theological virtues exercised with our human will and intellect, we can lift our hearts to be aware of and participate in the divine realities. The more intentionally we participate in liturgical prayer, the more efficacious it will be in our lives:

But in order that the liturgy may be able to produce its

---

[3] Vatican II, *Sacrosanctum Concilium*, §2.

full effects, it is necessary that the faithful come to it with proper dispositions, that their minds should be attuned to their voices, and that they should cooperate with divine grace lest they receive it in vain.[4]

We may even discover that our participation in the Liturgy allows divine grace to overflow into our senses and affect our minds and bodies. The testimonies of the saints tell us about extraordinary experiences of ecstasy, supernatural knowledge, prophecy, healing, and other heavenly happenings in the course of the liturgy. Altogether this means that liturgical prayer can be unimaginably sublime and truly a taste of heaven.

On the other hand, the liturgy can be disappointingly simple, grounded in the bland experience of our poor, human limitations. We are sleepy, distracted; we misspeak the words or even struggle with the language; we accidentally omit certain parts or embarrassingly repeat others. Sometimes it feels like an entirely ordinary experience with little real impact on our lives. When anointing a dying patient or celebrating a Mass with children, the responses may be inadequate or missing completely. Children scream during their own Baptisms, which should be the greatest moment of their lives, and parents spend all their attention fussing over how to make them stop, rather than witnessing the sublime reality that is taking place. The Church is human and divine, and so are the Sacraments, and so is our prayer. But the meaning of the Incarnation is precisely that the divine can become fully human without loss of divinity and even so can raise up the human to make it divine without loss of our humanity.

---

[4] Vatican II, *Sacrosanctum Concilium*, §11.

An Intimate Encounter

One consequence of this is an unspeakable intimacy with God. In order to fill every part of us with divinity, He must enter into every part of us. We have been talking until this chapter about how this happens primarily through individual prayer. Now we are talking about how it happens through community prayer, and in a particular way through the Liturgy. The most vulnerably intimate human acts are redeemed by the Liturgy. The humiliating incapacity of a dying man in all his nakedness and helplessness is redeemed though the dignity of the Sacraments of Anointing, Reconciliation, and Viaticum. The intimacy of sexual intercourse is touched and divinized through the Sacrament of Holy Matrimony in which it plays an essential role. The shame and regret of sin are touched and transformed by the Sacrament of Reconciliation. The helplessness of infancy is dignified by the great Sacrament of Baptism and, in the Eastern Rites, also through Confirmation and the Eucharist. The awkwardness and uncertainties of adolescence are touched, in the Roman Rite in most dioceses, through the Sacrament of Confirmation and, earlier in history, through first Holy Communion. Furthermore, our daily life is touched, morning, noon, and night, light and dark, home and abroad, in every phase of consciousness, health, youth, and old age through the Liturgy of the Hours or through perpetual Eucharistic adoration or other visits to the Blessed Sacrament. The Liturgy is the way that the Lord through the Church brings His divinity and the whole heavenly Kingdom in contact with the full range of our humanity.

A Human Encounter

Conversely, from our side of the relationship, we are invited and urged to bring our full humanity into the celebration of the Sacraments. We are invited to stir our minds to recognize, in faith, the heavenly realities present in the Liturgy. We also repeatedly make the choice to be present, to lift up our hearts above the things of this world and to remain consciously and actively in the Lord's presence through an act of the will. Our emotions can be stirred, our memories stimulated, our thoughts elevated as we participate in liturgical prayer according to our own proper roles.

This is the meaning of the full, active participation that the Second Vatican Council sought to foster through the liturgical reforms. Our participation should be a full offering of ourselves, in our reason, imagination, memory, feelings, body, and will. In short, we must offer our hearts. The words of the Liturgy facilitate this, as the Second Vatican Council urged in repeating the principle of St. Benedict already expressed in the early sixth century, "that our minds are in harmony with our voices."[5] Pope Benedict XVI drew our attention to this point as he focused particularly on the liturgical command, "Lift up your hearts":

> "Sursum corda", let us lift up our hearts above the confusion of our apprehensions, our desires, our narrowness, our distraction. Our hearts, our innermost selves, must open in docility to the word of God and must be recollected in the Church's prayer, to receive her guidance to

---

[5] St. Benedict, *RB 1980: The Rule of St. Benedict in Latin and English with Notes*, trans by Timothy Fry (Collegeville, MN: The Liturgical Press, 1981), 19.7.

God from the very words that we hear and say. The eyes of the heart must be turned to the Lord, who is in our midst: this is a fundamental disposition.[6]

To refer back to the principles already expressed in this book, this encounter with the Lord is a high point in our human-divine relationship. It unfolds with words, images, and ideas, but also especially in silence. "This principle—that without silence one does not hear, does not listen, does not receive a word—applies especially to personal prayer as well as to our liturgies: to facilitate authentic listening, they must also be rich in moments of silence and of non-verbal reception."[7] Though rich with words and images, the liturgy can also leave us feeling the absence of God as the words and images fade into the background, and we stretch our hearts to encounter a God who remains fundamentally mysterious to us. We experience this hidden God as a kind of darkness. That darkness comes in various ways.

Revealed and Hidden in the Liturgy

Sometimes God is hidden through the external experience of poor circumstances. Throughout the liturgy, our senses are faced with concrete realities which can be beautiful and moving. They can be the height of human art, architecture, and artisanship in ancient churches and magnificent vestments. They can touch

---

[6] Pope Benedict XVI, Wednesday General Audience, September 26, 2012, (at http://w2.vatican.va/content/benedict-xvi/en/audiences/2012/documents/hf_ben-xvi_aud_20120926.html).

[7] Pope Benedict XVI, Wednesday General Audience, March 7, 2012, (at http://w2.vatican.va/content/benedict-xvi/en/audiences/2012/documents/hf_ben-xvi_aud_20120307.html).

the transcendent in music with heavenly polyphony or reverent monastic chant. They can be choreographed and directed by excellent emcees with seamless execution. They can also be drab, dissonant, stumbling, and almost comical as human beings with all their limitations seek to carry out the details of divine worship. Masses celebrated in concentration camps and solitary confinement have glorified God and invited divine grace into the most desperate circumstances. In their external exigencies, no one could call them beautiful or inspiring, but in their inner realities they were perhaps most like the first Mass that took place "on the night before He was to suffer."[8]

Sometimes we face the darkness of a hidden God through our own interior distractions and failed efforts to experience the divine realities. We are bound to encounter the limitations of our humanity in sleepiness or distraction. We may even be disturbed at the kinds of thoughts or feelings that come forth unwanted. When this occurs, it is simply another opportunity to offer our poor humanity to a God who loves us. We should neither imagine that we deserve to be in His presence nor excuse ourselves on that account. Rather, we must try to accept gratefully that we are paupers in a heavenly court:

> But you have come to Mount Zion and to the city of the living God, the heavenly Jerusalem, and to innumerable angels in festal gathering, and to the assembly of the first-born who are enrolled in heaven, and to a judge who is God of all, and to the spirits of just men made perfect, and to Jesus, the mediator of a new covenant, and to the

---

[8] Roman Canon.

sprinkled blood that speaks more graciously than the blood of Abel. (Heb 12:22–24)

Exposing Our Poverty in Confession

It might be surprising to some that one of our liturgical prayers necessitates the recounting of our sins. The Sacrament of Confession has been one of the most powerful experiences of prayer for many people, including many canonized saints. In Confession, we place ourselves before the Divine Judge who is all mercy. We have the opportunity to go into the deepest places of sin in our hearts and expose those places to the healing power of divine mercy. Despite the frequent protest that one can confess one's sins to God directly, the human mediation of the priest in the Sacrament of Confession provides an irreplaceably powerful experience of the concreteness of God's forgiving and healing love. Building on that experience, it can give us the courage in our private prayer to go with God down into those dark and fearful places in our hearts. The Church's liturgical prayer is designed for this experiential reinforcement that, just as the words of absolution can be spoken over our darkest sins, so our Heavenly Father always welcomes home His wayward children with open arms, no matter what we have done or how often we have strayed.

For this reason, the saints have advised that we not cover over or dress up our sins. When we can confess in naked poverty, we open our hearts more fully to God's healing love, and we also glorify God more for the greatness of His mercy. As St. Bernard preached, "the more one lessens the fault, the more one diminishes the glory of him who forgives it."[9] At the same time, Pope Francis often challenged priests to make the Confessional safe enough for this kind of vulnerability. "Confession is not a matter of sitting down in a torture chamber."[10] He also instructed them saying, "It is not necessary to ask questions."[11] These exhortations from the Holy Father challenge the priest to enter into the liturgical prayer of confession with a merciful heart like that of our Savior. Priests need to have a prayerful presence in the Confessional in order to bear the Lord's merciful heart to the faithful and welcome their vulnerable participation in this powerful form of prayer.

Though many may not think about the Sacrament of Confession in this way, it is a liturgical prayer. The priest is not a counselor, but rather a liturgical minister, presiding over a Sacrament of mercy that leads the penitent into a deeper encounter with the Sacred Heart of Jesus. Viewing the Sacrament in this way can help us enter into it more efficaciously. The liturgical prayer of Confession really begins from the time of preparation before entering into the Confessional. The examination of conscience and the preparation of one's confession of sins is reminiscent of the biblical parable of the Prodigal Son (see Luke 15:11–32). The son's confession really began with a decision to return to his father and was then followed by a preparation of the words he

---

[9] Bernard of Clairvaux, Sermon 16 no. 11, in *The Works of Bernard of Clairvaux, Vol. 2, Part 1: Song of Songs I*, trans. Kilian Walsh (Kalamazoo, MI: Cistercian Publications, 1981), 122.

[10] Pope Francis, Audience from November 13, 2013, (at http://w2.vatican.va/content/francesco/en/audiences/2013/documents/papa-francesco_20131113_udienza-generale.html).

[11] Pope Francis, Address to Capuchin Friars, February 9, 2016, (at https://w2.vatican.va/content/francesco/en/homilies/2016/documents/papa-francesco_20160209_omelia-frati-cappuccini.html).

would speak to his father. Though he never had the chance to complete his rehearsed speech, he did not complain about that when he was raised up to his place in the family with all of his dignity restored by the Father's merciful love. We can keep this parable in mind for inspiration and encouragement as we prepare to speak our sins to the Father in the Sacrament of Confession.

Confession continues in the presence of the priest-minister. The traditional Confessional screen can be a great help in reducing the distractions that naturally come when the Sacrament becomes too focused on the human encounter with the priest. Though the priest is a necessary part of the Sacrament, he is always present in the person of Christ. The confessional screen can help to keep the mystical reality of Christ's presence in the mind of the penitent even as the humanity of the priest rightly and necessarily still comes through in his physical presence and his voice. The importance of a physical, human presence is still so important that the Church has discerned the Sacramental invalidity of Confessions through telecommunication such as the telephone or video conferencing.

The Confession that begins with remote preparation continues all the way through the completion of a penance after leaving the Confessional. The penance can never be seen as a form of earning forgiveness or even making up for sins. This is no more possible for us than it was for the Prodigal Son. The only way to let God into the deepest and darkest parts of our hearts is by accepting His unconditional love and mercy as a completely free gift that could never be repaid. Seen in this light, the penance can be completed in the warm afterglow of gratitude for the absolution of our sins. In this way, after we encounter God through the priest in the Confessional, we can bring that encounter into the intimate privacy of our own personal prayer and extend it into our actions.

Lift up Your Hearts: Vulnerability

> For me, prayer is a surge of the heart; it is a simple look turned toward heaven, it is a cry of recognition and of love, embracing both trial and joy.[12]

We lift our hearts and remain in the heavenly court especially through vulnerability. We learn to bring our whole lives, unadorned, before the Lord. We learn to open our deepest secrets, fears and even sins. We accept the poverty of our humanity and still boldly hold our deepest desires before God like little children. We allow ourselves to fall in love with the Divine Bridegroom. He always initiates this love. He invites us into the heavenly love song through the Liturgy of the Hours and then consummates that love bodily through the Eucharist, which is the "Sacrament of the Bridegroom and of the Bride."[13] The more we take the risk of vulnerability in liturgical prayer, the more "the liturgy may be able to produce its full effects."[14]

The liturgy always begins with a penitential rite that invites us to vulnerability by calling us before all else to remember our sins. It teaches that vulnerable contrition is the best way for us to prepare to celebrate the sacred mysteries. We do not start

---

[12] St. Thérèse of Lisieux, *Manuscrits autobiographiques*: C 25r, quoted in CCC 2558.

[13] John Paul II, *Mulieris Dignitatem*, §26.

[14] Vatican II, *Sacrosanctum Concilium,* §11.

by remembering our accomplishments or all the praiseworthy things we have done. We do not remember our faithfulness or the impressive regularity of our prayers. With shame and vulnerability, we remember our sins. We do not try to justify that we somehow deserve the unimaginable gift of entering into and even communing with the divine presence. Rather, at the heart of the introductory rites, we open our hearts vulnerably to receive divine mercy.

Vulnerability then follows again as we participate in the Liturgy of the Word. We hear the way that God has longed for us, sacrificed for us, and prepared us for His coming. We sing the psalms expressing our human experience in suffering and longing for a Savior. We reflect on the essential mysteries of our faith in the epistles, and then we hear the very voice of God in the proclamation of the Gospel. The ordained minister likewise seeks to proclaim the good news in such a way that it would open hearts vulnerably to a more fervent availability to God. The Eucharistic Liturgy, in making present the suffering, death, and Resurrection of Christ, further inspires a vulnerable surrender to grace as the divine lover becomes substantially present to each of the worshippers through the Sacrament of His Body and Blood.

The Holy Spirit: Artisan of Vulnerability

The Holy Spirit is the One who, in Christ, reveals to us the deepest inner mysteries of God:

For the Spirit searches everything, even the depths of God. For what person knows a man's thoughts except the

spirit of the man which is in him? So also no one com-
prehends the thoughts of God except the Spirit of God.
Now we have received not the spirit of the world, but the
Spirit which is from God, that we might understand the
gifts bestowed on us by God. (1 Cor 2:10–12)

The Spirit of God exposes the inner mysteries and makes God
vulnerable to our senses and understanding in a particular way
through the Sacraments. Each of the Sacraments has an epiclesis
in which the liturgical minister calls down the Holy Spirit to
make divine realities present in limited, created forms. The Holy
Spirit takes from the ancient realities of Christ's life and makes
them mysteriously, sacramentally present to us: "These things I
have spoken to you, while I am still with you. But the Counselor,
the Holy Spirit, whom the Father will send in my name, he will
teach you all things, and bring to your remembrance all that I
have said to you" (John 14:25–26). The "remembering" Christ
speaks about here, as well as the command, "Do this in memory
of me" which He spoke at the Last Supper, is a remembering that
also makes present. After all, none of us heard the words of Jesus
or witnessed the Last Supper two thousand years ago. We could
only ever participate in it supernaturally. That is the work of the
Holy Spirit, to make those mysteries present, again, to us.

On the other side, it is also the Holy Spirit who searches the
depths of our own hearts. Sometimes through spiritual consolation, sometimes through inexpressible groaning, He moves us to
be more vulnerable before the Lord. Our vulnerability in prayer
is thus a movement on our part but also it is a movement of the
Holy Spirit within us. We need to act, but we also need to let
Him act. So long as we do not resist the vulnerable movements

that emerge from our hearts, the Holy Spirit will help us unfailingly to enter more deeply into the sacred mysteries. In doing so, He will also form in us the mind and heart of Christ.

Indeed, over time we are steadily transformed by the Holy Spirit through liturgical prayer:

> The liturgy in its turn moves the faithful, filled with "the paschal sacraments," to be "one in holiness"; it prays that "they may hold fast in their lives to what they have grasped by their faith"; the renewal in the Eucharist of the covenant between the Lord and man draws the faithful into the compelling love of Christ and sets them on fire. From the liturgy, therefore, and especially from the Eucharist, as from a font, grace is poured forth upon us; and the sanctification of men in Christ and the glorification of God, to which all other activities of the Church are directed as toward their end, is achieved in the most efficacious possible way.[15]

An Objective, Communal Prayer Involving the Whole Church

The power of the Liturgy has already been expressed as well as the way we can personally enter it more deeply and reap its fruits through vulnerability. We must recognize, however, that the Liturgy is always an inherently communal prayer. It is the prayer of the Church. It is the Church, with her ordained ministers especially configured through liturgical prayer in the Sacrament

---

[15] Vatican II, *Sacrosanctum Concilium*, §10.

of Holy Orders, that makes liturgical prayer possible. It is not merely a human invention but rather a gift of divine institution. The liturgy provides a venue for our subjective, personal encounter with Christ, but it does so through the objective, communal celebration and re-presentation of the mysteries of Christ's life. It always anchors us in objective truth, never letting our prayer be swept away into entirely subjective experiences. It always solidifies our relationship with the community of believers at the same time as it strengthens our relationship with the Lord.

One concrete benefit of this is that it provides a way for us to pray together. We learn the same words and gestures in the Liturgy and so we can praise the Lord with one mind and one voice. Furthermore, the words we pray together, with their objective value coming from Scripture and the prayers of the saints, conform our minds and hearts to Christ. Thus we pray not only with those physically present but with those mystically present from ages past. The faith of the mystical communion of saints lifts us up especially in liturgical prayer. Indeed, the power of the prayer is not determined by the one with the weakest faith but rather it is set by the faith of the Church herself, "look not on our sins, but on the faith of your Church."[16] In this way, no one person brings others down by personal doubts and distractions, but rather all are lifted up by the faith of the Church.

We can experience this reality when we are having a bad day, when we had a sleepless night or when our faculties are diminished by age—whether young or old. Though our own faith may feel weak, we can allow ourselves to be carried by others. How beautiful to reflect on the experience of Blessed Karl Leisner

---

[16] Roman Missal.

who was supported by a circle of prisoners as Bishop Gabriel Piguet laid hands on him in the Dachau concentration camp and ordained him a priest. How moving to think of his one and only Mass that he surely could not have offered without the help of others.[17] Likewise, St. Maximilian Kolbe managed to celebrate Mass daily for his Franciscan brothers as they established a mission in Japan. His health prevented him even from standing, but supported like Aaron, with a brother at each side (see Exod 17:12), he was able to confect the Eucharist and bring heaven to earth for the nourishment and sanctification of the mission.[18]

On other occasions we may feel that we are carrying the others who are present. This is often the experience in a nursing home, prison, or mental hospital. Even in a monastery, when Mass is celebrated early in the morning, the celebrant may seem to be the only one fully awake, and even that may be questionable. In those cases, it is the Church herself who provides, while each one offers what he can with as much love and devotion as he can muster, unabashed at giving the dregs of his humanity to the God who was not ashamed to drink of those dregs out of love for us.

Liturgical Modesty: Veiled Vulnerability in Public Prayer

How does the communal nature of liturgical prayer affect personal vulnerability? Vulnerability in liturgical prayer can open

---

[17] Otto Pies, *The Victory of Father Karl*, (New York: Farrar, Straus and Cudahy, 1957).

[18] Jerzy M. Demánski, O.F.M. Conv., *For the Life of the World: St. Maximilian and the Eucharist* (Libertyville, IL: Academy of the Immaculate, 2014).

us to the joy of encounter, the sweetness of falling in love, the tears of sorrow or the fire of passion and zeal. We can cry out for the salvation of others, lament at the blasphemies committed against God, or surrender humbly before the divine mysteries that confront us. At the same time the Liturgy allows for and even facilitates a whole range of human responses; its understated qualities allow each one to be moved uniquely even as all pray the same prayers simultaneously. Romano Guardini expressed this as liturgical modesty:

> Then the liturgy is wonderfully reserved. It scarcely expresses, even, certain aspects of spiritual surrender and submission, or else it veils them in such rich imagery that the soul still feels that it is hidden and secure. The prayer of the Church does not probe and lay bare the heart's secrets; it is as restrained in thought as in imagery; it does, it is true, awaken very profound and very tender emotions and impulses, but it leaves them hidden. There are certain feelings of surrender, certain aspects of interior candor which cannot be publicly proclaimed, at any rate in their entirety, without danger to spiritual modesty. The liturgy has perfected a masterly instrument which has made it possible for us to express our inner life in all its fullness and depth, without divulging our secrets—"secretum meum mihi." We can pour out our hearts, and still feel that nothing has been dragged to light that should remain hidden.[19]

---

[19] Romano Guardini and Joseph Ratzinger, *The Spirit of the Liturgy: Commemorative Edition* (San Francisco: Ignatius Press, 2018), 287.

The challenge is for us to learn how "to express our inner life in all its fullness and depth."[20] That challenge is met in the Liturgy, but the knowledge and expansion of our inner life must develop also in our private prayer.

Ultimately, in our lives of prayer, there will be a movement of increasing vulnerability, always oscillating between private prayer and public prayer; between liturgy and personal devotion. It will be purified by times of hiddenness and silence, and also renewed through spiritual consolations. We will never escape our human poverty, nor is prayer ever anything other than a personal relationship with God, lived out in our humanity.

Communal Movements of Prayer

The Liturgy guides us to pray in particular ways at particular moments. We are exhorted to call to mind our sins, invited to offer prayers of intercession, urged to make thanksgiving, and led in personal petition. There will naturally be some discontinuity between our minds and our voices at these different points in our liturgical prayer; however, it is still effective as we take parts of the liturgical prayer into our own personal times of meditation. For example, we renew the relatively short time we can spend at Mass praying to the Lord by extending it in the time that can be spent adoring the Eucharist outside of Mass. Likewise, we take time for personal reflection on the Scriptures, examination of conscience, and longer times of thanksgiving and intercession outside the Mass.

---

[20] Guardini and Ratzinger, *The Spirit of the Liturgy*, 287.

Furthermore, as we take up different movements of prayer together with the Church, we express a range of emotions, such as joy, sorrow, hope, suffering, or longing. Even though we may not personally feel one of these emotions at a given point in the liturgy, we can unite ourselves with those who do. The ancient wisdom of the desert fathers still guides us in that regard. One of the desert fathers was asked by a young monk if he could simply pray the psalms each day that best expressed his own mood. He was instructed clearly how important it was to pray all the psalms. When a psalm expressed a different mood, the monk should learn to unite himself by praying with and for those who were going through that particular experience. It is good for us to remember that someone is happy even when our hearts are broken. Likewise, in the midst of our joy, we can ask that it be extended to those who are struggling with despair.

In liturgical prayer we experience most intensely that we are not made to be individual supermen who transcend the limits of humanity and no longer need anyone else. Rather we are called into ever deeper relationships with everyone as we grow in our relationship with God. As God has revealed to us, He Himself is a communion of Persons. Thus, as He transforms us more into Himself through prayer, He likewise transforms us into a deeper communion with others as well:

> Man became the image of God not only through his own humanity, but also through the communion of persons, which man and woman form from the very beginning. . . . Man becomes an image of God not so much in the

moment of solitude as in the moment of communion.[21]

God prevents the possibility that authentic prayer could ever become a merely selfish project of personal sanctification. It necessarily opens our hearts. We experience this particularly through liturgical prayer. At the same time, the Holy Spirit deepens our interiority through the Liturgy. Even as we all together confess our sins, we can be particularly moved by our own personal sinfulness. At another moment of communal thanksgiving, my heart may be set on fire in personal thanksgiving for what the Lord has done in my life. This experience of prayer together, even when it takes place in radically personal and private ways, further deepens our union with each other. There is a way one may even feel more deeply bonded with someone who was present at Mass when one received one's personal vocation. I will likely feel a stronger bond with the priest celebrant of a Mass in which God spoke to me personally and I felt the power of His mercy. The Christian faithful have a special bond with a community and even the physical church building where they received Sacraments of initiation or were united in Holy Matrimony. The powerful bonds that come through intense, personal, vulnerable participation in liturgical prayer will be even deeper than those that come from merely human expressions such as holding hands or singing together.

How Do I Enter In?

As already mentioned, we bring our humanity with us into litur-

---

[21] Pope St. John Paul II, Audience of November 14, 1979, no. 3, in Waldstein, *Man and Woman He Created Them*, 163.

gical prayer, just as we do with all prayer. We find ourselves falling asleep, thinking about the events of our day, planning the hours to come, disturbed by bad singing, distracted by the accoutrements of the Church, overly focused on the mechanics of the prayer or simply uncomfortable in the heat, cold or hardness of the pews. In these circumstances, the most important thing for us to do is simply to keep lifting our hearts to the Lord, no matter how difficult it may be or how it feels. It is important to do that gently, without doing violence to ourselves internally, but persistently, with hopeful expectation that God will meet our uplifted hearts with His grace and blessing.

When we lift our hearts to the Lord we may first need to gather up and recollect ourselves and then look up to Him. We should not waste time wondering what we have missed or lamenting our situation. Rather, we do best to recollect ourselves in one of several ways, allowing ourselves to be guided by the Holy Spirit. We can take a cue from the text of the prayer, reading, or song that is currently being proclaimed. We can make a theological meditation and remember the reality of the Mass and how Christ makes Himself present in the priest, the faithful, the Word, and above all the Blessed Sacrament. We can remember that all the angels and saints are present during the Liturgy and imagine our favorite saint sitting next to us or even presiding at the Mass. We can even start from our latest distraction and find a way to bring that into the Mass by turning it into a petition or a reason for repentance.

As the Catechism describes it, our prayer gradually becomes very simple and contemplative—a continually burning fire of love, with words, images, ideas, and interior movements of surrender being like kindling that keeps the fire burning.[22] This remains true during liturgical prayer as well, in which a single word or phrase of the liturgy, a single idea from the homily, or a single image from our memory can become the fuel for an extended fire of contemplation. Beautiful churches and symbolically meaningful vestments and vessels help here as well. Although the intricacy and beauty could distract us, it can also bring us back from distraction as a glance can remind us that heaven is near.

Having said that, we must become convinced that our efforts matter. Even if we felt that nothing connected and no fire was lit, we rightly exercise the theological virtues of faith, hope, and love when we trust that God is present and is pleased with our efforts. We look forward to new heavens and a new earth, and we allow the experience of dryness and darkness to do its purifying work as we forget what lies behind and strain forward to what lies ahead (Phil 3:13). In the process, God transforms us from within and stretches our hearts to be able to receive more of Himself.

---

[22] CCC 2717.

8

Prayer with Word and Sacrament

Personal Prayer

L ITURGICAL PRAYER is the source and summit of the Church's life and the highest form of prayer.[1] At the same time, liturgical prayer should naturally flow into personal prayer and vice versa. As expressed by the Second Vatican Council:

> The spiritual life, however, is not limited solely to participation in the liturgy. The Christian is indeed called to pray with his brethren, but he must also enter into his chamber to pray to the Father, in secret; yet more, according to the teaching of the Apostle, he should pray without ceasing.[2]

Here the Council Fathers introduced two important concepts,

---

[1] Vatican II, *Sacrosanctum Concilium*, §10.
[2] Vatican II, *Sacrosanctum Concilium*, §12.

namely, prayer in secret and prayer without ceasing. In fact, many of the forms of personal prayer tie the two naturally together.

In this chapter and the next chapter, we will describe and comment on how to grow in forms of personal prayer by drawing on the concepts developed in the first part of the book. Namely, we remember that prayer is fundamentally relational and human. For this reason, we can only approach God in our human poverty, opening our hearts to Him vulnerably as we receive Him in His own vulnerable self-revelation. Furthermore, because our human limitations prevent our full comprehension of His Divinity, our prayer is always marked by aspects of silence and darkness as we relate to God in faith and hope. In all of this, the beginning and the end of our prayer is summarized in a deepening, contemplatively transforming movement into the mystery of human-divine love.

In this chapter we examine two of the more essential forms of personal prayer, specifically, Eucharistic adoration and *lectio divina*. They are more essential because their focus is on the Eucharist and the Word of God. We could say they are only one degree removed from the Liturgy of the Eucharist, which also focuses on the Word of God and the Sacrament. In a way they consist of taking the elements of liturgical prayer out of the public context and into one's inner chamber, extending the opportunity for divine intimacy. These two forms of prayer are the most universal.

Eucharistic Adoration

[The butterfly] circles the flame and then burns itself up entirely in it, and especially in this great octave of sacramental love [Corpus Christi]. Ah, my daughter, eat and drink and inebriate yourself. Fly, sing, jubilate, exult, keep a feast with your Divine Spouse.[3]

We must begin this chapter with the highest form of devotion, which is also more than a devotion, namely Eucharistic adoration. This personal, devotional prayer is also truly a form of liturgical prayer. Because the Eucharist comes only from the Church's Liturgy, there is always a liturgical dimension to Eucharistic adoration. Furthermore, the widespread practice of the worship of the Eucharist outside the Mass has led to the development of liturgical rites of Exposition and Benediction and liturgical prescriptions for how the Eucharist can remain exposed in the monstrance for the adoration of the faithful. The adoration of the Blessed Sacrament exposed in the monstrance is truly a form of liturgy. In fact, the requirement that someone must always be present when the Eucharist is exposed makes more sense when thinking of the adoration of the Blessed Sacrament as a liturgy, because, for a liturgy (meaning literally "work of the people") to be carried out, there must be at least one person who remains present. In light of this, the practice of perpetual adoration, which has spread broadly throughout the world like never before, is particularly spectacular, because it means that where there is perpetual Eucharistic adoration, there are perpetual liturgies taking place that are shared among whole parishes and communities. And, because the liturgy is always efficacious, *ex opere operato*, the mere presence of the faithful with Jesus exposed in the monstrance has a profound effect on renewing the Church and transforming the world.

---

[3] St. Paul of the Cross, L 1:251, June 15, 1740, quoted in Bialas, *The Mysticism of the Passion*, 352.

Eucharistic devotion is founded on the teaching of Jesus that the consecrated bread of the Mass is truly His Body and Blood (John 6:48–58). The Church has reaffirmed this throughout the centuries and highlighted this unique Eucharistic presence in a significant way at the Second Vatican Council. The Constitution on the Sacred Liturgy speaks of four ways that Jesus is present in the Mass: "He is present in the sacrifice of the Mass, not only in the person of His minister, 'the same now offering, through the ministry of priests, who formerly offered himself on the cross', but especially under the Eucharistic species."[4] The remark that He is *especially* present in the Eucharistic species points to a realism and concreteness that is not part of the other forms of His Presence. Moreover, the Eucharist remains the Body and Blood, Soul and Divinity of Christ beyond the time of the celebration of the Mass and has always been preserved in a special place with special reverence to administer to the sick. Furthermore, as long as the Eucharist has been preserved, It has been adored.

Because this is the only way that Jesus is *substantially* present, in His Body and Blood, substantially present and preserved in the consecrated host, it always holds a special place in the devotion of the Church and the devotion of the faithful. This makes sense naturally when viewed from a relational perspective. As much as we love to talk with a loved one on the phone, we always prefer to be with our beloved in person. In the Eucharist, the Divine Bridegroom remains bodily present to us. This is a great help for us as human beings, since we always start with our senses as our starting point for encounter. The opportunity to raise our eyes to the Eucharist—whether in the monstrance or in the Tabernacle—

---

4   Vatican II, *Sacrosanctum Concilium*, §7.

serves to focus our attention and lift our hearts at the same time. Furthermore, although we know that God is always with us, it always helps us to encounter Him in a concrete location. The widely appreciated pious practice of a visit to the Blessed Sacrament as we walk past a Church highlights the special quality of having Jesus in our neighborhoods and cities in this concrete way. For those of us who live in the same building with Him in our religious houses or rectories, we feel how special it is to have Jesus in our home. Recognizing the value of brief visits to the Blessed Sacrament and longer times of Eucharistic adoration, Pope Francis made a plea in his flagship document: "One concrete sign of such openness is that our church doors should always be open, so that if someone, moved by the Spirit, comes there looking for God, he or she will not find a closed door."[5] In the Eucharist, in a profound way, we can find God.

As we have emphasized earlier in speaking about our relationship with God in prayer, it is critical to approach prayer with a concreteness and realism. Our faith in the Real Presence of Christ in the Blessed Sacrament fully supports and encourages such concreteness. When we are in the presence of the Blessed Sacrament, we can say that is *really* Jesus! There He is! Eucharistic adoration gives us the opportunity to enter into a real communion of persons with Jesus in a spiritual way that also incorporates our senses. Gazing upon Him uses our physical eyes and orients our posture in prayer.

As we come before the real and visible Presence of the Almighty, we humble ourselves before Him through genuflection or even prostration. The Greek word for adoration—*proskyne-*

---

5   Pope Francis, *Evangelii Gaudium* (2013), §47.

sis—speaks to that posture. We prostrate before the Creator out of recognition that we are unworthy and sinful creatures, and He is pure goodness, beauty, truth, and the source of all Being. Our natural and initial gesture in coming before God is humble submission. At the same time, our prayer is not truly Christian until we allow Him to raise us up. We come to Him in humble submission and He raises us up to an intimate equality as the Latin word for adoration—*adoratio*—tells us. "The Latin word for adoration is ad-oratio—mouth to mouth contact, a kiss, an embrace, and hence, ultimately love. Submission becomes union, because He to whom we submit is Love. In this way submission acquires a meaning, because it does not impose anything on us from the outside, but liberates us deep within."[6]

Ultimately, we are also drawn not only to see but to "taste and see" the goodness of the Lord (Ps 34). We adore the Eucharist, which we also call "Holy Communion." "In the Eucharist, adoration must become union."[7] Amazingly, God is always drawing us into deeper intimacy, deeper communion with Himself where a much fuller contemplative union with Him can be realized. He dignifies us by the Love that He freely pours out on us and into us. He divinizes us as He fills us with Himself. Knowing that the ultimate desire of the Lord and His call to us is full Communion orients our prayer time in adoration. Our time in Eucharistic adoration always includes a dimension of longing. We are invited to

---

[6] Pope Benedict XVI, Homily at Closing Mass of World Youth Day at Marienfeld, Cologne, Germany, August 21, 2005 (at http://w2.vatican.va/content/benedict-xvi/en/homilies/2005/documents/hf_ben-xvi_hom_20050821_20th-world-youth-day.html).

[7] Benedict XVI, Homily at Closing Mass of World Youth Day at Marienfeld Cologne, Germany, August 21, 2005 (at http://w2.vatican.va/content/benedict-xvi/en/homilies/2005/documents/hf_ben-xvi_hom_20050821_20th-world-youth-day.html).

feel our thirst for Him and also to feel the deep longing thirst He has for us, which can truly be called *eros*. What divine madness has moved Him to become bread for us? He becomes so humble and small, so vulnerable, so that we can eat Him. Like a father who offers a finger to his baby or, even more poignantly, a mother who offers her breast, God makes it possible for us to eat Him and make Him a part of ourselves.

These reflections help us enter into our time in Eucharistic adoration with a more accurate realism. We can be distracted by the seemingly static quality of Eucharistic adoration. The Mass itself might seem like a more dynamic worship of Jesus in the Blessed Sacrament, but the truth is that there is nothing static about the Eucharist. It is a heart pulsating and burning with love for us. When we are able to make the act of faith to believe in this love, it moves us to respond with our own vulnerable love to God's passionate, vulnerable love. Our time with the Eucharist is always profoundly relational and intimate, and like any relationship, the intimacy is heightened and deepened when it is extended and savored with regularity. This speaks to the importance of a daily Eucharistic holy hour for developing the greatest intimacy with our Lord Jesus Christ.

At the same time, our personal prayer with the Eucharist in adoration follows the same principles as we have discussed throughout this book. We come with our own humanity, we experience our poverty, we meet the Lord in silence, and sometimes He feels painfully absent from us. At times we feel our humanity more acutely: we fall asleep, become distracted, and fidget in our place whether kneeling, standing, or sitting. When we fall asleep or get distracted, we need to be aware that there might be something we are avoiding and ask ourselves whether there is anything we need to bring to God. In any event, though, we should turn our gaze back to the monstrance, the crucifix, or the Tabernacle and focus on the Lord, expanding our awareness of our infinite relationship with Him. We repeat that movement of our gaze, of our hearts over and over. Each time we can make it an act of love.

We don't always remember what happens in Eucharistic adoration. Many times it feels like a dream state or we experience it as a blackout. We may simply feel held by Him or experience the deeper union into which He draws us. He is always infinitely closer to us than we are to ourselves. Our goal is to let Him draw us into a deeper union with Him. We do this by simply renewing our decision to be with Him as we fall into distraction or drowsiness, or as we lose attention or awareness of where we are or what we are doing. Without becoming frustrated at all, we can renew our love every time. We can behave like a little child who falls asleep in her father's arms and periodically wakes up to discover where she is. After surveying the situation for a moment, she just nestles in more lovingly, trustingly, and securely in an act of self-giving love for the one who holds her. She is entrusting her entire self to him. We do the same thing in prayer when we return our attention to the Eucharist, to the Scripture, or to the Rosary in these times.

Like that little child who receives so much while being held, we have a similar experience in prayer before the Eucharist. Sometimes there are experiences of forgiveness, of a change of heart, of healing, or of enlightenment. Sometimes there is a sense of resolution. More often however, there is the experience of surrender and rest. Sometimes the experience of surrender and rest occurs in the wake of insight, resolution, or healing. Regardless of what is occurring in prayer, the focus should always be on the Lord rather than the healing, resolution, or whatever else we are doing. The most powerful effects will occur as we focus on Him, so we should devote ourselves to adoring Him, loving Him, and praising Him, even when we might be showing Him some areas of our life where there is some pain or difficulty.

As we discussed in earlier chapters, even when we are in great desolation and our feelings tell us that God is far away, it is important to make an act of love anyway. Our decision to stay with Jesus in the Blessed Sacrament, to continue directing our attention to Him, to abide with Him is itself an act of love even when we do not feel it. Feelings are concomitant but not determinant. Even if we don't feel ready for praise and adoration because we feel only dryness and lack of devotion, we can simply accept our psycho-spiritual state and offer ourselves to Him as we are. In this case, it is especially helpful to be in the presence of the Eucharist. There is a way that the mystery of the Eucharist draws us out of ourselves. We realize the greatness of God and also the intimacy He desires to have with us. The Eucharist draws us right into Its Source in the heart of the Trinity. God pours Himself out by giving Himself to us in the Eucharist, and in this way, He beckons us to pour ourselves out in response to this amazing love. We repeat our expressions of self-outpouring love again and again as we assume the normal dispositions of prayer in humility, contrition, affection, etc. All of it is oriented to the one reality of giving glory to God.

Lectio Divina

I would like in particular to recall and recommend the ancient tradition of *Lectio divina*: the diligent reading of Sacred Scripture accompanied by prayer brings about that intimate dialogue in which the person reading hears God who is speaking, and in praying, responds to him with trusting openness of heart (cf. Dei Verbum, n. 25). If it is effectively promoted, this practice will bring to the Church – I am convinced of it – a new spiritual spring-time. As a strong point of biblical ministry, *Lectio divina* should therefore be increasingly encouraged.[8]

Just as Sacred Scripture is the soul of theology,[9] it also naturally becomes the soul of our own prayer. Whether we make reference to it explicitly or not, Sacred Scripture has formed the prayers of the liturgy and all the devotional prayers that the Church recognizes. Although Catholics are often criticized for a diminished knowledge of Sacred Scripture, the reality is that they usually know much more than they realize. Because the readings from Scripture are heard in every Mass and form the substance of the Liturgy of the Hours, and because quotations from Sacred Scripture fill the writings of the saints and the devotional prayers they gave us, Catholics are formed deeply by God's Word.

At the same time, spending time explicitly with the Word

---

[8] Pope Benedict XVI, Address to Participants in the International Congress for the 40th Anniversary of the Dogmatic Constitution on Divine Revelation "Dei Verbum," September 16, 2005 (at http://w2.vatican.va/content/benedict-xvi/en/speeches/2005/september/documents/hf_ben-xvi_spe_20050916_40-dei-verbum.html).

[9] Second Vatican Council, *Dei Verbum* (1965), §24.

of God in Sacred Scripture is one of the most ancient forms of Christian prayer. Sacred Scripture held a fascination for the Fathers of the Church as evidenced by their writings. One can reconstruct a significant percentage of the Bible simply by collecting quotes from Patristic writings. This deep devotion to Sacred Scripture was the centerpiece of monastic prayer as it developed in the third and fourth centuries. This monastic preoccupation with prayerful reading of Scripture spread widely in the western Church through the Rule of St. Benedict, who prescribed for his monks four to six hours of *lectio divina* (sacred reading) each day.

The name "*lectio divina*" came to refer to a specific form of prayer due to the writings of Guigo the Carthusian.[10] He described *lectio divina* as a form of prayer that involved four stages: *lectio* (reading), *meditatio* (meditation), *oratio* (prayer), and *contemplatio* (contemplation). The basic movement is to start with Scripture (*lectio*), and it will lead you gradually to rest in a loving union with God (*contemplatio*).

Since the Second Vatican Council, *lectio divina* rose rapidly in prominence, not simply as a practice for monks but warmly encouraged for all Christians. It is recognized as a way of prayer that opens the one praying to a transforming union with God in contemplation. Pope St. John Paul II recognized the importance of praying with the Scripture: "There is no doubt that this primacy of holiness and prayer is inconceivable without a renewed listening to the word of God. . . . It is especially necessary that listening to the word of God should become a life-giving encounter, in the ancient and ever valid tradition of lectio divina, which draws

---

[10] Guigo II, *Ladder of Monks and Twelve Meditations*, trans. Edmund Collegde and James Walsh (Kalamazoo, MI: Cistercian Publications, 1981).

from the biblical text the living word which questions, directs and shapes our lives."[11] Pope Benedict XVI and the Synod Fathers encouraged all Christians to practice it and gave instructions on how to do that.[12] Pope Francis also encouraged its practice and gave further instruction on it as well.[13]

We will give a brief summary here of the practice of *lectio divina*, but recognizing that many books have been written on the subject,[14] we will focus on how *lectio divina* may be practiced in accord with some of the dimensions of prayer as we have described them earlier in this book.

Lectio (reading)

Lectio divina starts with reading the Sacred Scripture, because it is the Word of God. It would be impossible to overemphasize this point. Sacred Scripture is the Word of God. As stated at the outset of our book, God *wants* to communicate with us, and He makes His Word extremely accessible to us. He is not trying to hide His love from us or disguising Himself in such a way as to cause us to doubt His sincerity. He makes His Word known to everyone and He truly speaks through Sacred Scripture. St. Augustine said simply, "When you read the Bible, God speaks to you; when you pray, you speak to God."[15] For this reason, although other texts can be read prayerfully and communicate God's word to us in

---

[11] Pope St. John Paul II, *Novo Milennio Ineunte* (2001), §39.

[12] Pope Benedict XVI, *Verbum Domini*: Post-Synodal Apostolic Exhortation on the Word of God in the Life and Mission of the Church, September 30, 2010, §§86–87.

[13] Francis, *Evangelii Gaudium*, §§152–153.

[14] A particularly helpful guide can be found in Michael Casey, *Sacred Reading: The Ancient Art of Lectio Divina* (Liguori, MO: Triumph Books, 1996).

[15] St. Augustine, *Enarrationes in Psalmos*, 85, 7: PL 37, 1086, quoted in Benedict XVI, *Verbum Domini*, §86.

some way, no other text can compare with Sacred Scripture for communicating the Word of God. This becomes the foundation for our conversation with Him, and as we open ourselves to His Word in Scripture, we can steadily move from a Level I to a Level III conversation, from a merely transactional to a deeply transformational conversation.[16]

At first, we may read the Word of God simply to take in the story or gather together the data of God's actions in history (Level I transactional conversation). In theological reflection we may start to fashion particular arguments or see what conclusions we can draw from Sacred Scripture (Level II positional conversation). The goal of *lectio divina*, however, is a Level III transformational conversation. Namely, we want to approach our reading of Scripture in a way that lets God reveal Himself to us on His own terms. Rather than doing a bible study or using the Bible for "proof texting" certain beliefs, we can pray best with Scripture if we come to it as a lover who wants to know her beloved more deeply.

When reading Scripture, every word is important, just as lovers delight in the way the beloved speaks, not just the content. Why is this word used? Why is this parable given first? Why are certain points repeated? Bible studies, commentaries, and a wide variety of tools for biblical analysis are particularly useful for examining the questions that come up in our reading. These tools play an important role in helping us to hear what God wants to say to everyone through His Word, lest we fall into the trap of an "individualistic approach."[17] As Pope Benedict XVI clarified,

---

[16] See Chapter 1.
[17] Benedict XVI, *Verbum Domini*, §86.

"the sacred text must always be approached in the communion of the Church."[18]

When we read the Word of God with faith, we are reading it with an attitude of hearing how God is speaking to us. We can do this best if we read slowly and savor the words. It is valuable to notice the nuances and even read out loud to ourselves and reread the passage several times. These are the words of life. These are the words of divine love. Because the reading we do with *lectio divina* is so different than any other kind of reading we do, we generally need to read the passage several times to slow our minds down and transition away from the fast-paced, information-centric approach the world generally takes toward reading.

On a practical note, the Gospels tend to be the easiest passages for us to understand, and they are generally the most familiar. Furthermore, the Church, guided by the Holy Spirit, has taken the effort to divide up the Gospels into small passages offered to us as a part of the daily liturgy of the Holy Mass. These make excellent candidates for *lectio* because they are readily accessible, sufficiently brief, and available for each day. Other approaches for choosing passages are also possible, including a *lectio continua* that proceeds in a continuous fashion through a particular book of the Bible. Also fruitful can be an approach like that used in the Ignatian Spiritual Exercises in which passages are chosen to facilitate a particular spiritual movement in the heart of the exercisant.

Using the words of Pope Benedict XVI, we can summarize this first step of *lectio divina*: "It opens with the reading (*lectio*) of a text, which leads to a desire to understand its true content: what

---

[18] Benedict XVI, *Verbum Domini*, §86.

does the biblical text say in itself? Without this, there is always a risk that the text will become a pretext for never moving beyond our own ideas."[19]

Meditatio (meditation)

> Next comes meditation (*meditatio*), which asks: what does the biblical text say to us? Here, each person, individually but also as a member of the community, must let himself or herself be moved and challenged.[20]

While being careful not to manipulate the text of Sacred Scripture to say what we want, in this stage of our prayer, we want to open ourselves to the living Word of God, who continues to speak to us. "Scripture does not belong to the past, because its subject, the People of God inspired by God himself, is always the same, and therefore the word is always alive in the living subject."[21] As members of the People of God, the Word is speaking today to each of us. When we approach the Word with this kind of faith, we can sincerely ask ourselves, "What is God saying to me through this passage?" This question forms the heart of our meditation.

As we have discussed at length earlier in this book, the answer to this question comes to us in a real way, but always through the obscurity of faith and mediated through our human faculties and human limitations. Distractions inevitably arise as we begin to meditate on the passage of Scripture. Stilling our hearts, calming our minds, and entering into a silence that is open to hearing God

---

[19] Benedict XVI, *Verbum Domini*, §87.
[20] Benedict XVI, *Verbum Domini*, §87.
[21] Benedict XVI, *Verbum Domini*, §86.

are all as necessary in *lectio* as in any other kind of prayer. In *lectio* the passage we are reading can help us with this. By focusing on a meaningful word or phrase that is short enough to memorize, we may gently repeat it in our minds to slow down our thinking and focus our attention on God. As various disturbances, random thoughts, tangents, or even physical interruptions interfere, this word or phrase can be an anchor for us. It also serves as a reminder for us that can rapidly bring back our meditation and recollection even hours later. St. Francis de Sales described it as a "nosegay" that we could "sniff" later in the day, and it would return us quickly to the garden of paradise which we had entered in our time of prayer.[22]

How do we select a word or phrase to focus on in our prayer? In a sense, any phrase will do. St. Benedict insisted on this saying: "What page, what passage of the inspired books of the Old and New Testaments is not the truest of guides for human life?"[23] At the same time, we should let ourselves be guided by the Holy Spirit. It is good to listen for a word or phrase that seems to catch our attention, raise a question in our mind or stir something in us. Pope Francis gave a series of questions to guide us in this regard:

> Lord, what does this text say to me? What is it about my life that you want to change by this text? What troubles me about this text? Why am I not interested in this? Or perhaps: What do I find pleasant in this text? What is it about this word that moves me? What attracts me? Why does it attract me?[24]

---

[22] St. Francis de Sales, *Philothea, or An Introduction to the Devout Life*, trans. John C. Reville (Charlotte, NC: TAN Classics, 2010), part 2, chap. 7.

[23] *Rule of St. Benedict*, 73:3.

[24] Francis, *Evangelii Gaudium*, §153.

One of the key points in Pope Francis's questions is related to the topic reiterated through this book, namely that prayer is a relationship. I do not want to focus merely on the text in a detached way, I want it to mediate a relationship. In other words, "What is the Lord saying to *me*?" To add one question to the Holy Father's list, a very useful reflection can be, "How do I see God's love for me in this passage?" This is based on the all-important theological conclusion of Christianity, "God loves me." Furthermore, because His love is infinite, He loves me now and He is loving me through this text. So, I can ask confidently, "How does He want to express His love for me today through this passage of Scripture?" This question focuses our attention in a helpful way on the relational aspect of prayer and also saves us from reducing the Scripture to mere precepts or to a moral instruction. Scripture is not primarily answering the question, "What am I supposed to do?" so much as it is communicating to me who God is, who I am, and how He loves me. This is an important guide for our prayer.

The stage of meditation is where the work takes place in *lectio divina*. This may be more intense at some times while at other times our prayer may be very simple. Guigo the Carthusian illustrated *lectio divina* using the image of eating. He described reading as placing the food in our mouths and meditation as chewing. Chewing is not only work, but involves the joy of tasting as well, and digestion already begins to take place while the food is still in our mouths. The same could be said about meditation. Our meditation sometimes reveals beautiful truths as God speaks clear words into our personal lives. Sometimes we have insights about God or discoveries in Sacred Scripture. Prayer is always moving towards a synthesis of our knowledge of God and contemplation of Being that is simple and unitive, and sometimes we make a concrete step towards that contemplation in our meditation.

Sometimes the meditation is much more arduous, requiring us simply to ruminate, to chew and chew on the word. In these cases, the Scripture feels more like beef jerky, but it is necessary to chew until slowly it yields to our persistence, even sometimes not revealing its riches until the very end of a difficult prayer time or sometimes not at all. At other times, prayer comes quickly and it would be no more appropriate to keep chewing on Scripture than to chew on a piece of chocolate that dissolves quickly in our mouths. At that point it is more appropriate to swallow (*oratio*) and savor the experience (*contemplatio*).

Oratio (prayer)

> Following this comes prayer (*oratio*), which asks the question: what do we say to the Lord in response to his word? Prayer, as petition, intercession, thanksgiving and praise, is the primary way by which the word transforms us.[25]

After reflecting on the Word, slowly chewing on the questions of what God is saying to us, how He is professing His love for us, and ways that He is challenging us or directions in which He is guiding us, it is appropriate for us to give our response. Our response can take a variety of forms. Pope Benedict XVI quoted from the passage of St. Paul's letter to Timothy summarizing the forms of prayer as "petition, intercession, thanksgiving and praise" (1 Tim 2:1). The significance of that fourfold division

---

[25] Benedict XVI, *Verbum Domini*, §87.

of prayer is ancient, taught as a model in the Christian tradition going back at least to St. John Cassian.[26]

Fundamentally our prayer takes the form given to us by Our Lady in her response to the angel, "Let it be to me according to your word" (Luke 1:38). It is an acceptance of God's love, a surrender to His will, expressing gratitude for His grace and asking Him to share this grace with others as well. When our prayer is particularly dry or when God seems hidden or silent, our prayer may just be a surrender to whatever God is doing beyond our understanding. When our meditation has been rich, we may find ourselves moved into a prayer that is simple and leaves us in gratitude, wonder, and love before the God who loved us first.

Guigo the Carthusian illustrated the step of prayer as swallowing. Swallowing is a form of commitment. We are ready to make the food we are chewing on completely a part of ourselves. Likewise, our *oratio* is a form of commitment, accepting the word I have been chewing on as truly a word for me. Swallowing is a risk even greater than the risk of chewing. We make ourselves vulnerable as we let this word from the outside of us come into us and become part of us.

Contemplatio (contemplation)

> Finally, lectio divina concludes with contemplation (*contemplatio*), during which we take up, as a gift from God, his own way of seeing and judging reality, and ask ourselves what conversion of mind, heart and life is the Lord asking of us? In the Letter to the Romans, Saint Paul

---

[26] Ramsey, *John Cassian: The Conferences* 1.9.9.

tells us: "Do not be conformed to this world, but be transformed by the renewal of your mind, that you may prove
what is the will of God, what is good and acceptable and
perfect" (12:2). Contemplation aims at creating within
us a truly wise and discerning vision of reality, as God
sees it, and at forming within us "the mind of Christ"
(1 Cor 2:16). The word of God appears here as a criterion for discernment: it is "living and active, sharper than
any two-edged sword, piercing to the division of soul and
spirit, of joints and marrow, and discerning the thoughts
and intentions of the heart" (Heb 4:12).[27]

Pope Benedict XVI defined the last stage of *lectio divina*, contemplation, as a process of transformation in which we become
like God. As St. John promised, "We shall become like him for we
shall see him as he is" (1 John 3:2). Contemplation participates
in this vision through faith. As we have shown, there are contemplative dimensions to all prayer as a personal relationship with
God who draws us into His Mystery. Likewise, the contemplative
dimension of *lectio divina* is a culmination of the initial contemplative stirrings in the reading and searching of the Scriptures,
passing through the meditative moments, bursting into prayer
and the full flowering of contemplation. Such contemplation can
be very dark for our senses and intellects, but it is a loving union
and a vision through faith. That is the loving union that comes
about through the process of reading, meditating, and "swallowing" God's word in *lectio divina*. It brings about a transformation
and an obscure vision of the divine. In the stage of *contempla-*

---

[27] Benedict XVI, *Verbum Domini*, §87.

tio, our primary activity is simply to abide in Him, savoring the sweetness of loving union.

In his teaching on *lectio divina*, Guigo the Carthusian described the fourth step of *lectio divina* as digestion. After taking food, chewing, and swallowing, we are left with a stage that is more passive. This stage does not take conscious effort, but actually benefits more from not doing anything. After having a meal, simply resting in order to digest it is a very healthy thing. This is similarly true in *lectio divina*. After our encounter with God, we can simply rest in His Presence. The digestion of our encounter with Him and His Word spoken to us changes us from the inside, similar to the subtle way that the digestion of natural food changes us. A transformation takes place slowly and steadily as we develop a more "truly wise and discerning vision of reality, as God sees it."[28] This is a path to better living according to the logic of the Gospel and it is also a preparation for heaven, for that ultimate union with God when we will see Him as He is.

---

[28] Benedict XVI, *Verbum Domini*, §87.

9

Devotional Prayers

I N THIS CHAPTER, we examine the Jesus Prayer—a way of ceaseless prayer that is especially popular in the Byzantine Eastern Rite churches. We then explore prayer to the saints, especially the Blessed Virgin Mary, to whom we can draw close with the Marian Rosary. Thirdly, there is a plethora of devotional prayers of varying popularity, and we look at some general concepts and principles for incorporating those into a contemplative prayer life in the following section. We conclude this chapter by exploring the dynamics of intercessory prayer and how to approach that in a more contemplative way.

The Jesus Prayer

The "Jesus Prayer" has its origins in ancient monasticism. The wisdom of the desert fathers was gathered together and organized by St. John Cassian in his two classic works, *The Institutes* and *The Conferences*. St. John Cassian recorded excellent teaching on the capital sins and the battle with demons as taught by those experts who were tried and tested through their spiritual battles in the

Egyptian desert. A strategy they employed for resisting demonic temptation was the use of Scripture, following the example of Jesus's temptations in the desert. As faithful practitioners of *lectio divina,* the desert fathers had many scriptures at their fingertips, but they also offered a simplified approach with a single scripture passage from Psalm 70: "God, come to my assistance. Lord, make haste to help me." We encounter this verse of Scripture most regularly now in the Liturgy of the Hours. Each of the liturgical hours of prayer begins with this verse of Scripture. The desert fathers encouraged regular and even repetitious use of it to battle demons and keep one's attention focused on the Lord.

The repeated invocation of a verse of Scripture continued in the Christian tradition of prayer, especially in Eastern Christianity. It became a response to the desire to live out the command of St. Paul to pray without ceasing (1 Thess 5:17). Over time, the single verse from Psalm 70 was replaced with a variant of the publican's prayer, "God, be merciful to me a sinner!" (Luke 18:13). The name of Jesus was inserted, and several variants emerged, such as "Lord Jesus Christ, Son of God, have mercy on me, a sinner," or simply, "Lord Jesus Christ, have mercy on me." By repeating this simple prayer many times, even thousands of times a day, the prayer moves from the lips to the mind and from the mind to the heart.

The Jesus Prayer is part of a larger spiritual category called hesychasm, which blossomed and has been sustained especially in the Christian East. Pope St. John Paul II summarized hesychasm as "a method of prayer characterized by a deep tranquillity of the spirit, which is engaged in constant contemplation of God by invoking the name of Jesus."[1] And he gave the primary claim of hesychasm: "to emphasize the concrete possibility that man is given to unite himself with the Triune God in the intimacy of his heart, in that deep union of grace which Eastern theology likes to describe with the particularly powerful term of 'theosis', 'divinization.'"[2] The indwelling presence of God and our deepening union of wills with Him in our hearts is the contemplative union that we have been emphasizing throughout this book.

The method of the Jesus Prayer became popularized through a simple book that contains much wisdom, *The Way of a Pilgrim*.[3] It is the account of a simple, Russian pilgrim who was stirred by hearing the call to pray without ceasing and set out on a quest to learn how to do that. After consulting several masters and receiving some definitions of unceasing prayer, he finally found a spiritual director who gave him concrete guidance: pray the Jesus Prayer twelve thousand times a day. His experience is instructive for us. First he received a concise explanation of how to pray the Jesus Prayer:

> The ceaseless Jesus Prayer is a continuous, uninterrupted call on the holy name of Jesus Christ with the lips, mind, and heart; and in the awareness of His abiding presence it is a plea for His blessing in all undertakings, in all places, at all times, even in sleep. The words of the Prayer are: "Lord, Jesus Christ, have mercy on me!" Anyone who becomes accustomed to this Prayer will experience great

---

[1] Pope St. John Paul II, Angelus Address August 11, 1996, in *L'Osservatore Romano*, August 21, 1996.

[2] Pope St. John Paul II, Angelus Address August 11, 1996, in *L'Osservatore Romano*, August 21, 1996.

[3] Bacovcin, *The Way of a Pilgrim and The Pilgrim Continues His Way.*

comfort as well as the need to say it continuously. He will become accustomed to it to such a degree that he will not be able to do without it and eventually the Prayer will of itself flow in him.[4]

To restate this in terms we have used earlier in this book, the Jesus Prayer involves a vulnerable attention to the presence of God. It is vulnerable because it opens the interior ("the mind, and heart") to God and opens up our poverty to Him ("it is a plea"). It involves the imagination in a way that can be meditative (the R.E. French translation says, "forming a mental picture"[5]), but it is also intended to seep its way down into our faculties in a more habitual, contemplative way, so that we can be aware of Christ's "abiding presence" and implore His grace constantly "in all undertakings, in all places, at all times, even in sleep." Although it starts with a possibly more complex meditation, it moves towards simplicity and effortlessness, "to such a degree that he will not be able to do without it," such that "eventually the Prayer will of itself flow in him."

From the outset, the Jesus Prayer is directed toward simplicity. Like *lectio divina*, it may begin with some meditation, but the use of the mind and the will is only an initial stage until the prayer becomes interiorized, that is, contemplative. The focus of the meditation is on God's constant loving presence. Furthermore, the meditation is focused on driving out other thoughts that naturally come up:

---

[4] Bacovcin, *The Way of a Pilgrim*, 9.

[5] R. M. French, trans., *The Way of a Pilgrim and The Pilgrim Continues His Way*, 2nd ed. (New York: Harper, 1991), 9.

If after a few attempts you do not succeed in reaching the realm of your heart in the way you have been taught, do what I am about to say, and by God's help you will find what you seek. The faculty of pronouncing words lies in the throat. Reject all other thoughts (you can do this if you will) and allow that faculty to repeat only the following words constantly, "Lord Jesus Christ, have mercy on me." Compel yourself to do it always. If you succeed for a time, then without a doubt your heart also will open to prayer. We know it from experience.[6]

The intention of the teacher is that the Jesus Prayer begin as a repetitious, vocal prayer, while the mind is imagining the presence of Jesus. Part of the repetition of the prayer, however, is also a rejection of other thoughts. The goal is a simple, loving attention to the presence of Jesus and a simple, vulnerable awareness of our own poverty as sinners. The process of rejecting other thoughts should be gentle, but persistent, until slowly the heart opens up to the prayer. The opening of the heart may be slow and laborious or more rapid. Over time, the trend is that the prayer opens the heart more and more quickly to the merciful presence of God. That corresponds with the Pilgrim's experience as well:

> I did as the elder suggested, and on the first day I barely completed the assigned number by late evening. At first I felt tired in reciting the Prayer constantly; my tongue seemed numb and my jaw was tight. There was both a pleasant sensation and a slight pain in the roof of my mouth. My left thumb, with which I counted the beads,

---

[6] Bacovcin, *The Way of a Pilgrim*, 9.

was sore, and there was an inflammation in my wrist extending to the elbow which produced a pleasant sensation. All this seemed to attract and compel me to greater accomplishment, and I spent five days faithfully reciting twelve thousand Prayers a day, experiencing both joy and longing for the Prayer.[7]

The physical difficulties will also be accompanied by some mental difficulties. Boredom, doubts about the value of this prayer, sleepiness, and other distractions inevitably come. As expressed earlier in this book, we need to respond to these struggles with renewed faith, hope, and love. The prayer itself, "Lord Jesus Christ, have mercy on me," helps us to lift our hearts again to the Lord and refresh our sense of His loving presence. Each repetition of the prayer can be an act of faith, hope, and love. Each decision to focus on God by rejecting other thoughts is a concrete act of love for God. Slowly this prayer exercise opens the heart to God's grace and can lead to the experience known as the "warming of the heart":

> After some time I felt that the Prayer was somehow entering the heart by itself. The words of the Prayer seemed to be formulated according to the rhythm of the heartbeat, that is (1) Lord, (2) Jesus, (3) Christ, etc. I stopped vocalizing the Prayer and began to listen attentively as the heart spoke, and I remembered the words of my late elder in describing this joy. Then I felt a slight pain in the heart and such love toward Jesus Christ that I wished I could throw myself at His feet, lovingly embrace them,

---

7 Bacovcin, *The Way of a Pilgrim*, 12.

and thank Him for this great consolation which He gives in His mercy and love to His unworthy and sinful creatures through His name. Then I experienced a kind of blessed warmth in the heart which spread through my whole breast.[8]

Several things took place in this movement of the pilgrim's prayer. For one, we see that the vocal prayer settled into a habitual disposition so that he no longer spoke, but "began to listen attentively as the heart spoke." This is the vulnerable, attentive listening we spoke of earlier and the contemplative silence that develops from deep prayer. There is also an experience of interior freedom and self-discovery: "I felt that the Prayer was somehow entering the heart by itself." Furthermore, the pilgrim experiences what St. Ignatius called "spiritual consolation" in the form of the warming of the heart: "I experienced a kind of blessed warmth in the heart which spread through my whole breast." That was accompanied by an insight that St. Ignatius would identify as coming from God because it came along with the experience of spiritual consolation, namely, "I felt a slight pain in the heart and such love toward Jesus Christ that I wished I could throw myself at His feet, lovingly embrace them, and thank Him for this great consolation which He gives in His mercy and love to His unworthy and sinful creatures." This self-awareness as a sinner and deeper insight about God's mercy is a clear fruit of the pilgrim's prayer.

The pilgrim also witnessed to the telltale fruits of interior transformation that accompanied his prayer. It helped him love

---

[8] Bacovcin, *The Way of a Pilgrim*, 17.

more deeply and more universally: "If I happened to meet people during the day they all seemed as close to me as if they were my kinsmen, even though I did not know them."[9] It also helped him embrace his crosses with joyful abandon:

> Sometimes I walk seventy or more versts [~45 miles] a day and I do not get tired; I am only conscious of praying. When the cold air chills me, I begin saying the Prayer with greater intensity and I warm up. When hunger begins to overcome me, I begin saying the name of Jesus Christ more frequently and I forget that I wanted to eat. When I become sick and feel rheumatic pain in my back and legs, I pay greater attention to the Prayer and I do not feel the pain. When someone offends me, I remember how sweet the Jesus Prayer is and the offense and anger disappear and I forget everything. I walk in a semiconscious state without worries, interests, and temptations. My only desire and attraction is for solitude and ceaseless recitation of the Jesus Prayer. This makes me happy.[10]

This teaching on the Jesus Prayer is a helpful balance between kataphatic (imageful) and apophatic (imageless) prayer. The prayer is focused on communion with Jesus and a loving awareness of His Presence. Although it shifts inner attention away from thoughts and moves towards an interior, silent, loving awareness of God, it does not seek to create an inner void or simply to empty the mind like some forms of eastern, non-Christian prayers. The approach of the Jesus Prayer to ignore extraneous thoughts is a

---

9 Bacovcin, *The Way of a Pilgrim*, 14.
10 Bacovcin, *The Way of a Pilgrim*, 15.

kind of asceticism, letting even good thoughts go, but it is not simply rejecting thought as such. It is explicitly choosing God over any other thoughts, thereby asserting His place at the top of our value hierarchy. Furthermore, the Jesus Prayer is clearly directed to a more contemplative, simple, prolonged act of love and a more intuitive knowledge of God. At the same time, it allows for some meditation to picture God and some feelings of love for Him to stir our awareness of His Presence.

As Prefect of the Congregation for the Doctrine of the Faith, Cardinal Joseph Ratzinger issued a very helpful document clarifying some of the distorted forms of meditation that can draw people away from authentic Christian prayer and how to identify what they are lacking:

> Some use eastern methods solely as a psycho-physical preparation for a truly Christian contemplation; others go further and, using different techniques, try to generate spiritual experiences similar to those described in the writings of certain Catholic mystics. Still others do not hesitate to place that absolute without image or concepts, which is proper to Buddhist theory, on the same level as the majesty of God revealed in Christ, which towers above finite reality. To this end, they make use of a "negative theology," which transcends every affirmation seeking to express what God is and denies that the things of this world can offer traces of the infinity of God. Thus they propose abandoning not only meditation on the salvific works accomplished in history by the God of the Old and New Covenant, but also the very idea of the One and Triune God, who is Love, in favor of an immer-

sion "in the indeterminate abyss of the divinity." These and similar proposals to harmonize Christian meditation with eastern techniques need to have their contents and methods ever subjected to a thorough-going examination so as to avoid the danger of falling into syncretism.[11]

The Jesus Prayer combines a psycho-physical preparation for prayer (disciplining our minds to let extraneous thoughts go) with a focus on Jesus Christ that can lead to authentic Christian contemplation. The practice of the Jesus Prayer can be of great assistance when our minds are not capable of making more complicated meditations. As our internal prayer becomes simpler, the Jesus Prayer easily stirs our hearts into a loving awareness of God's presence. Also, in infirmity it can be a great companion to direct our minds and hearts to God when our suffering bodies want to draw all our attention to themselves. The Jesus Prayer can be a great path for recollection and a preparation for other forms of prayer such as the Liturgy of the Hours or the Mass. It can also help us gather our inner faculties when we start a holy hour of Eucharistic adoration.

The Rosary and Marian Prayer

To this point, we have focused exclusively on prayer to God who is Father, Son, and Holy Spirit. Because this is the source and summit of all prayer, ultimately leading to union with God and transformation into Him, this is the natural focus of a book on prayer. Having said that, we do nothing alone. Our relation-

---

[11] Joseph Ratzinger, *Orationis Formas*, no. 12.

ships with friends and family who pray with us and teach us
to pray obviously directly impact our growth in prayer. And, as
mentioned earlier in our chapter on the liturgy, we always pray
together with the whole Church, who is truly a Mother of our
faith and whose faith makes all Christian prayer possible. Furthermore, our Mother the Church consists of all the saints of
all times, and so we are always part of and praying with a larger
family than merely those who are currently living on earth.

Our relationships with these saints are real relationships, even
though we may never have met them in the flesh. The stories,
places, and relics of these saints facilitate a human, embodied
encounter with them and the grace of the Holy Spirit makes
them spiritually present to us in the mystical Body of Christ. Our
friendships with the saints generally develop organically, including saints chosen for us or by us as our baptismal or Confirmation
patrons. We also find that saints have a way of choosing us, which
happens in a whole range of wonderful and unexpected ways.
Our relationships with the saints and with various contemporary
members of the Body of Christ could be described as a constella-
tion that locates us in our own unique place in the heavens.

There is one who stands out in the heavens, however, who is
venerated beyond all other saints and to be venerated in a unique
way by all the redeemed, namely the Blessed Virgin Mary. She is
Mother of God, Mother of the Church, and Mother of each one
of us. She is the first disciple and the first to be redeemed. In that
way she is a model for us and shows us in her glorified flesh the
end result of love and fidelity to Christ. She lived a fully human
life, including the holocaust of faith and hope, as she remained
at the foot of the Cross. She lived a life of prayer, demonstrated

most vividly in her dialogue with the angel Gabriel and most movingly in her loving presence to her crucified Son. For these reasons, we look to her example and we ask for her guidance.

But she is also much more than a good example. Because she is the one who received the eternal Son fully into her womb and gave Him to us, she can be seen as the mediatrix of all graces and the co-redemptrix with Christ her Son. God made her cooperation an essential part of the redemption and so she is a mother to us in the order of grace.[12] We also read this in the words of Jesus from the Cross, "Behold your mother," which have been understood to apply to each of Jesus's beloved disciples, namely, to each one of us. We can also see that she who was the Mother of the historical body of Jesus is also the Mother of the mystical Body of Jesus, because she is simply the Mother of Jesus, who is God and man. And so we not only look to her example, we also receive directly through her hands and through her womb, through her face and through her heart, the grace we need to complete our journey of faith until we share fully in her glorification in heaven.

We always benefit by calling on her in our prayer. It is powerful and efficacious to make a simple invocation at the beginning of our prayer time asking our Mother to lead us to her Son. Even if we do not do this, however, all our prayer actually takes place in her, because we never receive Jesus without Him first passing through her. Explicitly acknowledging her and beseeching her assistance simply helps us conform ourselves to her, and so receive Him more purely and perfectly through her Immaculate Heart. This was the straightforward logic of St. Louis de Montfort in his Marian consecration. Referencing St. Augustine's insight, he

---

[12] Vatican II, *Lumen Gentium*, §60.

reiterated that we are in the womb of Mary until we are born into eternal life.[13] Like a baby in the womb, we receive all our nourishment through our mother. We simply choose to make that relationship explicit by choosing for ourselves what God has already chosen for us, namely, to allow all grace to pass to us through Mary and likewise to allow all we do to pass through Mary on its way to God and to others. And so we ask that she who gave our Savior to us would also give us to our Savior.

There are many ways to pray with Mary, but the most popular in the Roman Catholic Church has been the Rosary. In his beautiful apostolic letter *Rosarium Virginis Mariae*, which provides a moving and rich catechesis on praying the Rosary, Pope St. John Paul II proclaimed candidly, "The Rosary is my favorite prayer. A marvelous prayer! Marvelous in its simplicity and its depth."[14] He continued on in that letter to make concrete suggestions on how better to pray the Rosary, including the use of scripture verses, repetition of the mysteries interspersed with the Hail Mary, use of images, singing the doxology and even five new mysteries of light. He gave explanations of the prayers of the Rosary and offered meditations on each of the set of mysteries. But perhaps most importantly, he set the tone of the whole Rosary by explaining how it helps us to meditate on the Face of Christ through the eyes of Mary. Thus, the Rosary is contemplative! "Contemplating the scenes of the Rosary in union with Mary is a means of learning from her to 'read' Christ, to discover his secrets and to understand his message."[15]

---

[13] St. Louis-Marie Grignion De Montfort, *The Secret of Mary*, Reprint Edition (Charlotte, NC: TAN Books, 1998), no. 14.

[14] Pope St. John Paul II, *Rosarium Virginis Mariae* (2002), §2.

[15] St. John Paul II, *Rosarium Virginis Mariae*, §14.

Furthermore, Pope St. John Paul II makes it clear that the Rosary is more powerful than just intercession or imagination. Rather, he asserts that "the Rosary mystically transports us to Mary's side,"[16] and so it brings us spiritually and truly into the great mysteries of Christ's birth, life, death, and resurrection. This is the soul of the Rosary, as he draws from the teaching of Pope St. Paul VI:

> The Rosary, precisely because it starts with Mary's own experience, is an exquisitely contemplative prayer. Without this contemplative dimension, it would lose its meaning, as Pope Paul VI clearly pointed out: "Without contemplation, the Rosary is a body without a soul, and its recitation runs the risk of becoming a mechanical repetition of formulas, in violation of the admonition of Christ: 'In praying do not heap up empty phrases as the Gentiles do; for they think they will be heard for their many words' (Mt 6:7). By its nature the recitation of the Rosary calls for a quiet rhythm and a lingering pace, helping the individual to meditate on the mysteries of the Lord's life as seen through the eyes of her who was closest to the Lord. In this way the unfathomable riches of these mysteries are disclosed."[17]

Many papal encyclicals and many books have been written on the Rosary. It is a prayer that is as accessible to three-year-olds as to the greatest saints. It is easy to learn and simple to pray, but one can never outgrow the Rosary. Its meditative quality makes

---

[16] St. John Paul II, *Rosarium Virginis Mariae*, §15.
[17] St. John Paul II, *Rosarium Virginis Mariae*, §12.

it infinitely deep as it transports the one praying into divine mysteries that are infinitely deep. In this regard, it fits well with the themes of prayer we have outlined in this book. It follows relational paths of development similar to other forms of prayer. It can feel exciting at first as we come to know our Lady and entrust ourselves to her motherly love. It can put us to sleep or feel boring as it becomes part of our daily prayer routine. We can experience God's silence and our own poverty as we struggle to enter contemplatively into the mysteries on any given day.

What we find, however, is that if we take up the Rosary as a daily prayer, reciting it faithfully and making efforts to enter, even in simple ways, into the mysteries, we will steadily develop a relationship with Mary. In developing a relationship with her, we also begin to take on her virtues. St. Louis de Montfort listed those virtues as the following: angelic sweetness, ardent charity, blind obedience, constant mental prayer, divine wisdom, heroic patience, lively faith, profound humility, surpassing purity, universal mortification.[18] Others could also be named, but even this impressive list is sufficient to motivate us to draw close to her. Furthermore, as we draw close to Mary, we always draw close to Jesus Who is never separate from her. As depicted in countless works of art, He is always in her arms or at her side, even as they are glorified in their bodies in heaven. She is always the Gate of Heaven and to draw close to her is to draw close to the whole Trinity.

Like any relationship, our relationship with Mary requires daily attention. As we have said in regard to devotion to the

---

[18] St. Louis-Marie Grignion De Montfort, *True Devotion to Mary: With Preparation for Total Consecration*, trans. Frederick William Faber, Tan Books Catholic Classics Series (Charlotte, NC: TAN Classics, 2010), 55.

Blessed Sacrament and making a Eucharistic holy hour, daily recitation of the Rosary will be most effective in drawing out the grace of this prayer and leading us closer to Jesus through Mary. Through daily recitation, we become less distracted by the mechanics of the prayer and more able to enter in a simple way into the mysteries or simply draw close to Mary our Mother and enjoy her maternal, feminine love for us.

While the Rosary has a particular structure, there are many ways to enter into it internally. One way is by reciting the prayers with a simple attention to Mary's presence and an openness to her love. One could think of holding her hand in holding the beads of the Rosary. Similarly, the very prayers that are spoken could provide the meditation that takes us into her presence. One could imagine entering into the angel Gabriel's angelic love for Mary in taking up his heavenly greeting "Χαῖρε, κεχαριτωμένη" or "Hail, Full of Grace" (Luke 1:28). Likewise, one could allow great love and honor to fill the heart when repeating Elizabeth's ecstatic exclamation, "Blessed are you among women and blessed is the fruit of your womb" (Luke 1:42). Similarly, the prayers of the Our Father and the doxology wrap each decade of the Rosary into a Trinitarian encounter. Taking up the words of the Son, by the power of the Holy Spirit, we are able to say "Our Father." And in giving glory to God, we glorify each Person of the Blessed Trinity by name in the conclusion of each decade of the Rosary. In this way, the prayers of the Rosary can, themselves, lift our hearts to the Lord and bring us into loving surrender to God and tender affection for our Blessed Mother. This way of praying the Rosary would be quite similar to the Jesus Prayer, although with the obvious elaboration that we are directing attention and affection to God through our relationship with Mary.

Another way of praying the Rosary would be a meditation on each mystery. While repeating the individual prayers of the Rosary with one part of our mind and perhaps with our voices, we can direct another part of our mind to meditating on the particular mystery associated with each decade. In this we ask Mary to lead us into each of the mysteries, helping us to behold them through her eyes and to be transformed by them in the grace that flows through her heart. As Pope St. Paul VI said, we are mystically transported into the mysteries when we pray them in the Rosary. Similar to *lectio divina,* we allow our encounter with the mysteries to touch our hearts, speak to our difficulties, heal our wounds, inspire our action, and move us to thanksgiving and deeper surrender. Similar to the Ignatian style of entering into the biblical scene in prayer with Scripture, the mysteries of the Rosary invite us to enter into the scene with Mary not only to behold like a movie from the outside, but even to interact from the inside with the particular events in the life of Christ her Son.

The Rosary can also be prayed primarily as intercession for others. Like the Jesus Prayer, it acknowledges that we are sinners in need of God's mercy: "Pray for us sinners." Furthermore, we ask for prayer at the only two guaranteed moments of our lives, "now and at the hour of our death." Because these two moments are guaranteed, they are the times most in need of grace. Above all, we want to live in the grace of God *now.* All the grace that we do not faithfully respond to now, however, we can save up for our last opportunity to receive it—the hour of our death. We pray for ourselves in this way and we also pray for others. Carrying intentions into the Rosary, especially including the Holy Father's intentions, is a great way to pray for others. We can attach a particular name or prayer request to each bead or each decade. There are countless stories of those who have had extraordinary, saving encounters with Mary during their lives or even after their deaths, sustained by Rosaries prayed earlier in life or prayed for them by loved ones.

Although one might argue that the repetition of the Rosary is excessive, repetition helps us in our human frailty. We do not pray as we ought and so if we pray each Hail Mary with a tenth of our attention and affection, after a decade we will have prayed one Hail Mary well. Similarly, meditation requires some time to develop, and a single Hail Mary would be insufficient space to take us into the mysteries and allow us to soak them in. Repetition also helps us to detach from the words and helps make the words a part of us so that they flow out of our breath and heartbeat. Our prayer becomes more apophatic, letting go of images and stimulating only an affection of the heart or a willed adherence to the Lord. We find ourselves simply carried into the Heart of Christ through the Heart of Mary.

For those who have lost the practice of the Rosary or never developed a habit of praying it, the best way is simply to start. By offering the prayers and persevering in it daily, the resistance can break down and the prayer can flow more freely from the heart. What starts with our efforts will find support and even greater energy in the Blessed Virgin's efforts, since she is far more ardent in bringing us to her Son than we are in seeking Him out.

Various Devotional Prayers

The Catechism of the Catholic Church lists three expressions of prayer: vocal prayer, meditation, and contemplative prayer. These three categories follow a progression in our spiritual lives. Even small children can recite vocal prayer, while meditation requires more growth and contemplation is the full flowering of the life of prayer. At the same time, these should not be seen as three levels in such a way that we would "graduate" from one and move on to the next. Rather they are better seen as adding layers or new dimensions to our prayer. The Catechism is clear about the ongoing importance of vocal prayers and points to the example of Jesus who continued to use vocal prayers throughout His life even to His last breath:

> Vocal prayer is an essential element of the Christian life. To his disciples, drawn by their Master's silent prayer, Jesus teaches a vocal prayer, the Our Father. He not only prayed aloud the liturgical prayers of the synagogue but, as the Gospels show, he raised his voice to express his personal prayer, from exultant blessing of the Father to the agony of Gethsemani.[19]

Indeed, reciting novenas, chaplets, and prayers composed by the saints is a beautiful way of praying. Of course, the words alone are not efficacious. As the Catechism teaches, they must be united with some intention, even a habitual intention, to lift the heart and mind to God, to become vulnerable, and to unite with Him in love:

---

[19] CCC 2701.

Through his Word, God speaks to man. By words, mental or vocal, our prayer takes flesh. Yet it is most important that the heart should be present to him to whom we are speaking in prayer: "Whether or not our prayer is heard depends not on the number of words, but on the fervor of our souls."[20]

Some may have the misimpression that vocal prayers are less important or less valuable than meditation, as if the person who speaks to God or recites the prayers of the saints is less advanced than the person who sits in prolonged silence. But judgments of holiness cannot be made from such external impressions. The Catechism reinforces the value of vocal prayers, even seeing in them the beginnings of contemplative prayer as we also have suggested:

> Because it is external and so thoroughly human, vocal prayer is the form of prayer most readily accessible to groups. Even interior prayer, however, cannot neglect vocal prayer. Prayer is internalized to the extent that we become aware of him "to whom we speak." Thus vocal prayer becomes an initial form of contemplative prayer.[21]

Similarly, it is sometimes said that asking God for things is a more childish or less advanced form of prayer. To the contrary, Pope Francis taught clearly against this:

> None of us is obliged to embrace the theory that someone advanced in the past, namely, that the prayer of sup-

---

[20] CCC 2700.
[21] CCC 2704.

plication may be a weak form of faith, while the more authentic prayer would be pure praise, that which seeks God without the burden of any request. No, this is not true. The prayer of supplication is authentic; it is spontaneous; it is an act of faith in God who is Father, who is good, who is almighty. It is an act of faith in me, who am small, sinful, needy. And for this reason prayer, in order to ask for something, is quite noble.[22]

The possibilities and limitations of rote prayers follow the guidelines provided earlier in this book. When we offer a novena or read lengthy prayers, we must learn to do it in a more contemplative way, simply using the prayers of the saints and spiritual masters as words to express our own hearts. Like people who buy greeting cards to express their feelings for friends and loved ones, the Church has a wealth of precomposed prayers to help us express our hearts to the Lord. Expressing our hearts in this way also has the effect of forming our hearts, and ultimately can inform and shape our own spontaneous prayers as well. Furthermore, it can form the way we remain with God in a loving, silent contemplation. After a period of loving silence, we might return to the prayers we were offering.

Our prayer should follow the path of vulnerability and help us experience and enter into our own poverty more deeply. Sometimes the humble prayers of the saints, like St. Thomas Aquinas's prayers before and after Mass, summon us to a deeper humility than we might have reached on our own. Likewise, prayers

---

[22] Pope Francis, General Audience, December 12, 2018 (at http://w2.vatican.va/content/francesco/en/audiences/2018/documents/papa-francesco_20181212_udienza-generale.html).

such as the Litany of Humility or the Litany of Trust can touch on areas of our hearts that resist surrender and move us to give ourselves to God more fully. The Litany of the Sacred Heart of Jesus or the Litany of Jesus Christ, Priest and Victim, can fill our minds with ideas and images that stimulate our meditation and help us to fight against the temptation to doubt in God's presence, power, or infinite love.

Pope Benedict XVI wrote about the value of using the prayers of the saints and other prayers for public devotion:

> For prayer to develop this power of purification, it must on the one hand be something very personal, an encounter between my intimate self and God, the living God. On the other hand it must be constantly guided and enlightened by the great prayers of the Church and of the saints, by liturgical prayer, in which the Lord teaches us again and again how to pray properly. Cardinal Nguyen Van Thuan, in his book of spiritual exercises, tells us that during his life there were long periods when he was unable to pray and that he would hold fast to the texts of the Church's prayer: the Our Father, the Hail Mary and the prayers of the liturgy. Praying must always involve this intermingling of public and personal prayer. This is how we can speak to God and how God speaks to us.[23]

In this teaching, Pope Benedict XVI described the synergy that should develop between personal prayer and public prayer, between meditation and vocal prayer. He described a healthy balance that each of us must find in our practice of prayer. There

---

[23] Pope Benedict XVI, *Spe Salvi* (2007), §34.

is a value to reciting particular prayers every day. There is also a value in persevering in novenas and other prayers that continue across many days. In both cases, the insights and examples of the saints penetrate our lives more deeply. In sustaining prayer for many days, it requires us to solidify our commitment, making God a high enough priority that we make sure to make the time for Him each day in order to complete the repeated prayers. This can stretch us. Sometimes it is our failure to persevere that is the greatest benefit by the way it exposes our poverty and leads us back to God even more humbly in our need.

There is no standard requirement for how much or what kinds of devotional prayer one should include. Religious orders such as the Missionaries of Charity publicly recite a great quantity of devotional prayers every day. Other orders, such as the Benedictines, are traditionally extremely sparse in their public recitation of any prayers other than the Mass and the Divine Office.

A danger that must be avoided, of course, is the recitation of devotional prayers to the point that there is never any silence. It would be the equivalent of a relationship in which only one partner ever spoke. Likewise, recitation of devotional prayers could become superstitious unless there is a relationship with God and a sense that the prayers are directed to this loving God who sees us, listens to us, and cares for us.

Intercessory Prayer

Closely related to devotional prayers are the intercessory prayers that we offer for others. In fact, this is often the first thing people think of when they think of prayer and often the first kind of prayer that we learn as children, kneeling at our bedside with our parents. It may be expressed as simply as, "Dear God, please bless Daddy, bless Mommy, bless Gramma . . ." Though simple enough for a child's limited vocabulary and conceptual development, there is something profound in these little prayers. Such prayers imply it is possible to have a relationship with God that is natural and informal and that He lowers Himself to accept the squeaky voices of small children. In fact, when we hear such prayers, we often spontaneously understand that God accepts these sincere prayers from the pure hearts of small children more readily than He accepts the sophisticated prayers of adults that are often mixed with vanity and self-interest. One clear point we should make, then, is that we dare not "grow out" of such prayers that contain pure expressions of love for our fellow man enfolded in a sincere, infinite act of trust in our Heavenly Father. That was certainly the insight that guided the simple but profound teaching of the Doctor of the Little Way, St. Therese of Lisieux.

When we think of praying for others, though, we naturally encounter questions about how best to do this. Jesus told us clearly to be like the importunate widow, never tiring of asking for justice. He did not expect her to be sophisticated—only persistent to the point of being irritating (see Luke 18:1–8). Still, it begs the question whether there is a way to present a petition that is more pleasing to God or whether there are certain devotions that are "more powerful" than others. While the Church does acknowledge some differentiation of "effectiveness" between various prayers in her catalog of indulgences, one must be careful not to take an overly pragmatic, mathematical, or economical approach to this, as if a point system could be assigned to prayer.

Ultimately, prayer is a·mysterious reality that cannot be reduced to a strict system of measurement. Furthermore, even in the case of indulgences, there is an immeasurable requirement of an "interior disposition of complete detachment from sin, even venial sin."[24] Indeed, this requirement highlights the fact that prayer is relational, not merely functional.

A related question arises about remembering specific individuals and specific intentions in our prayer. The Church blesses this activity through the Mass, including several places where specific names can be spoken in the Eucharistic Prayer, not the least of whom are the Pope and the local bishop who are included in every Mass. Likewise, we see this in the prayers of the faithful, which were expanded in the new rite of the Mass following Vatican II. Though optional on weekdays, the Church requires the Prayers of the Faithful on Sundays. Additionally, the Church's canon law acknowledges that the Mass can be offered for a specific intention, for which a stipend may be received, along with the variety of other intentions that could be included by the priest or the faithful in the liturgical celebration. From this we see the value placed by the Church on intercessory prayer, including remembering individuals by name and the formulation of fitting petitions.

It often happens, however, that certain individuals find themselves elaborating long lists of prayers they wish to offer every day. There are clearly enough needs that we could formulate prayer intentions ad infinitum. Some people list the names of all those they wish to pray for and spend long periods of time going

---

[24] Cardinal William Wakefield Baum, The Gift of the Indulgence, January 29, 2000 (http://www.vatican.va/roman_curia/tribunals/apost_penit/documents/rc_trib_appen_pro_20000129_indulgence_en.html).

through their lists of names. That can also lead to the quandary of how these lists could ever be shortened. When should we ever stop praying for someone? Even after death, people may still need our prayers. Likewise, we are inclined to simplify lists by gathering the names into groups and praying for those groups, such as "for all priests," "for all mothers," "for all government leaders," etc. This may sound scrupulous, but it is a reasonable concern and for some people a serious concern.

One of those who was seriously concerned about this question was the Doctor of the Church, St. Therese of Lisieux. After receiving the request from the Mother Prioress to pray for a seminarian, she began to devote the bulk of her pious practices, prayers, and sacrifices to this seminarian. That was fine until she received a second seminarian to pray for. At that point she faced a dilemma, which she explained in her *Story of a Soul*, written to her Mother Prioress:

> Last year, at the end of May, it was your turn to give me my second brother, and when I represented that, having given all my merits to one future apostle, I feared they could not be given to another, you told me that obedience would double their value.[25]

Though she recognized the wisdom of the Prioress's response, she continued to reflect on this dilemma in prayer. After all, she actually had not only two seminarians to pray for but many others as well:

> As I have two brothers and my little sisters, the novices, the

---

[25] St. Therese of Lisieux, *The Story of a Soul*, trans. T. Taylor, 172.

days would be too short were I to ask in detail for the needs of each soul, and I fear I might forget something important.[26]

The answer came to her in prayer:

Simple souls cannot understand complicated methods, and, as I am one of their number, Our Lord has inspired me with a very simple way of fulfilling my obligations. One day, after Holy Communion, He made me understand these words of the Canticles: "Draw me: we will run after Thee to the odour of Thy ointments." O my Jesus, there is no need to say: "In drawing me, draw also the souls that I love": these words, "Draw me," suffice. When a soul has let herself be taken captive by the inebriating odour of Thy perfumes, she cannot run alone; as a natural consequence of her attraction towards Thee, the souls of all those she loves are drawn in her train.[27]

Inspired by the Holy Spirit, St. Therese solved this dilemma for us in a very sweet way, using the insight of our book that all prayer should incorporate contemplation. We simply need to gather all those we pray for into our hearts and then run to Jesus in our normal way of self-offering, contemplative prayer. This helps us understand the value of petitions and lists and names as well. Those are ways that we gather our petitions into our hearts, calling them to mind, even stirring some affection, and then we must carry them with us into our union of hearts with the Lord.

---

[26] St. Therese of Lisieux, *The Story of a Soul*, trans. T. Taylor, 173.
[27] St. Therese of Lisieux, *The Story of a Soul*, trans. T. Taylor, 173.

10

Charismatic Prayer

The Spiritual Gifts

MAKE LOVE YOUR AIM, and earnestly desire the spiritual gifts, especially that you may prophesy. For one who speaks in a tongue speaks not to men but to God; for no one understands him, but he utters mysteries in the Spirit. On the other hand, he who prophesies speaks to men for their upbuilding and encouragement and consolation. He who speaks in a tongue edifies himself, but he who prophesies edifies the Church. Now I want you all to speak in tongues, but even more to prophesy. He who prophesies is greater than he who speaks in tongues, unless someone interprets, so that the Church may be edified. (1 Cor 14:1–5)

St. Paul clearly emphasizes the superlative excellence of love. He does that both in his introduction to his great hymn on love in his first letter to the Corinthians when he says, "But earnestly desire the higher gifts. And I will show you a still more excellent way" (1 Cor 12:31), and also in the conclusion to that chapter: "Make love your aim, and earnestly desire the spiritual gifts" (1 Cor 14:1). At the same time, however, he does not make the pursuit of love exclusive. Rather, in both cases he couples it together with desire for the gifts of the Spirit when he says, "Earnestly desire the higher gifts," and "earnestly desire the spiritual gifts" (1 Cor 12:31; 1 Cor 14:1). He teaches us about the power that comes to Christians through the Holy Spirit to do things beyond mere human capacity, and he also orients that power to love. Unlike the devil who seizes power and uses it for his own self-exaltation, the spiritual power of Christians is received as a gift and must always be placed in the service of love.

Praying with the Spirit and Praying with the Mind

In his brief explanation of the spiritual gifts at the beginning of chapter 12 of his first letter to the Corinthians, St. Paul groups the spiritual gifts into two categories—those which build up the one praying and those which build up the Church. He places a preference on those which build up the Church. In this whole passage there is never an exhortation to exclude or eliminate certain gifts, but rather a hierarchy with personal growth in holiness as the proper foundation of ministry and then ultimately aiming toward the perfection of love. This growth in holiness deepens the contemplative dimension in all expressions of prayer. In particular, St. Paul urges the growth in personal holiness that can come through speaking "in tongues," which St. Paul describes as "utter[ing] mysteries in the Spirit" (1 Cor 14:3). These cannot be comprehended with the reason or immediately turned into words, but St. Paul still urges their importance by saying, "I want you all to speak in tongues" (1 Cor 14:5). This would be the lowest priority, but still important for our personal growth. After all, St. Paul explained that, "he who speaks in a tongue edifies himself" (1 Cor 14:4). The word "edify" means "to build up." We certainly all need to practice prayer that builds us up.

St. Paul explains further the complementarity between praying in the spirit and praying with the mind: "For if I pray in a tongue, my spirit prays but my mind is unfruitful. What am I to do? I will pray with the spirit and I will pray with the mind also; I will sing with the spirit and I will sing with the mind also" (1 Cor 14:14–15). St. Paul does not present the contrasting experiences of prayer "with the spirit" and "with the mind" as contradictory or in competition but rather in a relationship of complementarity. They are both good and they both build us up. St. Paul makes the additional point in this passage that prayer with the mind can also build others up.

We can understand the categories of prayer that St. Paul is describing based on all that we have already discussed through-out the earlier chapters of this book. We clearly understand that prayer engages the mind and even the emotions. At the same time, Christian prayer must repeatedly return to silent love. In being relational, prayer begins with a communication that moves toward a communion of love. In fact, when all is working well, our communion with God is deepened through periods of com-munication and periods of silent love. At times, advanced prayer includes, sometimes predominantly, a silence of the mind in addition to times of words, images, and insights. Sometimes silent prayer still retains a certain affective quality, such as a warming of the heart, and there is the intention of the will, but the mind is not "fruitful," meaning that there are no particular images and words that are part of our prayer. The prayer of communion in faith has gone beyond what can be captured in words or images and has become more contemplative. It can even be the case that the mind—the memory and the imagination—can be restless while the intellect and the will are focused on a transcendence of God (a "pure immaterial species"—see below) that cannot be translated into words and images. Dom John Chapman described it vividly:

> The intellect has become capable of perceiving pure immaterial species; it has before it God as pure Spirit, by means of infused species. So long as it looks at God, it cannot use its ordinary power of working by phantasms (abstractions). But what it sees cannot be translated into terms of phantasms; therefore it thinks it sees nothing at all . . .
>
> So: — The intellect is occupied without knowing it, and cannot work in the ordinary way. The will, however, always follows the intellect, and it loves and desires what the pure intellect is contemplating. The imagination has no idea what is going on. The will is occupied, and leaves it to itself; so the imagination runs off as it pleases. Hence an extraordinary state of things.[1]

---

[1] John Chapman, *Spiritual Letters* (New York: Burns & Oates, 2003), 252–54.

When Abbot John Chapman says that the soul "has before it God as pure Spirit" we could say that the person is "praying in the spirit." We see here in the realm of traditional prayer forms and traditional teaching on prayer a movement of prayer in faith beyond what the mind can comprehend. This builds up the person praying in deep, if also mysterious ways. St. John of the Cross even identified the way that deep roots of sin can be dried up in such prayer.[2] The great teachers on prayer advocate at the same time a "prayer with the mind" so that the Church can be built up. We are indebted to St. Augustine, St. Teresa of Avila, St. John of the Cross, and so many others for translating their experiences of prayer into words that our minds can understand (at least partially). It is still very good prayer when we are unable to "see" God, even with our minds, in those times when He seems hidden and silent and we can only persevere through faith. We recognize the value of such prayer in a way that is complementary to prayer "with the mind."

We can understand this prayer in terms of poverty and vulnerability as well. When the "imagination has no idea what is going on,"[3] there is a feeling of incompetence that can make us want to cry out humbly with the Apostles, "Lord, teach us to pray!" (Luke 11:1). When we enter a long period of prayer and afterwards cannot speak about anything that happened because it was not prayer with the mind, we can feel very silly and unproductive. Our union is in love, not in thought, "because he can certainly be loved, but not thought. He can be taken and held by love but not by thought. Therefore, though it is good at times to think of the

---

[2] St. John of the Cross, Dark Night of the Soul, bk. II, chap. 3, no. 1.
[3] Chapman, *Spiritual Letters*, 252.

kindness and worthiness of God in particular, and though this is a light and a part of contemplation, nevertheless, in this exercise, it must be cast down and covered over with a cloud of forgetting."[4] Even knowing this, however, we may still feel ridiculous when we can find no words to describe God after spending so much time in prayer. The author of the *Cloud of Unknowing* has learned to embrace his poverty when he can state it simply, "But now you put me a question and say: 'How might I think of [God] in himself, and what is he?' And to this I can only answer thus: 'I have no idea.' For with your question you have brought me into that same darkness, into that same cloud of unknowing."[5] In my human poverty, I must learn to accept prayer that seems useless, leaving me with nothing to show for it.

The Charismatic Renewal

Just as our discussions on prayer have not absolutized the value of praying in silence (contemplation) over and against praying "with the mind" (meditation), so also St. Paul encouraged the Corinthians to embrace both praying "with the spirit" and praying "with the mind" (1 Cor 14:15). They serve different purposes. Prayer in the spirit cannot be communicated for the edification of others unless it is accompanied by a special gift of interpretation (1 Cor 14:5). This does not cause St. Paul to discourage prayer in the spirit but rather to encourage prayer with the mind in addition to prayer in the spirit. As we just explored, we can see the connec-

---

4　James Walsh, ed., *The Cloud of Unknowing* (Mahwah, NJ: Paulist Press, 1981), 130–31.

5　Walsh, *The Cloud of Unknowing*, 130.

tion between "praying in the spirit" and the prayer in faith and silence to a hidden God that we described in earlier chapters. St. Paul discusses "praying in the spirit" as "speaking in tongues" in this passage, however. That leads us to ask ourselves, what is speaking or praying in tongues?

Since the development of the Catholic charismatic renewal in 1967, theologians, including Joseph Ratzinger, have agreed that the experience of "babbling" prayer heard at charismatic prayer services corresponds to the "speaking in tongues" spoken of by St. Paul in 1 Corinthians 14, etc., which was widespread in the early Church:

> Praying in tongues was very common in the early Church and is very common in the renewal. Some take up a position against tongues which logically denies its existence in the early Church and denies the possibility of its existence today. This position cannot be defended exegetically or theologically.[6]

This analysis was published as part of an extensive study of theologians in the 1970s and gathered together in a series of documents known as the Malines documents. The Malines documents received the magisterial approval of the Church in its original episcopal publication and still continues to enjoy the Church's explicit favor decades later in the approbation of Pope Francis: "In the Malines Documents, you have a guide, a

---

[6] *Theological and Pastoral Orientations on the Charismatic Renewal* aka The Malines documents, prepared at Malines Belgium, May 21-26, 1974. Published in English as Kilian McDonnell, ed., *Toward a New Pentecost for a New Evangelization: Malines Document I*, Subsequent edition (Collegeville, MI: Michael Glazier, 1993).

reliable path to keep you from going astray."[7] There have been many analyses and studies of the Catholic charismatic renewal throughout those decades and extensive support from the Holy See, which has acknowledged both the value of the renewal as well as the need for ecclesial supervision and discernment. Cardinal Ratzinger reasserted those points as Prefect for the Congregation of the Doctrine of the Faith when he wrote the foreword for the fourth Malines document in 1982:

> I also urge them to pay attention to the Cardinal's double plea, which deserves the greatest consideration: on the one hand, his appeal to those responsible for the ecclesial ministry—from parish priests to bishops—not to let the Renewal pass them by but to welcome it fully; and on the other, his appeal to the members of the Renewal to cherish and maintain their link with the whole Church and with the charisms of her pastors.[8]

The support for the renewal persisted throughout the pontificates of Pope St. Paul VI, Pope St. John Paul II, Pope Benedict XVI, and perhaps most enthusiastically in the pontificate of Pope Francis. Furthermore, the doctrinal analysis and support expressed in the above exhortation of the CDF Prefect Cardinal Joseph Ratzinger were still maintained by the CDF Prefect Cardinal Gerhardt Mueller thirty-four years later in his teaching on the relationship between the hierarchical and charismatic gifts in

---

[7] Pope Francis, Address to Participants in the 37th National Convocation of the Renewal in the Holy Spirit, June 1, 2014 (at http://w2.vatican.va/content/francesco/en/speeches/2014/june/documents/papa-francesco_20140601_rinnovamento-spirito-santo.html).

[8] Cardinal Leon-Joseph Suenens, *Renewal and the Powers of Darkness. Malines Document IV* (London: Darton, Longman and Todd, 1983), xi.

the life and mission of the Church.[9]

The Malines documents provided much wise counsel together with its extensive analysis of the experience of the Catholic charismatic renewal. It situated the experience of charismatic prayer and charismatic gifts in the context of the Church's ordinary sacramental and ecclesiastical structures. It warned against developments in prayer that would lead one outside the normal obedience to the teaching or governing authority of the Church. It identified the gifts as being a part of but not a substitute for the ordinary Christian life of works of mercy and the developments of prayer discussed throughout the great mystical tradition of the Church. The charismatic gifts including tongues, prophecy, and healing were not to be seen as measurements of holiness or necessary steps along the path of Christian life. At the same time, they were considered, already by the Second Vatican Council, to play an important role in the Church's mission: "These charisms, whether they be the more outstanding or the more simple and widely diffused, are to be received with thanksgiving and consolation for they are perfectly suited to and useful for the needs of the Church."[10] The decree on the laity reinforces this point:

> From the acceptance of these charisms, including those which are more elementary, there arise for each believer the right and duty to use them in the Church and in the world for the good of men and the building up of the

---

[9] Cardinal Gerhardt Mueller, Letter Iuvenescit Ecclesia to the Bishops of the Catholic Church Regarding the Relationship Between Hierarchical and Charismatic Gifts in the Life and the Mission of the Church, May 15, 2016 (at http://www.vatican.va/roman_curia/congregations/cfaith/documents/rc_con_cfaith_doc_20160516_iuvenescit-ecclesia_en.html).

[10] Vatican II, *Lumen Gentium*, §12.

Church, in the freedom of the Holy Spirit who "breathes where He wills" (John 3:8). This should be done by the laity in communion with their brothers in Christ, especially with their pastors who must make a judgment about the true nature and proper use of these gifts not to extinguish the Spirit but to test all things and hold for what is good (cf. 1 Thess. 5:12,19,21).[11]

We do not presume to provide an extensive analysis of the Catholic charismatic renewal here, but only enough to establish its validity and to provide pointers for additional explorations on the part of the reader. We are more interested in focusing on the approach to prayer offered by the renewal and understanding charismatic forms of prayer in light of all that has been said earlier in this book.

Charismatic Prayer Is Relational

In particular, we can see, in the prayer forms of the renewal, including praise, adoration, tongues, song, prophecy, and intercession for miracles and healing, the qualities we discussed earlier in this book, including vulnerability, faith, silence, hiddenness, and poverty. We will consider each of these elements, but we begin first with the relational quality of charismatic prayer.

The focus of charismatic prayer is especially on our intimate, personal relationship with Jesus Christ and the sonship that we share with Him through the Spirit of adoption. The same Spirit that gives us gifts is the Spirit that makes us sons, and as sons

---

[11] Second Vatican Council, *Apostolicam Actuositatem* (1965), §3.

we know the Father's tender and abundant generosity, "Son, you are always with me, and all that is mine is yours" (Luke 15:31). From the earliest days of the renewal, there was a strong focus on this relationship with Jesus Christ and everything in the Catholic faith fell into place for those "baptized in the Spirit" because of how it related to Jesus. The Scripture relates immediately to Jesus as being the same Word of the Father. Scripture was also viewed by those in the charismatic renewal as the love letters of Jesus to the believer. The Eucharist was immediately beloved because It was recognized as being Jesus Himself. The Blessed Mother, likewise, held a special place for charismatics because she is the Mother of Jesus. And charismatic prayer naturally led to service of the poor (as indicated by the third of the Malines documents[12]) because in the poor we find Jesus (see Matt 25:31–46).

This radical focus on a personal relationship with Jesus Christ has remained a hallmark of the charismatic renewal. This relationship is developed through praise songs that are personal and vulnerable, directly expressing our love for Jesus and our desire to have Him enter more deeply into our lives. One praise song aches for Him with the words, "Lord, I need you, oh, I need you. Every hour I need you."[13] The normal form of charismatic praise and worship also invites vulnerability through its physical expressions. By standing up, raising hands, and singing out, a person more fully and publicly commits to prayer and proclaims in a more radical and personal way the expressions of the Scrip-

---

[12] Cardinal Leon-Joseph Suenens and Dom Helder Camara, *Charismatic Renewal and Social Action: A Dialogue* (Ann Arbor, MI: Servant Books, 1979).

[13] Matt Maher, "Lord, I need you," *All the People Said Amen*, track 4 (Essential Records, 2013), AZ Lyrics. https://www.azlyrics.com/lyrics/mattmaher/lordineedyou.html.

ture-inspired song lyrics such as, "You give and take away, you give and take away, my heart will choose to say, Lord blessed be your Name!"[14] In this way, songs with lyrics of radical surrender and embracing the Cross provide a sobriety that balances the exhilaration that can go with boldly and publicly proclaiming Christ. In a prayer meeting, a Christian disciple has the opportunity for an expressive *parrhesia*, boldly professing "Jesus as Lord" as a manifestation of the Holy Spirit in the presence of other people. In that bold proclamation, he does not shrink from but even more courageously professes his personal discipleship as a way of the Cross.

Charismatic Prayer Moves toward Silence

At the same time as it involves loud and bold proclamations, the experience of charismatic prayer follows the same path of contemplative maturing as we find in other forms of prayer, described earlier. What begins with emotional intensity and continues to be open to such experiences also moves into times of dryness, silence, and hiddenness typical of other forms of Christian prayer. The song lyrics, "Open the eyes of my heart, Lord, open the eyes of my heart—I want to see you, I want to see you,"[15] capture the longing for more still that is found at the charismatic prayer meeting. Even the gifted, prophetic experience of words

---

[14] Matt Redman, "Blessed Be Your Name," *Blessed Be Your Name: The Songs of Matt Redman Vol. 1*, track 1 (Survivor Records, 2005), Genius. https://genius.com/Matt-redman-blessed-be-your-name-lyrics.

[15] Michael W. Smith, "Open the Eyes of My Heart," *Worship*, track 5 (Reunion Records, 2001), AZ Lyrics. https://www.azlyrics.com/lyrics/michaelwsmith/opentheeyesofmyheart.html.

and images, or the spiritual consolations that may accompany praise and worship, do not fully satisfy the deep longings of the disciple. In fact, they only open up deeper longings. For decades, charismatic prayer meetings have regularly incorporated periods of Eucharistic adoration including times of silence before the exposed Blessed Sacrament.

Praying in tongues

In the experience of God's hiddenness and the silencing of words and images in our minds, praying in tongues can come to the aid of the believer. Praying in tongues has been a hallmark of the charismatic renewal, although it has been repeatedly observed, as early as the first of the Malines documents, that it should be seen neither as necessary nor sufficient.[16] Prayer in tongues is simply one expression of prayer in the spirit. Prayer in tongues is certainly not praying with the mind, although while the mouth is making sounds according to some regular patterns known as a person's "prayer tongue," the mind can be free to wander and open itself to other gifts, such as prophecy or intercession.

We often have the experience that we run out of words before we run out of prayer. Rather than feverishly inventing new words or reciting lengthier prayer formulae, the one who prays in tongues can continue praying out loud without remaining attached to the words. This is beneficial for several reasons. If the one praying were to fall silent, it would leave the others wondering if he were still praying. Likewise, by continuing to make some sounds, it helps him to remain engaged in the prayer while moving beyond words to a deeper openness to the Holy Spirit. This can be part

---

[16] McDonnell, *Toward a New Pentecost for a New Evangelization*, 41.

of intercessory prayer or spontaneous praise or personal petition. It allows him to express himself vocally, while not getting caught up in formulating sentences and piecing together concepts. He may just linger on a feeling, an expression of love, or some other longing that cannot easily or effectively be put into words. All of this allows a prayer in faith to a hidden God.

Prayer meetings

> What then, brethren? When you come together, each one has a hymn, a lesson, a revelation, a tongue, or an interpretation. Let all things be done for edification. (1 Cor 14:26)

In the praise and worship found in a charismatic prayer meeting, one can even identify the kind of prayer movement that would be found in *lectio divina*—namely *lectio, meditatio, oratio*, and *contemplatio*. Prayer meetings always include a unified singing of songs with lyrics that are generally shaped by Sacred Scripture. This can be seen as a form of group *lectio*. This is typically followed by an eruption of spontaneous prayer that begins with simple repetitions of the lyrics of the song in a form of *meditatio*. Those eruptions of prayer may involve some elaboration or personalization of the ideas in a form of the *oratio* found in *lectio divina*. The prayer also takes on a unique quality by being offered in a group setting. While one listens to the others who are praying, the spontaneous expressions of prayer may also be influenced by others' exclamations or formulations. Then the prayer tends to move to a wordless form of prayer in tongues, similar to a movement of *contemplatio,* until it often settles into silence.

This wordless prayer of *contemplatio* is not unlike the grace of infused contemplation spoken of earlier in the book. In other words, often the precise fruit of praise and worship is God taking us into His contemplative gaze. It is in this contemplative gaze of love where the "anointing" comes, and people are enrapt by the presence and anointing of God and are given a supernatural gift of prayer.

In the silence, words can emerge, including words spoken from God in prophecy, quotations from Scripture, or images that rise up in one of the participants' minds. Sometimes a form of prayer in tongues emerges as an elaborated solo expression that calls forth an interpretive prophecy, as St. Paul noted in 1 Corinthians 14:5. Other times the prayer in tongues moves into a harmonious singing that is reminiscent of an orchestra initially tuning its instruments into a unified whole. The result is that the charismatic-prayer meeting often follows a form of collective *lectio divina* that opens the individuals to divine words of exhortation, encouragement, love, affirmation, and guidance while simultaneously forming a diverse group of believers into a unified body.

Throughout the tradition, one expression repeatedly used for prayer or song in tongues is "jubilation." St. Augustine spoke beautifully about the praise of God that cannot be expressed in words in a homily on Psalm 33:

> Do not search for words, as if you could find a lyric which would give God pleasure. Sing to him "with songs of joy." This is singing well to God, just singing with songs of joy. But how is this done? You must first understand that words cannot express the things that are sung by the heart. Take the case of people singing while harvesting in

the fields or in the vineyards or when any other strenuous work is in progress. Although they begin by giving expression to their happiness in sung words, yet shortly there is a change. As if so happy that words can no longer express what they feel, they discard the restricting syllables. They burst out into a simple sound of joy, of jubilation. Such a cry of joy is a sound signifying that the heart is bringing to birth what it cannot utter in words. Now, who is more worthy of such a cry of jubilation than God himself, whom all words fail to describe? If words will not serve, and yet you must not remain silent, what else can you do but cry out for joy? Your heart must rejoice beyond words, soaring into an immensity of gladness, unrestrained by syllabic bonds. *Sing to him with jubilation.* [17]

Here we read in St. Augustine how we can sing a song (and by extension say a prayer) that uses feeling and wordless expression "beyond syllabic bonds" to praise God. Sometimes there is confusion about the origin of praying in tongues being entirely divine as if the person were being possessed by the Holy Spirit. This would be a false understanding of this form of tongues. There is another miraculous form of "tongues" or "ears" that the Apostles experienced at Pentecost, described in Acts chapter 2. Likewise, the miraculous gift of interpretation or the miraculous facility to speak a language one has never studied would be different spiritual phenomena. But the prayer of tongues normally associated with the charismatic renewal could even be described as a human form of prayer that is utilized at will in order to

---

[17] St. Augustine, (Ps. 32, sermo 1, 7–8: CCL 38, 253–254) from November 22 in the Roman Breviary.

express intercession, thanksgiving, and praise for God beyond words, "with a simple sound of joy, of jubilation." It is a human form of prayer in the same way that we have discussed prayer throughout this book. Using the sounds from human vocal cords and with the affection of human hearts, this form of prayer opens up with a receptivity toward divine love and a readiness to receive divine gifts. It is certainly subject to the human free will and not normally an altered state or a form of ecstasy. Indeed, if it were not subject to the human will, St. Paul could not order those in the prayer meeting to do it more or less (1 Cor 14:5, 30–33).

Charismatic Prayer Calls Forth Deeper Faith

At first glance, the expressive prayer found in the charismatic renewal would seem to substitute signs and wonders for faith. Spoken words of prophecy and vocalized expressions of God's personal love for an individual seem to remove the need for faith, because the veil of mystery is lifted. These words spoken in the Spirit provide answers to the great question that most people praying have, such as, "What is God saying to me?" At the same time, the prophetic utterances are no more preserved from being doubted than our own personal prayer is. Even sudden healings that may not be explainable scientifically can never force someone to believe. Although these signs, wonders, and prophetic words can support and even convince the unbeliever at first (1 Cor 14:24–25), she must always freely take her own step in faith to believe or to keep believing in the truth of what is taking place.

Furthermore, like all extraordinary phenomena (visions, locutions, stigmata, levitation, etc.) the origins and meaning of the phenomena must be discerned through the normal processes of the Church (see *Iuvenescit Ecclesia* for more on this). These must be tested against public revelation (Sacred Scripture and the Church's teaching magisterium) and discerned by the fruits they produce in believers' lives. St. John of the Cross expressed his confidence that in extraordinary charismatic gifts, the grace is already communicated in the initial gift and so the receiver does not have to hold on to the effects. This would be similar to receiving a hug from a person. Having received the hug, the recipient accepts the communication of love, affection, and support and does not need to hold on to the physical feeling of the hug, but rather takes to heart the message it conveys. That process of taking the message to heart and letting go of the feeling is again an act of faith.

In addition to the faith that is called forth from the recipient, there is much faith needed also from the one who communicates the message. When a word or image of prophecy is spoken, the one who speaks it acts in faith. Receiving such a message may not require a particular level of faith or holiness, but it certainly requires faith to discern the authenticity and communicate it to others. The same is true for miraculous healings. A healing does not depend on the holiness of the one praying nor does the healing increase his holiness, but the acts of faith, hope, and charity needed to pray for a miraculous healing help him to grow in holiness. Furthermore, the process of asking for healings and handling the mixed effects of that prayer can lead to a fruitful purification of the one praying. God's choice to bestow miracles of healing is mysterious and challenges our faith and trust in Him. The uncertainty of the results also challenges the faith of the person who is praying, requiring him to vulnerably step out in faith and hope for the good of the other. Any temptations to self-aggrandizement and pride will be purified by repeated "failures."

Teaching authoritatively on what makes prayer authentically Christian, Cardinal Ratzinger highlighted the danger of "Messalianism," writing:

> These false fourth century charismatics identified the grace of the Holy Spirit with the psychological experience of his presence in the soul. In opposing them, the Fathers insisted on the fact that the soul's union with God in prayer is realized in a mysterious way, and in particular through the sacraments of the Church. Moreover, it can even be achieved through experiences of affliction or desolation.[18]

He also clarified that the forms of error that can arise in prayer can be diagnosed very simply, noting that the goal of prayer is to grasp the divine depths revealed in Christ, the Incarnate Word, and in the gift of His Spirit. "These divine depths are always revealed to him through the human-earthly dimension."[19] As much as we touch on that which is beyond the human-earthly dimension by encountering God in a love beyond words or in supernatural experiences, we always ultimately remain rooted in our humanity and return to it. It is always the foundation of our encounter with the sacred humanity of Christ which reveals the fullness of God to us.

---

[18] Ratzinger, *Orationis formas*, no. 9.
[19] Ratzinger, *Orationis formas*, no. 11.

The Gift of Prophecy

The Catechism encourages the use of special gifts of the Holy Spirit to assist our Christian ministry in CCC 2004, which explains and quotes from St. Paul's letter to the Romans:

> Among the special graces ought to be mentioned the *graces of state* that accompany the exercise of the responsibilities of the Christian life and of the ministries within the Church: "Having gifts that differ according to the grace given to us, let us use them: if prophecy, in proportion to our faith; if service, in our serving; he who teaches, in his teaching; he who exhorts, in his exhortation; he who contributes, in liberality; he who gives aid, with zeal; he who does acts of mercy, with cheerfulness" (Rom 12:6–8).

Each of the gifts mentioned in the passage from the letter to the Romans is important for Christians to reflect on and put into practice in our lives. We focus our attention here on the gift of prophecy because it is a particular experience and expression of prayer. What is prophecy?

> Paul places strongest emphasis on prophecy as the charism that is especially efficacious in building up the church (1 Cor 14:1–5). Prophecy is speech that is inspired by the Spirit, communicating a message that is not one's own but comes from God. It may include disclosure concerning the future (cf. Acts 11:27–29) or reading of hearts (1 Cor 14:25; cf. Acts 5:2–4), but more often it takes the

form of encouragement and consolation (1 Cor 14:3) or conviction of sin (1 Cor 14:24).[20]

In the normal use of our minds, we draw input from our feelings, our five senses, and our memory to form words and images in our imagination. Those words and images are abstracted and processed by various faculties of discursive reason, and eventually we may also express them through speaking, gestures, facial expressions, art, music, etc. When those words and images are also formed under divine influence, we call it the gift of prophecy. Normally the human and divine processes are intermixed in a way that makes it difficult to tease out exactly where one ends and the other begins. The divine influence can enter into any part of this process, from the most superficial level, which is actually external and involves influencing our senses, to the deepest level, which is purely spiritual and involves influencing our abstract reason (what the Scholastics call the "possible intellect"). In between these two extremes is an influence on our imagination. From these three levels we have the traditional descriptions: "sensory visions," "imaginative visions," and "intellectual visions."[21] These categories capture more than visual images and would include any of the five senses as well as words and more abstract concepts.

In prayer we experience this gift in various ways. We have a sudden insight and then we have to work to put it into words; an image comes to us about a situation we are praying over; we are moved to take a particular action to reach out to someone; a

---

[20] International Catholic Charismatic Renewal Services Doctrinal Commission, *Baptism in the Holy Spirit* (Locust Grove, VA: NSC USA, 2017), 53.
[21] Ralph Martin, *Fulfillment of All Desire* (Steubenville, OH: Emmaus Road, 2006), 312–328.

particular verse of Scripture comes to us—maybe the words or just the reference. Often these words and images rise up from our memory and imagination but come together in an unexpected way. Other times we are thinking through a problem in prayer and then we arrive at an insight that seems to fit perfectly. It is right on target. In these experiences, we can be very aware of our own thinking with our own ideas and images emerging, and yet we also have the sense of another Actor participating in our reflections. As we practice with this gift, we can become more sensitive to the Lord's work, and we can learn to support it better and interfere with it less.

The gift of prophecy can be at work in our prayer or also in our conversations or our ministries. It is a powerful gift to accompany preaching and teaching. It elevates the effect of conversations as we allow God to participate in our gestures and the formulations of our words. Ultimately, we want to allow our whole lives to be under the influence of divine grace. For this reason, St. Paul was especially enthusiastic about the gift of prophecy. He included it in every listing of the charisms of the Holy Spirit. He exhorted believers to "earnestly desire" (1 Cor 14:1; 1 Cor 14:39) this gift, and he said he desires it for all of us (1 Cor 14:4–5).

Naturally, prophecy always requires discernment. Although only God can infuse grace into our higher intellectual processes to create intellectual visions, our imagination, emotions, and senses can all be influenced by demonic forces. Thus, the more external the vision is, the less trustworthy it is. How do we know which words, images, and insights are trustworthy as being genuine prophecy? We must always test everything against the magisterial teaching of the Church. God will never contradict

Himself, and so He will never reveal anything contrary to the theological doctrine of the Church. Likewise, He will never call us away from fidelity to our vocational commitments. As we discussed earlier in the book, St. Ignatius provided other tools for discernment. In his "first week rules," he indicated simply that divinely inspired thoughts rise up from spiritual consolation, and these are the opposite of the demonically influenced thoughts that arise from spiritual desolation.[22] In other words, the spiritual force that is influencing our thoughts will also flow over into our other faculties so that we can recognize his action. Peace, joy, a heart inflamed with love, an increase in the theological virtues, etc., are some of the signs that accompany the influence of the good spirit. Darkness of soul, inner turmoil, restlessness, disturbance, despair, doubts, and a draw to low and earthly things are some of the signs that accompany the influence of the evil spirit.

While we must be careful about not falling into deception, prophecy can be a powerful gift when used appropriately. Whether it is a matter of personal guidance or divine encouragement or direction for major decisions, prophecy concretely manifests God's will in our lives through the radiance of His light in our souls. St. Teresa of Calcutta had visions of Jesus and Mary through her encounters with the poor on her train ride to Darjeeling. These visions, presumably imaginative, were the guiding light for her founding of the Missionaries of Charity.[23] Later in her life, she continued to make prophetic gestures and speak prophetically. For example, on one occasion she sought to visit her Sisters in Beirut during the Civil War in Lebanon.

---

[22] St. Ignatius of Loyola, *Spiritual Exercises*, nos. 316–17.

[23] St. Teresa of Calcutta, *Come Be My Light: The Private Writings of the Saint of Calcutta*, ed. Brian Kolodiejchuk (New York: Doubleday, 2007).

The President, who was a good Catholic, prevented her because of the extreme danger. She paused to reflect and pray and then asked him if he would allow it if there were a cease fire. She said she would pray to Our Lady and ask that gift from her for her feast day which was coming up the next day. The President was stunned and tried to dissuade her from putting such pressure on Our Lady, but Mother Teresa stood firm. Miraculously, there was indeed a cease fire the next day, and the President escorted Mother Teresa to her convent to care for the Sisters and the poor.[24]

Signs of Authenticity

When the gift of prophecy is authentic, it follows the same developments of prayer outlined earlier in the book. It is relational, requires faith, works through poverty, and even though God is speaking in some way, He remains hidden and silent to the prophet. On the contrary, when the prophet feels omniscient, greater than everyone else, filled with control and power, it is more likely that he is having a manic episode. The prophets in the Old Testament were always reluctant. Prophecy for them was a way of the Cross. They did not want to speak out the words they were receiving in prayer, but in the end they could no longer resist: "If I say, 'I will not mention him, or speak any more in his name,' there is in my heart as it were a burning fire shut up in my bones, and I am weary with holding it in, and I cannot" (Jer 20:9).

---

[24] *Mother Teresa*, directed by Ann Petrie and Jeanette Petrie (n.p.: Petrie Productions, 1986), DVD.

God honors our freedom, and He does not want to overpower us or use us. As a result, prophecy generally appears from within, mixed with our own thoughts. We must apply faith and discernment to decide what is of God and what is from ourselves or from the Enemy. At the same time, prophecy develops relationally. Each of us has a unique relationship with the Lord and receives words, images, and insights from Him according to our own particular "grammar" or "vocabulary." God is the same yesterday, today, and forever, and His interactions with us tend to be consistent. He works with our own aptitudes and natural abilities and communicates in consistent ways so that we can recognize His voice and heed His call. "The sheep follow him, for they know his voice," Jesus said simply (John 10:4). As we learn to recognize His voice in prophecy and as we are confirmed through faith by speaking out or acting out that prophecy, it deepens our relationship with Him, and we discover how personally He loves us.

When human reasoning can confirm the words we are receiving in prayer, it is comforting and gives us more ease and courage to speak out. On the other hand, prophecy can be harrowing when we believe we are hearing His voice but our human reasoning leads us to question what we are hearing. For example, one man was praying over a woman and seeking a word from God for her. She had expressed that she was having some health problems and was seeking prayer particularly for that. She did not elaborate on what the problems were. As the man began to pray, there emerged in his imagination a faint image of a particular kind of sugar cookie called a "Smiley" cookie. He had no idea what that could mean but after some continued prayer, he felt confirmed that he should share that image. He planned to interpret it by explaining that it denoted sweetness and joy and that the Lord wanted to affirm her in those qualities. The woman's husband was also praying with them, and as soon as the man said that he was getting an image of a Smiley cookie, both husband and wife laughed and looked at each other, surprised. The woman declared, "Those are my favorite. I have been trying to quit eating so many of them." It turned out that her health problems were sugar- and weight-related, and cutting back on Smiley cookies was one of the remedies she needed to employ. The experience of prayer communicated a grace for her to step forward in that.

While the prophecies sometimes require an act of faith to speak out, which then is immediately confirmed and appreciated, at other times the prophet does not get the satisfaction of knowing his words reached someone's heart. That happens in words spoken in prayer meetings or communicated individually to someone. In these times, the prophet experiences the hiddenness and silence of God. At the other times, the one praying wants very much to find a word or an image of encouragement or consolation, but there is simply nothing coming. The Christian is always reminded that God is not a jukebox and He does not perform on command. God has the big picture in mind, and He gives His gifts as they are truly needed, on His timescale and in His way. The gifts of the Spirit are always God's gifts and not our possessions. The Christian, even when he is richly gifted, must never lose sight of his natural human poverty. He is always a beggar before God.

11

Then We Shall Be Like Him

"I Thirst"

I T IS THE PRACTICE for the Missionaries of Charity to have the words "I thirst" painted on the wall over the crucifix in their convents. For one who prays, these words have great meaning. One could, of course, think at first of the desire for deeper and total union with God which prayer stirs up. Then looking at the crucifix, one remembers the thirst of Jesus on the Cross, a thirst which brought Him to drink again the fruit of the vine, which He had promised His disciples He would not do until He entered into His kingdom (Matt 26:29). By accepting to drink the cup of self-offering in Gethsemane, and then on Calvary actually drinking this cup of consummation, He also completed the fourth cup of the Passover meal begun the previous evening at the Last Supper.[1] He thereby inaugurated His sacrifice of love, the new

---

[1] Brant James Pitre, *Jesus and the Jewish Roots of the Eucharist: Unlocking the Secrets*

covenant, now consumed, indeed consummated, on the Cross.

Therefore, His thirst was much more than physical thirst! His thirst was the thirst of infinite Divine love experienced also humanly, which is so intense that it is unimaginable and by human standards unbearable! That is how God loves us, shown nowhere so vividly as on the Cross, which is why we so often pray before the Crucifix. We are also drawn by His thirsting love as we receive and pray before the fruit of the consummation of the Incarnation in the Paschal mystery: the Eucharist. He thirsts for us! That is how much He loves us. When we are parched with thirst in the desert of life and in the desert of love and prayer, that is how He loves us. He loves us in our thirst, and He loves us with an even more intense thirst than ours. Therefore, as we have shown, it is so helpful in prayer just to let Him love us. We have seen how this relationship with Him, opened up in prayer in all its moments, transforms us into His likeness for which we have been created. We have tried throughout this book not to offer simply a theory about prayer but to lead into and make attempts to describe the experience of prayer. In this last chapter, we will return to many things we have talked about, now showing how it deepens as a more habitual union with God is established. In doing so, we will point to some of the manifestations of the transformation into His likeness that can be experienced even now. We will also look forward to what has been revealed about the promise that then we will see Him as He is.

We will begin with a mysterious saying of Jesus which the Church offers as one of the Gospel readings for funeral Masses.

---

of the Last Supper (New York: Doubleday, 2011); Scott Hahn, *The Fourth Cup: Unveiling the Mystery of the Last Supper and the Cross* (New York: Image, 2018).

It usually brings us much comfort when we reflect on it: "In my Father's house are many rooms; if it were not so, would I have told you that I go to prepare a place for you? And when I go to prepare a place for you, I will come again and will take you to myself, that where I am you may be also. And you know the way where I am going" (John 14:2–4). This reminds us of what we have said about the infinite love God has for each one of us; namely, He loves each one as if each were the only one in the world. The Lord has an unrepeatably unique relationship with each one of us. As each one of us is transformed in our relationship with the Lord, each of us grows and changes in our likeness to Him. When we see Him as He is, as unique as each of us is, we will be settled in a room precisely fitted to who we are and whom we have become, and we will be like Him! It will be finding our way home and coming home in a way we longed for all through our lives, rarely tasted and never quite achieved. It will finally be accomplished when we see Him as He is and see ourselves as we are, and then we will see how much we are like Him.

Greater Interiority

It is our experience of prayer that we enter ever more deeply into a personal relationship with God, one that is infinitely personal because it is a relationship with God. What is an infinitely personal relationship with God like? The mistake is to let the word "infinite" cause us to imagine a relationship that is so far beyond us in our creaturely finitude and limitations. But we must think of what makes a relationship personal in order to truly experience what an infinitely personal relationship with God might be like.

The more personal a relationship is, the more interior, the more capable of increasingly deeper love it is. When it is more personal, it does not become unreachable or farther beyond us but more and more deeply interior. This is true even if our human relationships, the more intimate they are, still have an elusive quality. But that elusiveness should not cause us to give up and leave the relationship but rather cause us to be drawn more deeply and intimately into it. So, our relationship with God is capable of becoming more deeply interior than any human relationship can ever become. "Not as man sees does God see, because man sees the appearance but the Lord looks into the heart" (1 Sam 16:7b). God's greatness does not detach us from Him but makes a fuller intimacy with Him than with any other person possible because His greatness is His Love.

This helps us understand many things. We long to see His face! Pope St. John Paul II, nearer to the time of His death, began to exhort us with even greater urgency to seek the face of the Lord. This was disturbing because of the elusiveness of actually seeing His face, as we all know. As God replied to Moses's request to see His face, "You cannot see my face; for man shall not see me and live. . . . you shall see my back; but my face shall not be seen" (Exod 33:20, 23). Despite this, the psalmist still gives us words to express our protest: "You have said, 'Seek my face.' My heart says to you, 'Your face, Lord, do I seek.' Hide not your face from me" (Ps 27:9). We do have beautiful icons of Christ, which iconically take us into Christ, especially through the eyes of the image written on the icon. Likewise, more in the western tradition, statues of Jesus such as statues of the Sacred Heart or of the crucifixion, by their realism or by artistic forms of abstraction, can seem to lead us into a kind of seeing. Furthermore and most especially, in the Eucharist we truly gaze upon the Body, Blood, Soul, and Divinity of Jesus but still under the appearances of bread and wine.

One of the reasons for the Incarnation was to allow us to gaze upon the Son of God in His humanity, with a human face. St. Teresa of Avila and so many of the saints recognize the importance of bringing images from the life of the incarnate Lord into our prayer to nourish it, and not too quickly to try to reach a prayer free of images. We seem to need this possibility of somehow seeing His face. Yet interestingly, after His death and resurrection, when Jesus appeared, He warned Mary Magdalene against clinging to Him and soon ascended to the right hand of the Father (John 20:17). He does this even saying that it is necessary for Him to depart so that the Spirit can come (John 16:7). Once again, we are left with an inability to see His face. As Jesus told the Apostle Thomas, now we must see Him in faith, a faith which is a gift and therefore infused, which does not pass through the eye, the imagination, or reason; since nothing we can see can any longer be God or represent God, we must pass through darkness and silence into an interior seeing.

Even in His resurrection appearances, He is not readily recognizable to those who knew Him so intimately. Only slowly are they able to see His face in a way which seems to require faith from those who behold Him. Even then, some seem to see Him more gradually and apparently even differently than others. In His risen existence, even after a bodily resurrection including His full humanity, He can only be seen by going more deeply in faith into an interior seeing, a seeing of the heart. This is the direction our seeing must take us as we come more and more to see His face. After forty days of preparation, at the Ascension, even the face of the risen Lord is removed from the external senses. When the Spirit descends, He does so in a way reminiscent of the appearances of the risen Lord: though it is the one Spirit, each one upon whom the Spirit descends receives Him in an individual way, in individual tongues of fire (Acts 2:1–4). As they burst forth from the upper room, they speak in uniquely different languages, though they are still able to understand the other various languages being spoken (Acts 2:5–11). The appearances of the risen Lord lead those who see Him bodily risen to know Him in uniquely personal and more interior ways, a profound deepening of the relationship they have with Him. Likewise, the descent of the Holy Spirit upon an individual person always comes in a uniquely personal way, bringing unique gifts to each one, transforming each one in a uniquely personal way, and bringing the relationship into a deeper interiority and love, as simultaneously it leads each one filled with the Spirit out to all the others.

The same is true regarding hearing the Lord. What do we really expect to hear? What did we come out into the desert of prayer to hear? We have already noted that when we listen in prayer, we do not usually hear words in the same way we hear the words of another human being. This can be severely disappointing and even shakes the faith of many people. Why isn't He answering me? We have also described how more often He speaks in our thoughts and our voice in a way that seems not to have originated from ourselves and yet which we recognize as true and a part of ourselves. Or maybe we simply have an insight or feeling that brings us resolution. These are all ways the Lord speaks which take us more deeply into an interior communication, often in ways more interior than words. Prayer, as it deepens and becomes more personal, takes us further and further from regular spoken words heard from outside ourselves and more and more within ourselves into a deeper and deeper communion. Words become less necessary from our side as well as from the side of God, and we have less need for answers or information from God as we simply rest in the silence of loving communion. We never stop needing nourishment by word and sacrament, by Scripture and the Eucharist, but more and more we listen in a silent receptivity and commune from the heart. Yet even in this graced silence, the silence can intensify to the point that the individual no longer hears God in the silence. Such silence becomes purifying as faith deepens.[2]

When we do see His face and hear His voice, we will find how much we are like Him. This hearing and seeing interiorly takes us deeper into His likeness, which increases as we give our hearts more and more to Him in the most deeply and personally interior way. Truly, we enter into an interior of ourselves in which we have never been before but which somehow we already know, and where we become ourselves more deeply as we recognize Him in an interior, spiritual way. This side of death, even this profoundly gracious relationship is still filled with a painful longing, a longing that is as deep as it is loving. Our likeness to Him is beyond comprehension now, yet that likeness constitutes the deepest heart of ourselves. As this transformation into His likeness nears its completion, we pour ourselves out in an increas-

---

[2] Adrienne von Speyr, *The Boundless God*, trans. Helena Tomko (San Francisco, CA: Ignatius Press, 2004).

ingly simple and total way, in a Godlike way, since He is infinite
Love, an infinite, Self-emptying gift.

The Fruits of Interior Prayer

The more deeply personal our relationship with God in prayer,
the more we pour ourselves out in love. Let us look at the fruit
of this prayer.

Transparency

First of all, we become increasingly transparent, and all of reality,
particularly other persons and the providence of God, become
more transparent. We become transparent through love and vulnerability. The avoidance of vulnerability keeps us opaque and is
one of the chief obstacles to deeper prayer and to a deeper relationship with God. Without realizing it, we can be very afraid
of deeper love because we are afraid of vulnerability, ultimately
afraid of being wounded. How many of us avoid transparency at
all costs because we are afraid we will be objectified, judged, or
that others will not love us in those places where we are most
wounded and sensitive? Taking the risk to love others can be
hard for many, but to love God can be terrifying. To truly love
Him is not just to know Him as an idea or feel control over Him
by thinking we have comprehended Him; it is to take the risk
of encountering Him as a tremendous and fascinating mystery.
God's providence threatens us because we realize how little we
really understand what is going on when we see how pervasively
He knows and provides, but also how there is no place we can
escape from Him (see Psalm 139:7–12). This feeling of being

examined and known by Him can be terrifying (see Psalm 139:1–6) until we surrender to His provident love, nowhere understood more deeply than in His intimately personal and interior love for us. Then we want to be transparent, because that vulnerability is our greatest openness to His love. Then we understand the meaning of the words of Jesus at the Last Supper when He describes what this transparency opens up for us: "In that day you will know that I am in my Father, and you in me, and I in you" (John 14:20). Thus Divine transparency draws human transparency deeply and interiorly into it.

Through prayer, all of reality becomes somehow illuminated by the love of God. It is seen mostly by the eyes of the heart and mysteriously it pours over somehow into actual external sight. Sometimes we see how God is *in* all things, which at the same time are not themselves divine but are rather *given* by God. These gifts become transparent to us as the fruit of prayer and deepening interiority, and we learn to see the Giver in all things. What we hear has a transparent clarity: the singing of a bird, the voice of another person, the beauty of a piece of music. We see and hear the vulnerability of all life and the precious uniqueness of every single thing, of every single being. When we see the luminous beauty of all of creation, it becomes easy to believe that each precious creature, each precious moment will ultimately flow into God's eternity, where it will not disappear but will eternally be preserved as precious. Especially precious is the way each person, especially in vulnerability, becomes transparent to one who is transparent. In this transparency, each person's uniqueness appears so evidently as a gift. Then, in the privileged

I/Thou,[3] one-on-one encounter in mutual, intentional transparency, the personal beauty and gift of each person, especially in his or her interiority, is overwhelmingly sacred and the occasion of deep love. It is a sense of the giftedness, the graciousness, and the unique beauty of every creature and of all creatures.

Now we can see better why the Lord Jesus appears risen in a way that is even more transparent and interior than in His earthly life. In His Incarnation, in a way, He became more opaque. Though we could see Him, we could not see *into* Him. He did not appear to be God, but rather merely another human being. In His Resurrection this changed. He taught us to see more deeply, looking through His exterior qualities to see His divinity. The particular characteristics of His humanity (hair color, eye color, height, etc.) became more transparent and gave way to a deeper vision. He was recognized by His Love—the way He spoke a name ("Mary!") or acknowledged the fears of the Apostles ("peace be with you!"), the way He turned a long night of nothingness into a miraculous catch (John 21), the way He counseled with Scripture and gave Himself in bread (Luke 24). We realize that so much we couldn't see of God, that was hidden for us, we actually could not see because He is transparent! It is to lead us into deeper transparency that Jesus ascended to the right hand of the Father and sent the Spirit, not that He would become more abstract and hidden, but that He might be even more transparent in the Holy Spirit.

Praying unceasingly

Obviously, we pass in and out of vulnerability. But for the one

---

[3]   Martin Buber, *I and Thou*, trans. Walter Kaufmann, 36th ed. (New York: Charles Scribners, 1970).

who has prayed regularly, for extended periods of time and over a considerable length of time, vulnerability becomes somehow continuous, though it might be more remarkable at some times than at others.

The same thing happens to prayer. No more than we can will ourselves to be always or more deeply transparent can we will ourselves to pray continuously. Our cultivation of a prayerful disposition and an effort to be vulnerable and transparent is necessary but not sufficient to achieve unceasing prayer or the transparency which must have been an important dimension of what Christ meant when He told us that to enter the kingdom of heaven, we must each become like a little child (Matt 18:5). It is the disposition of childlike trust in God—surrender rather than unflagging effort—that opens us to receive the gift of unceasing prayer.[4]

That it is possible for us to pray constantly—or, rather, impossible for us alone but possible for God—is shown in two admonitions of St. Paul: "Rejoice always, pray constantly, give thanks in all circumstances. For this is the will of God in Christ Jesus for you" (1 Thess 5:16–18). How interior and how much a gift this is can be shown by what St. Paul says in another place: "Likewise the Spirit helps us in our weakness; for we do not know how to pray as we ought, but the Spirit himself intercedes for us with sighs too deep for words. And he who searches the hearts of men knows what is the mind of the Spirit, because the Spirit intercedes for the saints according to the will of God" (Rom 8:26–27).

---

4 Benedict J. Groeschel, *Praying Constantly: Bringing Your Faith to Life* (Huntington, IN: Our Sunday Visitor, 2010).

This unceasing prayer comes from the most interior place of each of us because it comes from the place deep in our hearts where the Spirit resides continuously through the grace of the Sacrament of Baptism. Confirmation confirms this intimate indwelling of the Spirit as does every Sacrament we ever receive. As St. Paul says, the unceasing prayer of the Holy Spirit comes when we are most helpless in prayer, not when we are confident of our methodology or feel we know exactly how to access the Spirit. When we are most helpless, in our weakness, the Spirit prays in us, often with groaning too deep for words (Rom 8:26). In vulnerability and helplessness, we realize that the Spirit is always praying in us, often in a way that is too transparent for us to know or hear until we cannot pray anymore on our own!

We see this same dynamic in the Eastern tradition of the Jesus Prayer, as we considered in Chapter 9. The express purpose of the Jesus Prayer is the cultivation of an unceasing prayer of the heart. Here again we see the importance of helplessness and weakness in the repeated invocation: "Lord Jesus Christ, Son of God, have mercy on me, a sinner." Notice how the disposition of this prayer, like the prayer when we recognize the Spirit groaning in our depths, is one of helplessness in need of God's mercy. The quiet repetition of this prayer carves out greater depths of humility within us, which we have already noted is the most apt disposition with which to enter into prayer. Some people pray this way for fifteen minutes or a half an hour to calm and recollect themselves before or after a busy day. It would not be presumptuous to seek to continue to pray this prayer not with the lips but from the heart, from the deep interior where the Spirit is, and to recognize that the Spirit will possibly begin to sustain this prayer continuously in us. As this happens, the Spirit actually "brings our minds, hearts and wills into a communion with the mind, heart and will of Christ."[5] We know that as our personal relationship with the Lord deepens, other gifts become habitual in us: grace, the virtues, sacrifice, prayer, an awareness of our sins, and an ever deeper dying to self. Let us first talk about the awareness of sin.

My sin is always before me

We are not talking here about scrupulosity or a Jansenistic preoccupation with being unworthy, which can often hide a perfectionistic control or a deep-seated pride. The awareness of sin we are speaking of is never felt without an awareness of Divine Mercy. Rather than Martin Luther's judgment that even when justified, we remain sinners, our faith teaches us that even though sinners, we are forgiven and loved. Thus the awareness of sin found most deeply in the greatest saints is not a self-preoccupied, self-centered sense of how great all our sins are, but an awareness of how great our sins are *in the face of the infinite mercy and love of God.* One who prays much has again and again found himself faced with the gravity and dangerous nature of his own sins, as measured against the infinite love of God for us.

One's sinfulness is also exacerbated by the transparency into which one has grown. My sins are always before me because I see the interior of myself. Transparency does not make me want to hide from others, lest they somehow see or know my sins, but makes me so aware of how poorly I have loved so that now

---

[5] Ralph Martin, *Hungry for God: Practical Help in Personal Prayer* (Cincinnati, OH: Servant, 2006), 123–24.

I only want to rely on His love. As we have seen and will rediscover over and over again, any prayer that makes me more and
more focused on myself needs to be refocused on God. My sins
being always before me in my transparency makes me more aware
of the Mercy of the Father shown through Christ. This perhaps
helps us understand why those who are most saintly and who
have even preserved their baptismal innocence feel most unworthy because, in full transparency, they are most vulnerably aware
of how truly infinite God's Mercy is. This mercy is seen in Christ
so transparently and in such a vulnerable and personal way that in
the depths of my own interiority, my sins hidden from everybody
else are glaring at me. From this we understand better the formulation of the Jesus Prayer in the East which primarily centers on
Divine Mercy. The more continuously we pray, the more humble
and grateful our prayer becomes.

It is the paradox that those who seldom go to Confession have
trouble finding sins to confess, while those who confess often
are aware of many ways they have not been what they have so
greatly desired to be. At the same time, the one who prays much
becomes more aware of the sins of omission, along with a healthy
remembrance of past sins. This breeds an eagerness to confess
frequently because the Sacrament of Confession is a celebration
of love and forgiveness, not an indictment for sin that is never
forgiven. Usually when one cannot believe a sin is forgiven, either
there is some aspect or significance of the sin that has not been
confessed or needs to be explored further, or the person is himself
unforgiving and judgmental of others and hence cannot believe
he himself has been forgiven. These dilemmas are always best
solved by bringing the sin and its memories before the Lord in

prayer, and letting Love illuminate what keeps forgiveness from being received. Indeed, all sin is a choice of self over love, and a choice of self over Him. A person who has entered deeply into a personal relationship with Christ becomes pained even to recognize times during the day when she has not been sufficiently aware of God's presence and love, tending instead to simply act on her own.

Self-denial and dying to self

Self-denial and sacrifice, after becoming less self-conscious, tend to become a steady disposition. Rather than needing to constantly monitor oneself to weed out selfishness or to fulfill promised acts of self-denial, one tends to make fewer resolutions and instead to more continuously and spontaneously allow oneself to live the crucified love of Jesus: dying to self and coming more alive in love for God and others. Like prayer and transparency, this becomes continuous. Dying to self, as it deepens and the awareness of it becomes more interior, is more and more forgetful of self for the sake of the Other and the others. There comes a revelation through the lens of the infinite love of God how selfish we really are, and how isolating and imprisoning this selfishness is, how self-focus keeps us superficial and petty and keeps us always feeling like we are running out of whatever it is we think we want. The interior reflection of who I really am frees me more from the demands of my own ego or self and allows the faculties wasted in disordered self-love to seek a more worthy object. My ability to love myself comes besides, after I love God and then other people, as Jesus showed in setting the priority of the commandments.

The many ways we have felt angry or cheated, rejected or misunderstood, isolated or forgotten, used or abused, only drive us deeper into victimhood, self-pity, and sadness. Our ego is expensive to keep fed, and makes extraordinary demands without ever being satisfied. When the ego becomes more and more inflated, the self is always imploding. Prayer, in which we open ourselves as totally as we can to the Lord and focus on Him, takes us to an interior seeing which allows us to see how demanding our own ego can be and how its insistence on being the center of the universe throws everything out of focus. The ego prevents transparency by the opaqueness of its self-inflation, and the self becomes less capable of relationship, especially personal relationships, so that all love really becomes self-love. There is no room for God because the ego has become our god.

Dying to oneself takes one more deeply into the interior and into an awareness of how human love participates in the infinite love of God because human love itself has an infinite quality, which makes it suited for a personal relationship with God, who is infinite. This love becomes habitual and in fact deepens through actual experiences of being used, rejected, misunderstood, or forgotten. Someone who focuses on victimhood and builds his identity around being a victim will never heal without reaching the point of forgiving, loving, and dying to self. Sadly, when we have been hurt, we feel justified in demanding that the one hurting us undergo the same thing. Prayer that takes us into communion with God in our own interior and allows us to die to self is the most effective way to heal. This happens as we realize none of us is owed anything; rather, all is gift. The more personal and interior our prayer becomes, the more habitual these dispositions become, and the more we see that love alone heals. Furthermore, we see that dying to oneself in the sense of self-giving love, especially on behalf of the ones who hurt us, is the greatest freedom we can ever know, the freedom of forgetting ourselves because we are overwhelmed with the love of God. This kind of self-forgetful freedom from our ultimate encounter with God has an eternal quality: "It would be like plunging into the ocean of infinite love, a moment in which time—the before and after—no longer exists."[6] We see the self-forgetfulness also in the description from St. Paul: "It is no longer I who live, but Christ who lives in me, and the life I now live in the flesh I live by faith in the Son of God, who loved me and gave himself for me" (Gal 2:20). In other words, I am no longer the center of my own life; now Christ is the center.

The more we die to ourselves and the more this becomes a habitual disposition, we can come to feel the burden of our own selves, and of our lives, and even the futility of so much from which we had drawn joy and satisfaction. In this poverty of spirit, one feels helpless and tired, and may even feel repugnance in the face of what life demands. This happens when we no longer feel the gratification that came from satisfying the ego or when we lose the feeling of growing in a sense of self-aggrandizement. As these gratifications dry up, there can be a sense of the heaviness in life, and even a desire for life to be over. Perhaps this experience is in part what Jesus referred to when He told Peter that one day he would be led where He would rather not go (John 21:18). This sense of just going through life, pouring oneself out in a way that feels very empty, can develop into a desire like that of

---

[6] Benedict XVI, *Spe Salvi*, §12.

St. Paul, who said, "My desire is to depart and be with Christ, for that is far better" (Phil 1:23).

Yet there is freedom in a sense of no longer being able to do what one did before, and finding that things work out as well or better when we surrender, because we know that is what we most need to do. All we can do, and all we need to do is just to show up. Then we do what we can. We can have peace in this, because we believe in God's provident love. We no longer want life on our own terms but want our life on God's terms alone, which obviously will be the best terms. Similarly, we want our death and eternal life only on His terms because we have seen His love and His will with an interior seeing, and we want nothing other than His love and will alone. The heaviness that we speak about is somehow illuminated by the love of the Lord, and our sufferings and burdens, even when great, already bear the promise of a fullness beyond imagining: "Truly, truly, I say to you, you will weep and lament, but the world will rejoice; you will be sorrowful, but your sorrow will turn into joy. When a woman is in labor, she has pain, because her hour has come; but when she is delivered of the child, she no longer remembers the anguish for joy that a child is born into the world. So you have sorrow now, but I will see you again and your hearts will rejoice, and no one will take your joy from you" (John 16:20–22).

Eternally new

When speaking of the fulfillment of the Paschal mystery in the outpoured blood of the Lamb Who was slain, in the revelation given to St. John the beloved, Jesus says: "Behold, I make all things new!" (Rev 21:5).

We are often uneasy or even terrified by what is new. We so often have great difficulty letting go of what has been for fear that it will be lost, even eternally lost. It is even difficult watching the passing of time, letting go of what we have or of what we never received. In order to allow ourselves to truly heal and to move forward, it is necessary to face and let go of our sins in order to receive the mercy and grace to move on. When once we have put our hand to the plow, we need the resoluteness not to look back (Luke 9:62). Clinging to and protecting what we have can lead to futility, and when we cling to what we once had, we can fall into despair.

Sometimes it is necessary to actually renounce what lies behind, not in the sense of denying it or letting it go definitively, but in the sense of allowing it to be carried forward in a new way. Behold, I make all things new! Each moment is filled with the Glory of God, bursting with what is new, with transformation! "Christ is alive! He is our hope, and in a wonderful way he brings youth to our world, and everything he touches becomes young, new, full of life. . . . Christ is alive and he wants you to be alive!"[7]

We are not speaking here in a merely secular way of "the new" as some natural, creative force which animates human desires and all of reality through change or renewal. The new is not some eternal energy coming from "the universe," but is the ever animating, rejuvenating, and transforming love of God. Indeed, God can be understood as He Who eternally makes all things new and Who has accomplished this in history through the outpouring of Divine Mercy and Love in the mystery of the Incarnation

---

[7] Pope Francis, *Christus Vivit*: Post-Synodal Exhortation to Young People and to the Entire People of God, March 25, 2019, §1.

consummated in the Paschal mystery of the Passion, death, Resurrection, and Ascension of Our Lord Jesus Christ.

How do we live aware of the new in each moment of our existence? How do we live and pray it? We must prayerfully search and find what is new, or better said, allow reality to reveal how God makes all things new. The greater the interiority, transparency, and prayerfulness with which we live, the more spontaneously and continuously evidently new all is.

By this newness, we speak of much more here than ordinary change, but rather of the transformation that comes from the very life of God coursing within every moment of being. We might even say that doing God's will means, one moment at a time, seeking out, reverencing, and responding to all that God is making new. This includes God providing for and transforming me, you, others, His Church, the world, and all of creation, from within:

> Christ's resurrection is not an event of the past; it contains a vital power which has permeated this world. Where all seems to be dead, signs of the resurrection suddenly spring up. It is an irresistible force. Often it seems that God does not exist: all around us we see persistent injustice, evil, indifference and cruelty. But it is also true that in the midst of darkness something new always springs to life and sooner or later produces fruit. On razed land life breaks through, stubbornly yet invincibly. However dark things are, goodness always re-emerges and spreads. Each day in our world beauty is born anew, it rises transformed through the storms of history. Values always tend to reappear under new guises, and human beings have arisen time

after time from situations that seemed doomed. Such is the power of the resurrection.[8]

In a bored and tired world where we seek what is different because it is different, where fads entertain and there is no reference point but the self, things seem cyclical and quickly lose appeal. The endless variety promised by the idea that there is no divine will or created structure to reality, but that all things are really a social construction brought about by ourselves or by myself, becomes arbitrary and ultimately meaningless.

Actually, what is truly new always has its origins and inspiration in God Who is ever the same and ever new. God making all things new is self-evident and transparent to one who is transparent. The new rising out of the heart of Him Who is ever ancient, ever new takes us ever deeper into the bottomless unknown of ourselves, of others, and of reality, ever deeper into interiority. One who prays in this way understands the Incarnation and why it is that Jesus gave Himself to us to eat in His Body, Blood, Soul, and Divinity—an offering made once and for all and ever new.

An abiding, transforming union

From ancient stories to modern-day witnesses, there are countless examples of those who have received a grace of conversion that evoked a deep, burning, abiding love for Jesus that is intimately personal. The authenticity of such testimonies of a sudden, burning, personal love for Jesus, often coming from very young persons, are powerfully convincing, particularly when the person underwent conversion from out of nowhere. This is reinforced

---

[8] Francis, *Evangelii Gaudium*, §276.

when there is no self-adulation but only gratitude to the Lord alone. Some of the rest of us, who have only undergone conversion through much struggle and backsliding, over many years, and have yet to feel such an abiding, spontaneous personal relationship with Him, may wonder why we lack such compelling ways of expressing our love for the Lord and lack such freedom in Him! Such conversion bears such rich fruit that only the envious or cynical could dismiss it. Indeed, for many years now, though one won't often read about it in the secular media, there has been a mighty army of such young persons forming, often gathering in voluntary missionary groups for evangelization and always intentionally and devoutly Catholic, who have as their first priority to grow in a deeply personal and communal relationship with Jesus Christ.

Or, consider the cloistered contemplative nun who speaks humbly and in hushed tones about experiencing an abiding intimacy with the Lord so intense that it sometimes smothers her. Though she never dares to claim having reached transforming union or mystical marriage as the mystics describe it, she is surely in such a union. She says it is impossible to describe because the experience defies verbalization. Though she feels her attempts to describe it are incoherent, she eloquently and rather innocently describes an intimacy with the Lord which is so close that "union" is the only way to describe it. But it is also "beyond," a beyond which is an abyss within, beyond any depth she has ever known, a "beyond" by which God is not distant but rather unknown. Drawn powerfully into the realm of the unknown, an understanding is infused of the Divine attributes, not within the reach of the intellect but unfathomable. Now the abyss is seen as an

abyss of His Being, an abyss of Love, an abyss of Beauty, though
there is sometimes a gripping fear and profound awareness of sin
and resistance to the way the Lord is drawing her. Because this
is untraveled land, there are no familiar signposts and no words
to convey what is happening. She feels lost, yet found, and there
is an assurance that only here in this Divine abyss is He truly
known, in utter sweet Simplicity. The tug to go deeper is always
in tension with human nature trying to hold back. Drawn into
this perfect love, she "sings His praise unceasingly." Rather than
wishing to draw attention to herself for having this grace, she is
shy someone will detect it and think that something is wrong
with her. No hypochondriac or passively dependent person, she
is often the elected superior of her religious community, and so
actively attends to practical matters—both temporal and spiritual;
indeed, her pace would exhaust most of us. Her profound and
abiding sense of her own sinfulness does not keep her from great
and humble joy at the love of her divine Spouse.

Far from otherworldly or abstract, she sees and never forgets
"His most blessed eyes, of human flesh," penetrating her consciousness "surely at the moment He is being fixed to the cross."
She can hardly believe the penetrating serenity of the eyes of
the Beloved, glistening through those tears of torture which are
heart-rending. Then, on Easter, during the Gloria, He suddenly
impresses "His Risen Glorified Presence throughout my weak
spirit." Now not His agonizing human flesh but "His Glorified
Being" becomes the infinite abyss of Intimate Beauty. She cannot
"bring on this initial impact," but if and when she disposes herself
"to Him He is there and immediately overwhelms" her. "He is the
eternal within time and space, yet ever at one with us in the Sim-

plicity of His Being." She reports having felt for years a union with Him, being one with Him, a oneness that comes to take on a nuptial reality. Then the abyss opens, an abyss of His Infinite Being which takes her into the Unknowable where she is "lost yet found . . . savoring His love while thirsting for more." This "untraveled" spiritual pathway is not only of Him into her but of her into Him, "the only One who truly is!"

Another contemplative nun writes in her journal how she had resolved deeply at the outset of her life, like St. Teresa of Calcutta, to "never say 'no' to God." Seeking to do His will in everything, she is drawn ever more deeply into Christ crucified, and she writes: "I feel that my Divine Master wishes that I suffer something for His glory! My poor nature shrinks at the thought of this . . . but His Divine Heart lets me understand that He will help me, He will be near to me . . . and with His Divine Hand He will give me the chalice in which He has left a few drops for me to drink for His love! And my heart is ready to do this . . . with His Divine help!!" Later, near the end of her life she writes: "O, My Sweet Master, let the overflow of Thy Heart enter mine, and entirely consume it that it may live only to love and glorify Thee! . . . O My King, all things are in Your Hands, and I ask only one thing, Thy Heart, Thy Love, that I may gain it all back to offer Thee."

Such persons are not always cloistered or consecrated religious but are also often found among the lay faithful, both single and married persons whom no one would suspect of having such an intimate and abiding relationship with the Lord because their lives seem so ordinary and unlikely to draw the attention of others. Their way of approaching life is not flashy, but concrete, simple, and loving. We have no difficulty believing that such persons are living a life of transforming union with the Lord. Priests and spiritual directors are privileged to know such persons. At the same time, this transforming union is what the Lord wants for all of us. He wants it for us in the beatific vision in heaven, and He also, to whatever degree possible, wants it for all of us now. In fact, the personal relationship the Lord always already has with each of His human sons and daughters is a union of transforming love. Recall St. Augustine: "You are closer to us than we are to ourselves."[9] He is closer to each one of us than each of us is to ourselves. He already is always in transforming union with each of us and has given to each of us the capacity to participate in the transforming unsion His infinite Love has established with each one of us. We must simply enter progressively into this union which is only possible through His grace and as His gift.

Yet, sadly, in our present culture which has tried to obliterate any sense of God, probably the majority of people, even if they believe somehow in some sort of God, would never dream of the possibility of a personal relationship with Him. Many others have some sense of a personal relationship with God, but it remains rather peripheral and unrealized. With all of these and with all of us, God has an infinite love which He desires us to reciprocate as best and as fully as we can. This is the reason for evangelization, that as God shares that love with each person, the response of love includes a sharing that awakens that love in others as well. Mother Teresa's fixation with the Thirst of Jesus that moved her to include those words next to every crucifix was matched by a fixation on quenching that thirst through love. Her own love was

---

[9]   See St. Augustine, *Confessions*, bk. III, chap. 6, no. 11.

not enough—she stirred love in every person she met and directed that love to quenching the thirst of Jesus. The new evangelization is not about spreading information but spreading love, the God-sized self-emptying love that has been given to us in Jesus Christ.

Such love leads us within, and we need Christ and the members of His Body, the Church, to show us this love in credible, contagious ways. The saints in heaven and the saints here on earth are the human witnesses of the Love that comes to us through our Lord Jesus Christ. It is God's intention that we know of and share in this Love even now, as we have said. Contemplative nuns, or youth who might seem like they are making some kind of cult out of Christianity may not touch everyone, but Love does. In fact, we believe that many more than we would imagine have reached a transforming union with the Lord, and may not even themselves know it. It seems that if we think of saints like St. Paul of the Cross, St. Therese of Lisieux, or St. Teresa of Calcutta, we see people who surely lived lives of transforming union. If they knew it at some level, they knew it in a dark faith, and thus perhaps we may call it a dark transforming union. These three saints, and many others we could name, lived for many years, even the majority of their lives, in dark faith, with very little consolation, but in union with the Lord.[10]

Recently, St. Teresa of Calcutta has been recognized as a person who lived in great joy and selfless service, changing the face of the world with her and her Sisters' service to the poorest of the poor. When Jesus called St. Teresa to this vocation, He actually called her not only to serve the poor but the poorest of the poor and particularly the dying. He called her to climb into the

---

[10] See Martin, *Fulfillment of All Desire*, 418–433.

holes where the poorest of the poor cower and are forgotten, in other words, to actually share the desolation, poverty, and hopelessness of the poor. She immediately began to do so and began a journey of struggle and often of spiritual desolation. She not only helped the poor but shared all their misery, as Christ took on Himself our misery, sin, suffering, and death. Usually, she experienced great spiritual darkness. When one of her former spiritual directors, Bishop William Curlin, was asked if he had known of her desolation, he showed a piece of paper, a note written to him by Mother Teresa and passed silently to him in chapel, on which she wrote, "Father pray for me! Where is Jesus?"[11] Yet beyond food and comfort, it was precisely the love of Jesus for each one that she wanted to bring to the poorest of the poor, and most especially to the dying whom she hoped might taste His selfless love before dying. It turns out her "doubts" were primarily the fear that she would one day say "No" to Jesus.[12] During her final days as she lay close to death, while looking at the face of Christ taken from the Shroud of Turin, she was heard to say: "Jesus, I have never refused you anything."[13]

Few of us can claim this! It seems clear that Mother Teresa was in the transforming union during much of her life, but a dark union, or a union by virtue of which the person is largely living in darkness with little or almost no consolation. Like St. Paul of the Cross, founder of the Passionists, in the last months or weeks of her life, St. Teresa was full of great joy such as she had never known during life. It seems that some like St. Therese of Lisieux endured terrible suffering and sometimes even doubted

---

[11] Mother Teresa, *Come Be My Light*, 307.
[12] Mother Teresa, *Come Be My Light*, 186.
[13] Mother Teresa, *Come Be My Light*, 331.

the existence of God and heaven though they probably already enjoyed transforming union. Such souls are united in a union with the Lord which transforms them by their sharing in abiding union with the passion of Christ, which in turn shares in the redemption of souls Christ brought about through His Cross. As Hans Urs Von Balthasar wrote: "No sequence is irreversible, the termination of a period of aridity or darkness is no guarantee that a fresh, and severer one is not to follow. The classification of purgative, illuminative and unitive ways should be used, as we have already insisted, with discretion. A Christian, who has been led in advanced unitive ways and has experienced a beatific, nuptial union with God, may conceivably at death feel himself abandoned by God."[14]

We Shall See Him as He Is

"It does not yet appear what we shall be, but we know that when he appears we shall be like him, for we shall see him as he is" (1 John 3:2). Transparency is when we see and hear from the interior, and interiorly we become like Him as our creation in the image and likeness of God becomes realized more and more deeply. We will never *become* God Who is Wholly Other, but we will realize our likeness to Him and the way we image Him as never before. Indeed, we will see it; for we shall see Him as He is! As He is love, the more we have loved and allowed ourselves to be transformed by His love, the more we will recognize ourselves in Him as He recognizes Himself in us. Each one who has been

---

[14] Balthasar, *Prayer*, 217.

transformed through prayer and repentance and who has grown into Godlike love has entered into an abiding union with Him that transforms each one of us ever more deeply into His likeness. Though our sin is always before us, we might come to pray unceasingly as we are drawn ever deeper into intimacy with the Lord, as we realize how infinite His mercy is and how personally He has extended salvation to each of us, loving each one as if that one were the only person in the world. This realization makes my sins all the more painful as it shows how infinitely the Lord loves me. Such love transforms us, sometimes darkly through union with Christ Crucified, sometimes also through the suffering of love but with an overwhelming luminosity which almost crushes us with His love as it blinds us with His light.

This union deepens our transparency and perfects it so that now the interior is the exterior. If we have come to love with a Godlike love, then, standing before Christ at the particular judgment, we will in our transparency see how much we have become like Him who is absolute transparency because He is infinite, self-giving love. We know, we see, and we act from the inside out, just like He does, and we see with the same love He does, and thus we are like Him, in ways that are mysterious. It is mysterious how we are like Him because our transparency has been transformed by His transparency. For those who have loved in a solely self-loving way, even rejecting His love, they will see with the pains of Hell how unlike Him and opposed to Him they have become. On the other hand, if we realize that we still need to be purified further in love in order to be like Him, we will rejoice at the purifying fire of love in purgatory.

If we have become like Him and see Him as He is, we will

forever remain in that abiding, divinely self-emptying love, in union with all those others who have been transformed by His love. Faith and hope will have been stretched beyond their outmost limits and burst into an eternal vision and full possession. This is the Blessed Vision of God where we are possessed in love by the Son who gives us the capacity to see the Father, as the Holy Spirit who draws each person in his unique individuality into the perpetual adoration and who imparts to us in the fullness of the personality God has willed for us the perpetual adoration and eternal love of God.[15] Then we will fully contemplate eternally what we contemplated partially from the first stirrings of our prayer: that we belong to Him and were made for Him, that we are truly His beloved sons and daughters.

---

[15] Adrienne Von Speyr, *Gates of Eternal Life* (San Francisco: Ignatius Press, 1983), 84, 125.

Appendix

Florilegium

As an appendix to this work on prayer, we follow the ancient practice of gathering the texts of various authors together in a bouquet for the reader's ongoing reflection. We hope this "florilegium" provides further teaching and inspiration, and even better, that the reading itself would move the reader to prayer.

Pope St. Clement I (35–99)
Bishop of Rome

"Who can describe the bond of God's love? Who is able to explain the majesty of its beauty? The height to which love leads is indescribable . . . In love the master received us, Jesus Christ our Lord, in accordance with God's will gave his blood for us, and his flesh for our flesh and his life for our lives."

St. Ignatius of Antioch (d. 108)
Bishop of Antioch

"My dear Jesus, my Savior, is so deeply written in my heart, that I feel confident, that if my heart would to be cut open and chopped to pieces, the name of Jesus would be found written on every piece."

St. Irenaeus of Lyons (130–202)
Bishop

"Jesus Christ, in His infinite love, has become what we are, in order that He may make us entirely what He is."

St. Dionysius the Great (200–268)
Patriarch of Alexandria

"The fact is that the more we take flight upward (to God) the more our words are confined to the ideas we are capable of forming; so that now as we plunge into that darkness which is beyond intellect, we shall find ourselves not simply running short of words but actually speechless and unknowing . . . Trinity! Higher than any being, any divinity, any goodness! Guide of Christians in the wisdom of heaven! Lead us up beyond unknowing and light, up to the farthest, highest peak of mystic scripture, where the mysteries of God's Word lie simple, absolute and unchangeable in the brilliant darkness of a hidden silence. Amid the wholly unsensed and unseen they completely fill our sightless minds with treasures beyond all beauty."

DIADOCHUS OF PHOTICE (5TH C.)
Bishop

"Anyone who loves God in the depths of his heart has already been loved by God. In fact, the measure of a man's love for God depends upon how deeply aware he is of God's love for him. When this awareness is keen it makes whoever possesses it long to be enlightened by the divine light, and this longing is so intense that it seems to penetrate his very bones. He loses all consciousness of himself and is entirely transformed by the love of God." (*On Spiritual Perfection*)

ST. ANTONY OF EGYPT (c. 251–356)
Monk

"Whoever you may be, always have God before your eyes; whatever you do, do it according to the testimony of the holy Scriptures; and in whatever place you live, do not easily leave it. Keep these three precepts and you will be saved."

ST. EPHREM (306–373)
Deacon

"We glimpse the beauty that is laid up for us when we gaze upon the spiritual beauty your immortal will now creates within our mortal selves."

St. Gregory of Naziaznus (329–390)
Patriarch of Constantinople, Doctor of the Church

"The first of all beautiful things is the continual possession of God."

.

St. Ambrose (340–397)
Bishop of Milan, Doctor of the Church

"Drink, then, from Christ, so that your voice may also be heard. Store up in your mind the water that is Christ, the water that praises the Lord. Store up water from many sources, the water that rains down from the clouds of prophecy. Whoever gathers water from the mountains and leads it to himself or draws it from springs, is himself a source of dew like the clouds. Fill your soul, then, with this water, so that your land may not be dry, but watered by your own springs."

St. Jerome (347–420)
Priest, Doctor of the Church

"When we pray we speak to God; but when we read, God speaks to us. . . . We must love Christ and always seek Christ's embraces. Then everything difficult will seem easy."

St. Augustine of Hippo (354–430)
Bishop, Doctor of the Church

"The entire life of a good Christian is in fact an exercise of holy desire. You do not see what you long for, but the very act of desiring prepares you, so that when He comes you may see and be utterly satisfied. Suppose you are going to fill some holder or container, and you know you will be given a large amount . . . Because you know the quantity you will have to put in it and your eyes tell you there is not enough room . . . By stretching it, you therefore increase the capacity of the sack, and this is how God deals with us. Simply by making us wait he increases our desire, which in turn enlarges the capacity of our soul, making it able to receive what is to be given to us." (*Tractates on the First Letter of John*)

"But if someone does not know You, how can he call upon You? For not knowing You he might call upon someone else instead of You. Or must You first be called upon in order to be known?" Scripture says: unless they believe in Him how shall they call upon Him? . . . Lord, let me seek You by calling upon You, and let me call upon You by believing in You." (*Confessions*, book 1)

"You respond clearly, but not everyone hears clearly. All ask what they wish, but do not always hear the answer they wish. Your best servant is he who is intent not so much on hearing his petition answered, as rather on willing whatever he hears from you. Late have I loved you O Beauty ever ancient, ever knew, late have I loved you! You were within me, but I was outside and it was there that I searched for you . . . You were with me but I was not with you." (*Confessions*, book 10)

St. Gregory of Nyssa (335–394)
Bishop, Doctor of the Church

"Saint Paul himself and all who have reached the heights of sanctity had their eyes fixed on Christ, and so have all who live and move and have their being in him." (A Homily on Ecclesiastes)

St. John Chrysostom (c. 349–407)
Patriarch of Constantinople

"Prayer and converse with God is a supreme good: it is a partnership and union with God . . . I do not mean prayer of outward observance but prayer from the heart, not confined to fixed times or periods but continuous throughout the day and night . . . Prayer is the light of the spirit, true knowledge of God, mediating between God and man. The spirit, raised up to heaven, clings to God with utmost tenderness. Like a child crying tearfully for its mother, it craves the milk that God provides. Prayer stands before God as an honored ambassador. It gives joy to the spirit, peace to the heart . . . it is the longing for God, love too deep for words . . . When the Lord gives this kind of prayer to a man, he gives him riches that cannot be taken away, heavenly food that satisfies the spirit. One who tastes this food is set on fire with an eternal longing for the Lord: his spirit burns as in a fire of the utmost intensity."

St. Cyril of Alexandria (378–444)
Patriarch of Constantinople

"Prayer is happy company with God."

St. Benedict of Nursia (480–547)
Father of Western Monasticism

"Listen and attend with the ear of your heart."

Pope St. Gregory the Great (540–604)

"The greatness of contemplation can be given to none but those who love."

St. Gregory of Agrigentum, (6th–early 7th c.)
Patriarch of Constantinople

"Now it is our supreme delight to behold him and contemplate his divine splendor with the eyes of our spirit. When we participate in and associate with that beauty, we are enlightened and this is our delight. We take delight in being saturated with the sweetness of the Spirit, in being clothed in holiness, in achieving wisdom. Finally we are filled with the joy that comes from God and endures through all the days of our earthly life." (Commentary on Ecclesiastes)

St. Columban (543–615)
Monk, missionary

"If you search by means of discussions for the God who cannot be defined in words, he will depart further from you than he was before. If you search for him by faith, wisdom will stand where wisdom lives, at the gates. Where wisdom is wisdom will be seen, at least in part. But wisdom is also to some extent truly attained when the invisible God is the object of faith, in a way beyond our understanding, for we must believe in God, invisible as he is, though he is partially seen by a heart that is pure." (An Instruction)

St. Isidore (560–636)
Bishop of Seville, Doctor of the Church

"If a man wants to be always in God's company, he must pray regularly and read regularly. When we pray, we talk to God; when we read, God talks to us." (The Book of Maxims 3.8)

St. Maximus the Confessor (580–662)
Monk

"A pure heart is perhaps one which has no natural propulsion towards anything in any manner whatsoever. When in its extreme simplicity such a heart has become like a writing tablet beautifully smoothed and polished, God comes to dwell in it and writes there His own laws."

St. Bede the Venerable (672–735)
Monk

"On hearing Christ's voice, we open the door to receive him, as it were, when we freely assent to his promptings and when we give ourselves over to doing what must be done. Christ, since he dwells in the hearts of his chosen ones through the grace of his love, enters so that he might eat with us and we with him. He ever refreshes us by the light of his presence insofar as we progress in our devotion to and longing for the things of heaven. He himself is delighted by such a pleasing banquet." (A Homily)

St. Anselm (1033–1109)
Benedictine Abbot of Bec, Archbishop of Canterbury

"Lord my God, you gave me life and restored it when I lost it. Tell my soul that so longs for you what else you are besides what it has already understood, so that it may see you clearly. It stands on tiptoe to see more, but apart from what it has already seen, it sees nothing but darkness. Of course it does not really see darkness because there is no darkness in you, but it sees that it can see no further because of the darkness in itself . . . If I fail to see this light it is simply because it is too bright for me . . . O supreme and inaccessible light, O complete and blessed truth, how far you are from me, even though I am so near to you! How remote you are from my sight, even though I am present to yours! You are everywhere in your entirety, and yet I do not see you; in you I move and have my being, and yet I cannot approach you; you are within me and around me, and yet I do not perceive you." (*The Proslogion*)

St. Bernard of Clairvaux (1090–1153)
Cistercian Abbot

"Love is sufficient of itself, it gives pleasure by itself and because of itself . . . I love because I love, I love that I may love. Love is a great thing so long as it continually returns to its fountainhead, flows back to its source, always drawing from there the water that constantly replenishes it. Of all the movements, sensations and feelings of the soul, love is the only one in which the creature can respond to the Creator and make some sort of similar return however unequal though it be." (A Sermon)

St. Francis of Assisi (1181–1226)
Founder of the Franciscans

"What do you have to fear? Nothing. Whom do you have to fear? No one. Why? Because whoever has joined forces with God obtains three great privileges: omnipotence without power, intoxication without wine, and to life without death."

St. Anthony of Padua (1195–1231)
Franciscan priest, Doctor of the Church

"He prays best who does not know that he is praying."

St. Clare of Assisi (1194–1253)

"Place your mind before the mirror of eternity! Place your soul in the brilliance of glory! And transform your entire being into the image of the Godhead itself through contemplation....I come, O Lord, unto Thy sanctuary to see the life and food of my soul. As I hope in Thee, O Lord, inspire me with that confidence which brings me to Thy holy mountain. Permit me, Divine Jesus, to come closer to Thee, that my whole soul may do homage to the greatness of Thy majesty; that my heart, with its tenderest affections, may acknowledge Thine infinite love; that my memory may dwell on the admirable mysteries here renewed every day, and that the sacrifice of my whole being may accompany Thine."

St. Albert the Great (1200–1280)
Dominican Bishop, Doctor of the Church

"The highest perfection, therefore, of man in this life lies in this: that he is so united to God that his soul with all its powers and faculties becomes recollected in Him and is one spirit with Him. Then it remembers naught save God, nor does it relish or understand anything but Him. Then all its affections, united in the delights of love, repose sweetly in the enjoyment of their Creator." (*The Union of the Soul with God*)

St. Bonaventure, (1217–1274)
Cardinal, Bishop of Albano, Italy; Franciscan Doctor of the Church

"We must suspend all the operations of the mind and we must transform the peak of our affections, directing them to God alone.

This is a sacred mystical experience. It cannot be comprehended by anyone unless he surrenders himself to it; nor can he surrender himself to it unless he longs for it; nor can he long for it unless the Holy Spirit, whom Christ sent into the world, should come and inflame his innermost soul." (*The Journey of the Mind to God*, ch. 7)

St. Thomas Aquinas (1225–1274)
Dominican priest, Doctor of the Church

"Nothing created has ever been able to fill the heart of man. God alone can fill it infinitely."

St. Catherine of Siena (1347–1380)
Dominican tertiary, virgin, Doctor of the Church

"You are a mystery as deep as the sea; the more I search, the more I find, and the more I find the more I search for you. But I can never be satisfied; what I receive will ever leave me desiring more. When you fill my soul I have an even greater hunger, and I grow more famished for your light. I desire above all to see you, the true light, as you really are." (*Dialogue on Divine Providence*)

Bl. Jan Ruysbroeck (1293–1381)
Priest

"Our work is the love of God. Our satisfaction lies in submission to the Divine embrace ... In eternity all creatures are God in God ... My words are strange but those who love will understand."

JOHANNES TAULER (1300–1361)
Dominican priest

"A good meditation, even when it is interrupted by occasional nodding, is much more beneficial than many outward religious exercises . . . Give yourself entirely to God, enter and hide in the hidden ground of your soul."

ST. IGNATIUS LOYOLA (1491–1556)
Founder of the Society of Jesus

"The flame of divine love never rises higher than when fed with the wood of the cross, which the infinite charity of the Savior used to finish his sacrifice. All the pleasures of the world are nothing compared with the sweetness found in the gall and vinegar offered to Jesus Christ. That is, hard and painful things endured for Jesus Christ and with Jesus Christ."

ST. TERESA OF AVILA (1515–1582)
Reformer of the Carmelites

"Love calls for love in return. Let us strive to keep this always before our eyes and to rouse ourselves to love Him. For if at some time the Lord should grant us the grace of impressing His love on our hearts, all will become easy for us and we will accomplish things quickly and without effort." (*De Libro Vitae*)

St. Philip Neri (1515–1595)
Priest, oratorian

"The greatness of our love of God must be tested by the desire we have of suffering for His love."

St. Jane Frances de Chantal (1572–1641)
Visitation sister

"Yield yourself fully to God, and you will find out! Divine love takes its sword to the hidden recesses of our inmost soul and divides us from ourselves. I know one person whom love cut off from all that was dearest to her, just as completely and effectively as if the tyrant's blade had severed spirit from body . . . I am speaking of course of great souled individuals who keep nothing back for themselves, but instead are faithful in love." (*Memoirs*)

St. John Eudes (1601–1680)
Priest

"He belongs to you, but more than that, He longs to be in you, living and ruling in you, as the head lives and rules in the body. He desires that whatever is in Him may live and rule with you: His breath in your breath, His heart in your heart, all the faculties of His soul in the faculties of your soul, so that these words may be revealed in you: 'Glorify God and bear Him in your body, that the life of Jesus may be made manifest in you.'" (*A Treatise on the Admirable Heart of Jesus*)

St. Margaret Mary Alacoque (1647–1690)
Visitation sister

"The divine heart is in an abyss of all blessings, and into it the poor should submerge all their needs. It is an abyss of joy in which all of us can immerse our sorrows. It is an abyss of lowliness to counteract our foolishness, an abyss of mercy for the wretched, and an abyss of love to meet our every need . . . For the Sacred Heart is an inexhaustible fountain and its sole desire is to pour itself into the hearts of the humble so as to free them and prepare them to lead lives according to His good pleasure." (A Letter)

St. John Vianney (1786–1859)
Priest, patron of priests

"Prayer is nothing else but union with God. When one has a heart that is pure and united with God, he is given the kind of serenity and sweetness that makes him ecstatic, a light that surrounds him with marvelous brightness. In this intimate union, God and the soul are fused together like two bits of wax that no one can ever pull apart. This union of God with a tiny creature is a lovely thing. It is happiness beyond understanding." (*Catechism on Prayer*)

St. Charles Borromeo (1538–1584)
Cardinal, Bishop of Milan

"Would you like me to teach you how to grow from virtue to

virtue and how, if you are already recollected at prayer, you can be even more attentive next time, and so give God more pleasing worship? Listen, and I will tell you. If a tiny spark of God's love already burns within you, do not expose it to the wind, for it may get blown out. Keep the stove tightly shut so that it will not lose its heat and grow cold. In other words, avoid distractions as well as you can. Stay quiet with God. Do not spend your time in useless chatter." (*Acta Ecclesiastica Mediolanensis*)

St. Mary Magdalene de Pazzi (1566–1607)
Carmelite nun

"The Holy Spirit which moves in itself is the substance of the Father and of the Word, and it proceeds from the essence of the Father and the good will of the Word; it comes into the soul like a fountain, and the soul is immersed in it. Just as two rushing rivers intermingle in such a way that the smaller loses its name and is absorbed into the larger, so the divine Spirit acts upon the soul and absorbs it. It is proper that the soul, which is lesser, should lose its name and surrender to the Spirit, as it will if it turns entirely toward the Spirit and is united." (*Writings on Revelation and Trials*)

St. Francis de Sales (1567–1622)
Bishop of Geneva

"Do not suppose, my daughters, that prayer is the work of the human mind; it is the special gift of the Holy Spirit, raising the powers of the soul about their natural strength, so that they may be united to God by sentiments and communications that all the discourses and wisdom of man cannot produce without him." (Address to His Spiritual Daughters of the Visitation)

ST. PAUL OF THE CROSS (1694–1775)
Priest, founder of the Passionists

"Love is a unifying virtue which takes upon itself the torments of its beloved Lord. It is a fire reaching through to the inmost soul. It transforms the lover into the one loved. More deeply, love intermingles with grief, and grief with love, and a certain blending of love and grief occurs . . . Conceal yourself in Jesus crucified, and hope for nothing except that all men will be thoroughly converted to his will. When you become true lovers of the Crucified, you will always celebrate the feast of the cross in the inner temple of the soul, bearing all in silence and not relying on any creature." (Letter)

ST. ALPHONSUS LIGOURI (1696–1787)
Bishop of Sant'Agata dei Goti, founder of the Redemptorists

"Acquire the habit of speaking to God as if you were alone with Him, familiarly and with confidence and love, as to the dearest and most loving of friends."

St. Bernadette of Soubirous (1844–1879)
Religious

"My Jesus, fill my heart with so much love that one day it will break just to be with you. My Jesus, you know I have placed you as a seal on my heart. Remain there always."

St. Therese of Lisieux (1873–1897)
Discalced Carmelite nun, Doctor of the Church

"Do not fear to tell Jesus that you love Him even without feeling it. That is the way to force Jesus to help you, to care for you like a little child too feeble to walk."

Pope St. Pius X (1835–1914)

"Holy Communion is the shortest and safest way to heaven."

Bl. Columba Marmion (1858–1923)
Benedictine Abbot

"Now prayer, the life of prayer, maintains, stimulates, animates and perfects those sentiments of faith, humility, confidence and love which together form the best predisposition for the soul to receive divine grace in abundance. A soul given to prayer profits more from the sacraments and other means of salvation than another whose prayer is without constancy and intensity. One may recite the Divine Office, assist at Holy Mass and receive the sacraments, but if the soul does not give itself faithfully to prayer it's progress will often be mediocre. Why is that? Because the principal author of our perfection and holiness is God Himself and it is prayer that keeps the soul in frequent contact with God; it establishes and, after having established, maintains, as it were, a furnace in the soul. Even if the fire of love is not always alive, at least it lies smoldering, and as soon as the soul is put in direct communication with the Divine Life, for example, in the sacraments, this fire is enkindled by a powerful breath, making it rise upwards and wonderfully increase. The supernatural life of the soul is measured by its union with God through Christ, in faith and love; this love must bring forward acts, but these acts, if they are to be produced in an intense and regular manner, require the life of prayer. It can be established that according to ordinary ways, our progress in Divine love practically depends on our life of prayer." (Address on Prayer)

St. Faustina Kowalska (1905–1938)
Religious sister

"God is very generous and does not deny His grace to anyone. Indeed He gives more than what we ask of Him. Faithfulness to the inspirations of the Holy Spirit—that is the shortest route. . . . O King of glory, though You hide Your beauty, yet the eye of my soul rends the veil. I see the angelic choirs giving You honor without cease." (*Diary*, 291)

St. Maximilian Kolbe (1894–1941)
Franciscan priest

"Let us give ourselves to the Immaculata (Mary). Let her prepare us, let her receive Him (Jesus) in Holy Communion. This is the manner most perfect and pleasing to the Lord Jesus and brings great fruit to us." Because "the Immaculata knows the secret, how to unite ourselves totally with the heart of the Lord Jesus . . . We do not limit ourselves in love. We want to love the Lord Jesus with her heart, or rather that she would love the Lord with our heart."

St. Teresa Benedicta of the Cross (Edith Stein, 1891–1942)
Discalced Carmelite nun

"The deeper one is drawn into God the more one must 'go out of oneself'; that is, one must go to the world in order to carry the divine life into it . . . The limitless loving devotion to God, and the gift God makes of Himself to you, are the highest elevation of which the heart is capable; it is the highest degree of prayer. The souls that have reached this point are truly the heart of the Church."[1]

---

[1] Edith Stein, *Self-Portrait in Letters, 1916–1942*, trans. Josephine Koeppel, O.C.D., CWES, vol. 5 (Washington, D.C.:ICS Publications, 1993), 54.

Pope St. John XXIII (1881–1963)

"I have looked into your eyes with my eyes. I have put my heart near your heart."

St. Pio of Pietrecina (1887–1968)
Capuchin priest

"Prayer is the best weapon we have; it is the key to God's heart. You must be to Jesus not only with your lips, but with your heart. In fact on certain occasions you should only speak to him with your heart."

Pope St. Paul VI (1897–1978)

"The Holy Spirit also gives you the grace to discover the image of the Lord in the hearts of men, and teaches you to love them as brothers and sisters. Again, He helps you to see the manifestations of His love in events. If we are humbly attentive to men and things, the Spirit of Jesus enlightens us and enriches us with His Wisdom, provided that we are imbued with the spirit of prayer."[2]

Pope St. John Paul II (1920–2005)

"Prayer joined to sacrifice constitutes the most powerful force in human history . . . In prayer you become one with the source of

---

[2] Pope Paul VI, *Evangelica Testificatio* (1971), §44.

our true light—Jesus Himself . . . Prayer, intimate dialogue with the One who is calling you to be his disciples, must come first. Be generous in your active life . . . and be completely immersed in the contemplation of God's mystery. Make the Eucharist the heart of your day."

The Constitution on The Sacred Liturgy
Vatican Council II (1963)

"Christ is always present to his church, especially in the actions of the liturgy. He is present in the sacrifice of the Mass, in the person of the minister it is the same Christ who formerly offered himself on the cross that now offers by the ministry of priests, and most of all under the Eucharistic species. He is present in the sacraments by his power, in such a way that when someone baptizes, Christ himself baptizes. He is present in his word, for it is he himself who speaks when the holy Scriptures are read in the church. Finally, he is present when the church prays and sings, but he himself promised: 'Where two or three are gathered in my name, there am I in their midst.'[3]

St. John of the Cross (1542–1591)

"Keep spiritually tranquil in a loving attentiveness to God, and when it is necessary to speak, let it be with the same calm and peace. (Maxim #3) The Father spoke one Word, which was His Son, and this Word He always speaks in eternal silence, and in

---

[3] Vatican II, *Sacrosanctum Concilium*, §7.

silence must It be heard by the soul. (Maxims #21) What we need most in order to make progress is to be silent before this great God with our appetites and our tongue, for the language He best hears is silent love. (Maxims #53) Endeavor to remain always in the presence of God, either real, imaginative, or unitive insofar as is permitted by your works. (Degrees of Perfection #2) Do not omit mental prayer for any occupation, for it is the sustenance of your soul. (Degrees of Perfection #5) Never give up prayer, and should you find dryness and difficulty, persevere in it for this very reason. God often desires to see what love your soul has, and love is not tried by ease and satisfaction. (Degrees of Perfection #9) He is humble who hides in his own nothingness and knows how to abandon himself to God. (Other Counsels #5)"

St. Elizabeth of the Trinity (1880–1906)

"May nothing trouble my peace or make me leave you, O My Unchanging One, but may each moment carry me further into the depths of Your Mystery. Through all nights, all voids, all helplessness, I want to gaze on You always and remain in Your great light. O my beloved Star, so fascinate me that I may not withdraw from Your radiance. I remain very little in the depths of my poverty. I see my nothingness, my misery, my weakness; I perceive that I am incapable of progress, of perseverance; I see the multitude of my shortcomings, my defects; I appear in my indulgence. I fall down in my misery, confessing my distress, and I display it before the mercy of my Master."

St. Teresa of Calcutta (1910–1997)

"How do we learn? Through prayer. We talk to God, listening then speaking, this is prayer. If we have not listened, we have nothing to talk about. So we must take the trouble to listen. For this we need silence of the mind, silence of the heart, silence of the eyes, silence of the hands."[4]

St. Augustine on Desire

"Why he should ask us to pray, when he knows what we need before we ask him, may perplex us if we do not realize that our Lord and God does not want to know what we want (for he cannot fail to know it) but wants us rather to exercise our desire through our prayers, so that we may be able to receive what he is preparing to give us. His gift is very great indeed, but our capacity is too small and limited to receive it. That is why we are told: Enlarge your desires, do not bear the yoke with unbelievers.

The deeper our faith, the stronger our hope, the greater our desire, the larger will be our capacity to receive that gift, which is very great indeed. No eye has seen it; it has no color. No ear has heard it; it has no sound. It has not entered man's heart; man's heart must enter into it.

In this faith, hope and love we pray always with unwearied desire. However, at set times and seasons we also pray to God in words, so that by these signs we may instruct ourselves and mark the progress we have made in our desire, and spur ourselves on to

---

[4] Mother Teresa, *Where There Is Love, There Is God*, 18.

deepen it. The more fervent the desire, the more worthy will be its fruit. When the Apostle tells us: Pray without ceasing, he means this: Desire unceasingly that life of happiness which is nothing if not eternal, and ask it of him who alone is able to give it." (Letter to Proba, Ep. 130, 8, 15, 17-9, 18: CSEL 44, 56-57, 59-60)

SILVAN ROUSE (1922–2014)
Passionist priest

"The emptiness of things spiritual helps us to cope with His Eternal Beauty and Love."

POPE BENEDICT XVI (B. 1927)

"The more ardent the love for the Eucharist in the hearts of the Christian people, the more clearly will they recognize the goal of all mission: to bring Christ to others. Not just a theory or a way of life inspired by Christ, but the gift of His very person. Anyone who has not shared the truth of love with his brothers and sisters has not yet given enough."[5]

---

[5] Pope Benedict XVI, *Sacramentum Caritatis* (2007), §86.

Bibliography

Acklin, Thomas. *The Passion of the Lamb: The Self-Giving Love of Jesus.* Cincinnati, Ohio: St. Anthony Messenger Press, 2006.

Allen, Woody. *Love and Death.* Beverly Hills: MGM Studios, 1975.

Aquinas, St. Thomas. *Catena Aurea: Commentary on the Four Gospels, Collected out of the Works of the Fathers: St. Luke.* Edited by J. H. Newman. Oxford: John Henry Parker, 1843.

———. *On Evil.* Translated by Richard J. Regan. Edited by Brian Davies. New York: Oxford University Press, 2003.

———. *The Summa Theologiae of St. Thomas Aquinas*, Second and Revised Ed. Translated by the Fathers of the English Dominican Province. 1920; Kevin Knight, 2017, http://www.newadvent.org/summa/index.html.

Baars, Conrad W. *I Will Give Them a New Heart: Reflections on the Priesthood and the Renewal of the Church.* Staten Island, NY: Alba House, 2007.

Bacovcin, Helen, trans. *The Way of a Pilgrim and The Pilgrim Continues His Way.* Reprint. Garden City, NY: Image, 1992.

Balthasar, Hans Urs von. *Creator Spirit.* Vol. 3 of *Explorations in Theology.* San Francisco: Ignatius Press, 1993.

————. *Prayer.* San Francisco: Ignatius Press, 1986.

Barron, Fr. Robert. "The Fire of His Love." *CATHOLICISM.* Episode 9. DVD. Directed by Matt Leonard. Des Plaines, IL: Word on Fire, 2011.

Baum, Cardinal William Wakefield. The Gift of the Indulgence, January 29, 2000. http://www.vatican.va/roman_curia/tribunals/apost_penit/documents/rc_trib_appen_pro_20000129_indulgence_en.html.

Benedict, St. *RB 1980: The Rule of St. Benedict in Latin and English with Notes.* Translated by Timothy Fry. Collegeville, MN: The Liturgical Press, 1981.

Benedictine Monk, A. *In Sinu Jesu: When Heart Speaks to Heart— The Journal of a Priest at Prayer.* Kettering, OH: Angelico Press, 2016.

Benedict XVI. *Deus Caritas Est,* 2005.

————. Address to Participants in the International Congress for the 40th Anniversary of the Dogmatic Constitution on Divine Revelation "Dei Verbum," September 16, 2005. http://w2.vatican.va/content/benedict-xvi/en/speeches/2005/september/documents/hf_ben-xvi_spe_20050916_40-dei-verbum.html.

————. Audience of March 7, 2012. http://w2.vatican.va/content/benedict-xvi/en/audiences/2012/documents/hf_ben-xvi_aud_20120307.html.

————. General Audience of May 24, 2006. http://w2.vatican.va/content/benedict-xvi/en/audiences/2006/documents/hf_ben-xvi_aud_20060524.html.

————. Homily at Closing Mass of World Youth Day at Marienfeld, Cologne, Germany, August 21, 2005. http://w2.vatican.va/content/benedict-xvi/en/homilies/2005/documents/hf_ben-xvi_hom_20050821_20th-world-youth-day.html.

———. with Peter Seewald. *Last Testament in His Own Words.* Translated by Jacob Phillips. New York: Bloomsbury, 2016.

———. Meditation on the Shroud during his Pastoral Visit to Turin, May 2, 2010. http://w2.vatican.va/content/benedict-xvi/en/speeches/2010/may/documents/hf_ben-xvi_spe_20100502_meditazione-torino.html.

———. Message for the World Day of Communication 2012. http://w2.vatican.va/content/benedict-xvi/en/messages/communications/documents/hf_ben-xvi_mes_20120124_46th-world-communications-day.html.

———. *Sacratemntum Caritatis.* 2007.

———. *Spe Salvi.* 2007.

———. To Participants in the International Congress for the 40th Anniversary of the Dogmatic Constitution on Divine Revelation Dei Verbum, September 16, 2005. http://w2.vatican.va/content/benedict-xvi/en/speeches/2005/september/documents/hf_ben-xvi_spe_20050916_40-dei-verbum.html.

———. *Verbum Domini*: Post-Synodal Apostolic Exhortation on the Word of God in the Life and Mission of the Church, September 30, 2010.

———. Wednesday General Audience, March 7, 2012. http://w2.vatican.va/content/benedict-xvi/en/audiences/2012/documents/hf_ben-xvi_aud_20120307.html.

———. Wednesday General Audience, September 26, 2012. http://w2.vatican.va/content/benedict-xvi/en/audiences/2012/documents/hf_ben-xvi_aud_20120926.html.

Bernard of Clairvaux. *The Works of Bernard of Clairvaux, Vol. 2, Part 1: Song of Songs I.* Translated by Kilian Walsh. Reprint edition. Kalamazoo, MI: Cistercian Publications, Inc, 1981.

Bialas, Martin. *The Mysticism of the Passion in St. Paul of the Cross.* San Francisco: Ignatius Press, 1990.

Bonaventure, St. *Bonaventure: The Soul's Journey Into God / The Tree of Life / The Life of St. Francis.* Translated by Ewert Cousins. Mahwah, NJ: Paulist Press, 1978.

Bro, Bernard. *St. Therese of Lisieux: Her Family, Her God, Her Message.* San Francisco: Ignatius Press, 2003.

Buber, Martin. *I and Thou.* Translated by Walter Kaufmann. 36th ed. New York: Charles Scribners, 1970.

Casey, Michael. *Sacred Reading: The Ancient Art of Lectio Divina.* Liguori, MO: Triumph Books, 1996.

Catechism of the Catholic Church. Washington, DC: United States Conference of Catholic Bishops, 2000.

Cavalletti, Sofia. *The Religious Potential of the Child: Experiencing Scripture and Liturgy with Young Children.* Translated by Patricia M. Coulter and Julie M. Coulter. 2nd ed. New York: Liturgy Training Publications, 1992.

Chapman, John. *Spiritual Letters.* New York: Burns & Oates, 2003.

Compendium of the Catechism of the Catholic Church. Washington, DC: United States Catholic Conference of Bishops, 2006.

De Montfort, St. Louis-Marie Grignion. *The Secret of Mary.* Reprint Edition. Charlotte, NC: TAN Books, 1998.

———. *True Devotion to Mary: With Preparation for Total Consecration.* Translated by Frederick William Faber. Tan Books Catholic Classics Series. Charlotte, NC: TAN Classics, 2010.

Dománski, O.F.M. Conv., Fr. Jerzy. *For the Life of the World: St. Maximilian and the Eucharist.* Libertyville, IL: Academy of the Immaculate, 2014.

Dressler, H., and R. J. Deferrari, eds. *Early Christian Biographies.* Vol. 15. Translated by M. E. Keenan. Washington, DC: The Catholic University of America Press, 1952.

Elbée, Jean C. J. d'. *I Believe in Love: A Personal Retreat Based on the Teaching of St. Thérèse of Lisieux.* 2nd ed. Manchester, NH: Sophia Institute Press, 2001.

Elizabeth of the Trinity, St. *The Complete Works of Elizabeth of the Trinity, Vol. 1.* Translated by Sister Alethea Kane, O.C.D. Washington, D.C: ICS Publications, 1984.

Ephrem the Syrian, St. *Hymns on Paradise.* Translated by Sebastian P. Brock. Crestwood, NY: St. Vladimir's Seminary Press, 1990.

Feingold, Lawrence. *The Eucharist: Mystery of Presence, Sacrifice, and Communion.* Steubenville: Emmaus Academic, 2018.

Francis. Address to Participants in the 37th National Convocation of the Renewal in the Holy Spirit, June 1, 2014. http://w2.vatican.va/content/francesco/en/speeches/2014/june/documents/papa-francesco_20140601_rinnovamento-spirito-santo.html.

———. Address to Capuchin Friars, February 9, 2016. https://w2.vatican.va/content/francesco/en/homilies/2016/documents/papa-francesco_20160209_omelia-frati-cappuccini.html.

———. Audience from November 13, 2013. http://w2.vatican.va/content/francesco/en/audiences/2013/documents/papa-francesco_20131113_udienza-generale.html.

————. *Christus Vivit*: Post-Synodal Exhortation to Young People and to the Entire People of God, March 25, 2019.

————. *Evangelii Gaudium*, 2013.

————. General Audience, December 12, 2018. http://w2.vatican.va/content/francesco/en/audiences/2018/documents/papa-francesco_20181212_udienza-generale.html.

Francis de Sales, St. *An Introduction to the Devout Life*. Dublin: M. H. Gill and Son, 1885.

————. *Philothea, or An Introduction to the Devout Life*. Translated by John C Reville. Charlotte, NC: TAN Classics, 2010.

————. *Treatise on the Love of God*. Blacksburg, VA: Wilder Publications, 2011.

French, R. M., trans. *The Way of a Pilgrim and The Pilgrim Continues His Way*. 2nd ed. New York: Harper, 1991.

Fry, O.S.B., Timothy, trans. *The Rule of St. Benedict in English*. Collegeville, MN: Liturgical Press, 2018.

Garrigou-Lagrange, O.P., Reginald. *The Three Ages of the Interior Life: Prelude of Eternal Life*. Translated by Sr. M. Timothea Doyle, O.P. Vol. 1. St. Louis, MO: B. Herder Book Co., 1947.

Gawande, Atul. *Being Mortal: Medicine and What Matters in the End*. New York: Metropolitan Books, 2014.

Glaser, Judith. *Conversational Intelligence: How Great Leaders Build Trust and Get Extraordinary Results*. New York: Routledge, 2016.

Groeschel, Benedict J. *Praying Constantly: Bringing Your Faith to Life*. Huntington, IN: Our Sunday Visitor, 2010.

Guardini, Romano. *The Lord*. Washington, DC: Regnery, 1954.

————. and Joseph Ratzinger. *The Spirit of the Liturgy: Commemorative Edition*. San Francisco: Ignatius Press, 2018.

Guigo II. *Ladder of Monks and Twelve Meditations*. Translated by Edmund Collegde and James Walsh. Kalamazoo, MI: Cistercian Publications, 1981.

Haggerty, Fr. Donald. *Contemplative Provocations*. San Francisco: Ignatius Press, 2013.

——. *The Contemplative Hunger*. San Francisco: Ignatius Press, 2016.

Hahn, Scott. *The Fourth Cup: Unveiling the Mystery of the Last Supper and the Cross*. New York: Image, 2018.

Healy, Mary. *Healing: Bringing the Gift of God's Mercy to the World*. Huntington, IN: Our Sunday Visitor, 2015.

The Ignatius Catholic Study Bible: The New Testament. Edited by Scott Hahn and Curtis Mitch. San Francisco: Ignatius Press, 2010.

Ignatius of Loyola, St. *Spiritual Exercises*. Translated by Louis J. Puhl. Westminster, MD: Newman Press, 1960.

International Catholic Charismatic Renewal Services Doctrinal Commission. *Baptism in the Holy Spirit*. Locust Grove, VA: NSC USA, 2017.

John Paul II, *Man and Woman He Created Them: A Theology of the Body*. Edited by Michael Waldstein. Boston, MA: Pauline Books & Media, 2006.

——. *Mulieris Dignitatem*, 1988.

——. *Novo Millennio Ineunte*. 2001.

——. *Rosarium Virginis Mariae*. 2002.

Kant, Immanuel, *Critique of Pure Reason: Unified Edition*. Edited by James W. Ellington. Translated by Werner S. Pluhar. Indianapolis, IN: Hackett, 1996.

Kavanaugh, Kieran, trans. and ed. *The Collected Works of St. John of the*

Cross, Revised Edition. Washington, DC: ICS Publications, 1991.

Kowalska, St. Maria Faustina. *Diary: Divine Mercy in My Soul.* 3rd ed. Stockbridge, MA: Marian Press, 2005.

Leclercq, Jean and Paul Guistiniani. *Camaldolese Extraordinary: The Life, Doctrine, and Rule of Blessed Paul Giustiniani.* Bloomingdale, OH: Ercam Editions, 2002.

Leon-Joseph, Cardinal Suenens, and Dom Helder Camara. *Charismatic Renewal and Social Action: A Dialogue.* Ann Arbor, MI: Servant Books, 1979.

Lilles, Anthony. *Fire from Above: Christian Contemplation and Mystical Wisdom.* Manchester, NH: Sophia Institute Press, 2016.

Loehr, Gina. *The Four Teresas.* Cincinnati, OH: Franciscan Media, 2010.

Maher, Matt. "Lord, I need you." *All the People Said Amen.* Track 4. Essential Records, 2013. AZ Lyrics. https://www.azlyrics.com/lyrics/mattmaher/lordineedyou.html.

Martin, Ralph. *Fulfillment of All Desire.* Steubenville, OH: Emmaus Road, 2006.

———. *Hungry for God: Practical Help in Personal Prayer.* Cincinnati, OH: Servant, 2006.

Martinez, Luis M. *When God Is Silent: Finding Spiritual Peace amid the Storms of Life.* Manchester, NH: Sophia Institute Press, 2014.

———. *Worshipping a Hidden God: Unlocking the Secrets of the Interior Life.* 2003. Reprint, Manchester, NH: Sophia Institute Press, 2014.

Matthew, Iain. *The Impact of God.* London: Hodder & Stoughton, 1995.

McDonnell, Kilian, ed. *Toward a New Pentecost for a New Evangelization: Malines Document I.* Subsequent edition. Collegeville, MI: Michael Glazier, 1993.

Mede, Jude. *A Source/Workbook for Paulacrucian Studies.* New Rochelle, NY: Don Bosco Publications, Saint Paul of the Cross Province, 1977.

Metz, Johannes Baptist. *Poverty of Spirit.* Westminster, MD: Newman Press, 1968.

Mother Teresa. *Come Be My Light: The Private Writings of the Saint of Calcutta.* Edited by Brian Kolodiejchuk. New York: Doubleday, 2007.

———. *Where There Is Love, There Is God: A Path to Closer Union with God and Greater Love for Others.* New York: Image, 2010.

Mueller, Cardinal Gerhardt. Letter Iuvenescit Ecclesia to the Bishops of the Catholic Church Regarding the Relationship Between Hierarchical and Charismatic Gifts in the Life and the Mission of the Church, May 15, 2016. http://www.vatican.va/roman_curia/congregations/cfaith/documents/rc_con_cfaith_doc_20160516_iuvenescit-ecclesia_en.html.

Murray, Paul, O.P. *In the Grip of Light: The Dark and Bright Journey of Christian Contemplation.* London: Bloomsbury, 2012.

Otto, Rudolf. *The Idea of the Holy: An Inquiry Into the Non-Rational Factor in the Idea of the Divine and Its Relation to the Rational.* Translated by John W. Harvey. Pantianos Classics: CreateSpace Independent Publishing Platform, 2017.

Paul of the Cross, St. *The Letters of Saint Paul of the Cross, Volume 1, 1720–1747.* Edited by Laurence Finn and Donald Webber. Chicago, IL: Passionist Provincial Office, 2000.

———. *The Letters of Saint Paul of the Cross, Volume 2, 1748–*

1758. Edited by Laurence Finn and Donald Webber. Chicago, IL: Passionist Provincial Office, 2000.

Paul VI, *Evangelica Testificatio*. 1971.

Petit, Jean. *Descending Fire: The Journal of a Soul Aflame*. Manchester, NH: Sophia Institute Press, 2001.

Petrie, Ann and Jeanette Petrie. *Mother Teresa*. DVD, n.p.: Petrie Productions, 1986.

Phillippe, Jacques. *Thirsting for Prayer*. New Rochelle, NY: Scepter Publishers, 2014.

Pieper, Josef. *Silence of St. Thomas*. 3rd ed. South Bend, IN: St. Augustine's Press, 1999.

Pies, Otto. *The Victory of Father Karl*. New York: Farrar, Straus and Cudahy, 1957.

Pitre, Brant James. *Jesus and the Jewish Roots of the Eucharist: Unlocking the Secrets of the Last Supper*. New York: Doubleday, 2011.

Pseudo-Dionysius. *Pseudo-Dionysius: The Complete Works*. Edited by J. Farina. Translated by C. Luibheid and P. Rorem. Mahwah, NJ: Paulist Press, 1987.

Ramsey, Boniface, ed. *John Cassian, The Conferences*. Ancient Christian Writers, vol. 57. New York: Paulist Press, 1997.

Ratzinger, Joseph. *Dogma and Preaching*. San Francisco: Ignatius Press, 2011.

———. Letter to the Bishops of the Catholic Church on Some Aspects of Christian Meditation – Orationis Formas, October 15, 1989. http://www.vatican.va/roman_curia/congregations/cfaith/documents/rc_con_cfaith_doc_19891015_meditazione-cristiana_en.html.

———. *The Message of Fatima*. 2006. http://www.vatican.va/

roman_curia/congregations/cfaith/documents/rc_con_cfaith_ doc_20000626_message-fatima_en.html.

———. *Theology of the Liturgy: The Sacramental Foundation of Christian Existence.* Vol. 11 of *Joseph Ratzinger Collected Works.* San Francisco: Ignatius Press, 2014.

Redman, Matt. "Blessed Be Your Name." *Blessed Be Your Name: The Songs of Matt Redman Vol. 1.* Track 1. Survivor Records, 2005. Genius. https://genius.com/Matt-redman-blessed-be-your-name-lyrics.

Sarah, Cardinal Robert, and Nicolas Diat. *The Power of Silence: Against the Dictatorship of Noise.* San Francisco: Ignatius Press, 2017.

Schaff, Philip, ed. *The Confessions and Letters of St. Augustin with a Sketch of His Life and Work.* Vol. 1 of *A Select Library of the Nicene and Post-Nicene Fathers of the Christian Church.* Peabody, MA: Hendrickson, 1994.

Second Vatican Council. *Apostolicam Actuositatem.* 1965.

———. *Dei Verbum.* 1965.

———. *Lumen Gentium.* 1964.

———. *Sacrosanctum Concilium.* 1963.

Smith, Michael W. "Open the Eyes of My Heart." *Worship.* Track 5. Reunion Records, 2001. AZ Lyrics. https://www.azlyrics.com/lyrics/michaelwsmith/opentheeyesofmyheart.html.

Speyr, Adrienne Von. *Gates of Eternal Life.* San Francisco: Ignatius Press, 1983.

———. *The Boundless God.* Translated by Helena Tomko. San Francisco, CA: Ignatius Press, 2004.

———. *The World of Prayer.* San Francisco: Ignatius Press, 1985.

Stein, Edith. *Self-Portrait in Letters, 1916–1942.* Translated by

Josephine Koeppel, O.C.D., CWES, Vol. 5. Washington, DC: ICS Publications, 1993.

Stinissen, O.C.D., Wilfrid. *The Holy Spirit, Fire of Divine Love.* San Francisco: Ignatius Press, 2017.

Suenens, Cardinal Leon-Joseph. *Renewal and the Powers of Darkness. Malines Document IV.* London: Darton, Longman and Todd, 1983.

Tanquerey, Adolphe. *The Spiritual Life: A Treatise on Ascetical and Mystical Theology.* Translated by Herman Branderis. 2 ed. Rockford, IL: Tan Books & Pub, 2001.

Therese of Lisieux, St. *St. Therese of Lisieux: Her Last Conversations.* Translated by John Clarke. Washington, DC: ICS Publications, 1977.

———. *The Story of a Soul.* Translated by Robert J. Edmonson. Unabridged edition. Brewster, MA: Paraclete Press, 2006.

———. *The Story of a Soul.* Translated by T. Taylor. London: Burns & Oates, 1912.

Walsh, James, ed. *The Cloud of Unknowing.* The Classics of Western Spirituality. New York: Paulist Press, 1981.